The Art of Moral Judgement

Kenneth G. Greet

The Art of
Moral Judgement

LONDON
EPWORTH PRESS

Preface

THERE is a smell of death about some of the text books on ethics. One feels that the printing presses have taken the stuff of life and squeezed all the juice out of it. This dullness of exposition stands in stark contrast to the heat and excitement of the sort of discussions on moral issues to which I frequently listen and in which I am often involved.

This book, then, comes out of the experience of verbal strife and intense debate about living issues. The lack of any pretension to literary polish may not be excused, but it can be explained by the fact that it has been written over a few weeks already full of engagements. Yet I hope that the frequent forays into the field of battle will have saved the text from any appearance of academic detachment.

I am indebted to many scholars, and have quoted from some of them. But often I have wished to interrupt the smooth flow of their arguments. In writing my own text I have had constantly in mind the sort of person who might be looking over my shoulder, and, during Part One of the book, I have allowed him to interrupt. I hope this technique will help to clarify some points, and that for those not accustomed to the discussion of ethical theory, it will lighten the load where the material is necessarily a little heavy.

I am grateful to my friends the Revd Gordon Wakefield, M.A., B.Litt., Editor of the Methodist Publishing House, the Revd John Stacey, B.D., Secretary of the Methodist Local Preachers Department, and Sister Margaret Siebold, B.A., Secretary of the Methodist Study Centre, for their kindness in reading the manuscript and making a number of helpful suggestions. My secretary, Miss Christine Gibb, kindly typed the manuscript and helped prepare the index.

I hope the book will be of interest to those who believe that questions of right and wrong are important, and that if we seek patiently and humbly, we shall sometimes find the answers. The questions printed in the Appendix are for the use of individuals or groups who may find it helpful to articulate their own views on some of the issues raised.

Westminster, 1969   KENNETH G. GREET

Contents

7

Acknowledgements

I AM INDEBTED to the various authors from whom I have quoted, and to the following publishers for permission to use passages from the works referred to in the footnotes where their names occur:

Allen & Unwin Ltd., Bell & Sons Ltd., Chapman & Hall Ltd., Chatto & Windus Ltd., Clarendon Press, W. Collins, Sons & Co. Ltd., Darton, Longman & Todd Ltd., Eyre & Spottiswoode Ltd., Faber & Faber Ltd., Fontana Books, Victor Gollancz Ltd., Robert Hale Ltd., Hodder & Stoughton Ltd., Hutchinson Publishing Group Ltd., Independent Press Ltd., the Institute of Economic Affairs, Longmans, Green and Co. Ltd., Oxford University Press, Pelican Books, Routledge & Kegan Paul Ltd., the Society for Promoting Christian Knowledge, the Student Christian Movement Press Ltd., Studio Vista Ltd. (formerly Vista Books), University Tutorial Press Ltd., Nicholas Vane Ltd., Weidenfeld & Nicolson Ltd.

If I have inadvertently infringed any copyright I hereby tender my apologies.

1 Introduction: raising the questions

A GROUP of Christians at a weekend conference were discussing a number of intensely complex moral problems. When they had produced several widely divergent judgements on such questions as the use of nuclear weapons, the legalization of marijuana, abortion, euthanasia, and whether it is ever permissible to tell a lie, one of them asked, 'Who is to say which view is right and which is wrong?' At this point an elderly lay preacher who happened to be sitting in on the discussion said, with an apparent complacency which obviously irritated the group, 'May I suggest that it is all there in the Ten Commandments?' This drew from the group leader the sharp retort, 'No you may not, because it isn't.'

The retort was justified. The lay preacher's suggestion is not only demonstrably false, but it begs most of the questions which have to be raised by those who think deeply about right and wrong. Granted that the Decalogue contains a number of basic directives, by no stretch of the imagination can it be regarded as covering all the varied situations in which we have to decide our course of action. Moreover, it may properly be asked whether the Ten Commandments are all to be taken literally. What about 'Remember the sabbath day, to keep it holy'?[1] If, as the next two verses suggest, the day is to be kept holy by abstaining from all work, are Christians who work on the seventh day of the week committing an offence? Or again, we may ask whether it is allowable to make exceptions to any of the Commandments. For example, is killing always wrong? And, for that matter, does the simple prohibition of killing apply only to human life, or does it extend to animals? Must we all be vegetarians?

[1] Exodus 20:8.

It is unlikely that the lay preacher in the group would be satisfied with this rejoinder to his doubtless well-intentioned suggestions. It is therefore tempting to imagine the probable course of a further exchange between the lay preacher and the group leader.

L.P. It does seem to me we are making rather heavy weather of the whole subject. We really all of us know what's right and what's wrong, and there's no need for all this hair-splitting argument. Living the good life all boils down to keeping a few simple rules.

G.L. Would you care to mention what these simple rules are, then?

L.P. Well, let's take just one to be going on with: 'Always tell the truth.' What's wrong with that? There surely can't be any doubt about what it means.

G.L. It certainly is an excellent rule, but there are in fact a number of questions to be raised about it. Assuming that I know what the truth is, are you sure it is always right to tell it? Or to put the question in the form it more frequently takes, 'Is it not sometimes right to tell a lie?'

L.P. I don't see that good can ever come from doing evil.

G.L. But that really begs the question. What do you mean by 'good' and 'evil'?

L.P. Can't we be rather more specific, and set the question down within the context of a real situation?

G.L. That is exactly what we ought to do, and I will now attempt it. Here are a couple of situations, either of which can be imagined without difficulty. If a man whose mind is unhinged is about to jump off a window ledge twelve floors above street level, and I know he is addicted to tobacco, would I be justified in saying, 'Here, have a cigarette,' even if I could only hold out an empty packet? I should be acting a lie, but it might be the only way of saving the man's life, and maybe the lives of others down below. Or suppose – and this, alas, is all too easy to imagine – there has been a terrible motor accident. While the firemen are sawing a little girl out of the wreckage, she says to me, 'Is Mummy all right?' I know that her mother is dead. What do I say?

L.P. Well, in the latter case, I really am not sure. I should want to know what the future effect might be on the little girl of my telling her a lie.

G.L. But you cannot know that. The position surely is that you must take a risk. It might be right to tell the truth, or it might not.

L.P. I am not really sure.

G.L. And that is the point. The only way in which you could be sure that in all such circumstances the truth must be told is by putting forward the notion that the primary concern of morality is that I should be technically correct, with no blots on my record. But such an idea surely robs the word 'morality' of all meaning.

L.P. The incidents you've described are rather unusual. Surely most of the time its easy enough to understand and apply the simple rule about always telling the truth.

G.L. I am sorry, but I cannot agree. Long ago Pontius Pilate asked, 'What is truth?' and whether he was speaking sincerely, cynically, or despairingly, he certainly asked a pertinent question. Supposing I say, 'It is raining cats and dogs'; am I telling the truth?

L.P. Yes, of course you are. You are using a metaphor which everyone understands. It's not the literal meaning of the words which matters, but the sense they convey to the hearer.

G.L. Leaving aside the fact that the metaphor may not be understood by everybody, is it really the case that the truth or otherwise of what I say is determined by the sense it conveys to my hearer? Very often when the minutes of a meeting are read someone will object, 'This is not what I said at all; in fact I said exactly the opposite.' The recorder probably replies, 'I apologize. What I put down was what I *understood* the speaker to mean.' Was the speaker, whose original statement was completely in accord with the facts, really guilty of untruth because the person listening misinterpreted the sense of the words?

L.P. No, obviously not. A thing is true if it represents the facts as they are. Truth is, therefore, independent of both the person who seeks to express it and those who listen to what he is saying.

G.L. That seems perfectly clear if we think of a factual statement like, 'Last night the Maharishi gave a talk on BBC Television about transcendental meditation'. Such a statement can easily be verified and, if it is true, it remains true however many people misinterpret the statement. But supposing one viewer says, 'Transcendental meditation is a philosophy which embodies the ultimate truth about life,' and another says, 'It is a load of incoherent nonsense,' how shall we measure the degree of truth and falsehood in those two statements?

L.P. Perhaps the simple rule about always telling the truth is not as simple as it sounds. It should be amended to 'Always try to tell the truth'. It must be admitted that it is often very difficult, if not impossible, to know what the truth is.

G.L. This has been a useful dialogue for it has illustrated the fact that there is more to ethics than the assertion of a few simple basic rules of human conduct. It is evident that there are situations in life which require us to make exceptions to rules. There are also situations in which it is very difficult to know what judgement or action the application of the rule would dictate. Life is in fact too complex to be covered by a few basic rules. Every day we have to make decisions based not only on factual evidence, but on our interpretation of it. In other words, we have to make value judgements. An ethical judgement is concerned not only with the question whether a certain event occurred, but also with whether it ought to have occurred; not only with the ideas men hold, but also with the rightness or wrongness of those ideas.

There we may leave the imaginary dialogue. It has begun to open up some of the issues with which this book must deal, but has done no more than that. There are other more searching questions to be asked. Why should anyone be expected to take the Ten Commandments, or any other commandments, seriously? On the whole the modern world does not take kindly to orders imposed from above. Moral teaching stands little chance of acceptance unless it can be shown to be reasonable. Some of the ethical rulings of some parts of the Christian Church seem unreasonable to great numbers of people, especially when they find them contradicted by other parts of the Church.

How much truth is there in the contention that there is no specifically Christian ethic, and that Christianity is not so much an ethical system as a source of power which enables men to live up to standards already acknowledged by those to whom Christ came? Certainly the ethics of the Old Testament at its highest represent a very demanding standard. What is the source of this strong moral sense? If we say, 'Faith in God', how can we explain the moral sensitivity of some who profess no religion? Is a thing right because God commands it, or must the religious man say that God commands it because it is right, thus positing the view that there is some objective morality which is independent of religious belief?

Assuming that there is a specifically Christian morality, what is its basis? This was one of the questions raised by the writers of the report entitled *Sex and Morality*[1] which evoked such a furore of discussion at the end of the year 1966. Judging by the comments of some of the critics, the question itself was improper and unnecessary. Those who belong to the 'it's all there in the Ten Commandments' school had a field day. If they could have laid their hands on the original tablets of stone, they would no doubt have hurled them with a good conscience at the heads of those who prepared the Report. But when the tumult had subsided, the question remained, and it insists upon an answer. It was set down in the context of a highly emotive subject, but the language in which it was asked was measured and precise. Here is how the question was briefly elaborated:

Is the [Christian moral] system to be thought of as valid for all men in all times and all places, because it is deduced from a divine revelation, through scripture and tradition, of man's true nature? Alternatively, is the Christian system of morality a 'dynamic' or 'evolutionary' system which has to be worked out afresh by each generation in the light of their own understanding of Christ, paying due regard to the conditions obtaining in their time and place? These two alternatives give us a striking, but over-simplified, picture of the present controversy over Christian morals as the advocates of the 'New Morality' tend to envisage it. Neither alternative completely represents a position we hold. Nevertheless we have assumed that new knowledge must be taken into account in arriving at a Christian moral judgement; and it could be asked, 'Is this really legitimate? Is not the Church officially and irrevocably committed to the doctrine of immutable moral rules?'

In fact we have to deal with a number of separate questions of general principles ... We may distinguish the following:

(i) Does morality derive from God's will or from man's judgement?

(ii) Is morality static or revisable?

[1] Presented to the British Council of Churches, and published by the S.C.M. Press.

(iii) Is it best embodied in rules or ideals?

(iv) Does it bear mainly on actions, or on motives and dispositions?

(v) How much liberty of interpretation rests with particular cultural groups or individuals?[1]

There is nothing new about these questions, but together with others which are closely related to them, they are being asked with an urgency which makes the attempt to find more satisfactory answers one of first importance. Some of the reasons for that urgency and for the widespread moral confusion of our time are examined in Chapter 5. One reason is that the modern world confronts us with issues of unprecedented complexity. Very often the comparatively simple criteria of former times no longer seem applicable. Some of these issues are considered in the second half of this book. First of all, however, the attempt is made to define the nature and scope of ethics, and to look at some of the broader questions which fall within the field of ethical discussion to which this chapter has referred.

[1] op. cit., p. 17.

2 The nature and scope of ethical enquiry

What is ethics really about?

IN THE INTRODUCTORY chapter we plunged straight into the heart of an ethical discussion and proceeded to table a number of questions which require an answer. We recognized, but did not stop to ponder, the significance of the basic fact that we are all accustomed to using the terms 'right' and 'wrong'. Ethics may be defined, briefly and simply, as the study of right and wrong.

Like most brief and simple definitions of great subjects, this one is really quite inadequate. The word 'ethics' derives from the Greek word ἔθος which means 'custom' or 'habit'. (The Latin equivalent is *mores*, from which we get our word 'morals'.) Ethics, then, is concerned with men's habits and customs, and with whether those habits and customs are good or evil.

Now, however, we have introduced two other terms. Do the words 'right' and 'wrong' mean the same as 'good' and 'evil'? The word 'right' comes from the Latin *rectus*, which means 'according to rule'. But rules have some reference to the ends or results to be achieved. The rules incorporated in the Highway Code, for example, are designed to secure the desirable end of safety on the roads. The word 'good' (connected with the German *gut*) in ethical discussion may be applied to ends or results (though, as is clear from the discussion on p. 12, this is not always done). Thus I may say that it is right for me to take a certain drug because I am assured that this will rid me of a painful sickness and restore me to health: the restoration to health being the good result which flows from the right action.

It is a comparatively simple matter to describe the meanings normally attached to the basic vocabulary of ethical discussion.

The problems really begin when we start to explore the deeper significance of these terms. If ethics were merely descriptive, the field of enquiry would still be vast, but the task of amassing factual information would be fairly straightforward. The matter could be treated historically and accounts could be written, as indeed they have been, about the various ideas of right and wrong which have been entertained by different societies through the ages. Comparisons could be made between the behaviour patterns of one century and those of another. Ethical study, however, is not merely descriptive; it is prescriptive. As we said at the conclusion of the dialogue in the previous chapter, it is concerned not only with what is, but also with what *ought* to be. It is a fact, for example, that some people in this country want capital punishment to be restored. Such a fact falls very properly within the field of descriptive ethics. But equally ethics must be concerned with the question whether capital punishment *ought* to be restored.

Ethical judgements and scientific judgements

From what has just been said, it is obvious that the judgements of ethics differ from those of science. It might be said that the latter are concerned with facts, and the former with beliefs. The distinction is not really as clear-cut as that, but we will let the statement stand for the moment. If we look again at the question of capital punishment, we can discover by means of an opinion poll how many people out of a given number believe that the death sentence should be reintroduced, and how many hold the contrary view. Provided the enquiry is properly conducted, the figures represent an indisputable fact which has been scientifically established. If, however, I say that the retentionist view is wrong, this is a statement containing a value judgement which science cannot either prove or disprove. I am saying that human life has an absolute value, and that to hang a murderer is merely to add one evil to another.

This does not mean, of course, that scientific enquiry has no contribution to make to the processes of ethical judgement. On the contrary, particularly on an issue like capital punishment, a clear understanding of objective facts is essential to the making of an intelligent judgement. But knowledge of the facts does not by itself determine the kind of conclusion at which we arrive. Two people, equally knowledegable about the facts, can arrive at opposing judgements. Science may observe the fact that they differ, but it is helpless as an arbiter in the dispute about which of the two views is right.

It is possible to exaggerate the difference between ethics and science. As it stands, the bare statement that 'the assertions of the latter can be verified and those of the former cannot' is misleading. Michael Keeling quotes Professor W. T. Williams of the University of Southampton to show that 'even the experimental sciences are dependent to some extent on the workings of intuition.'[1] Although I have spoken of facts as if they were simple things, often they are not. It is frequently very difficult to determine what the facts of the case really are. It may be even more difficult to estimate the consequences of certain actions. A man may say, 'I know what the facts are, but as to the consequences which will flow from the juxtaposition of those facts, I am very uncertain.' That uncertainty may render the task of forming a moral judgement well-nigh impossible.

Aristotle described ethics as 'an inexact science'. It would probably be more accurate to describe it as an art rather than a science. Certainly, the phrase 'the art of moral judgement' accords very well with the facts of life as they relate to the experience of working out the rights and wrongs of various situations. To describe ethics as an art rather than a science is not by any means to suggest that it is less important than the scientific disciplines. The meaning and significance of life are not exhausted by what the experimental sciences tell us about it.

No intelligent person will feel obliged to oppose science as such. It is, after all, merely a method of looking at life and studying its many-sided phenomena. Our debt to scientists and to the use of scientific method is immeasurable. But any scientist who makes the arrogant claim that the whole of life's experience can be weighed and measured is merely revealing his ignorance.

When all this has been said, however, we are left with a big question about the real nature of ethical judgement, and, indeed, about the value of ethical study itself. If there is no way of proving that one view is right and another wrong, are we not left in a

[1] Michael Keeling, *Morals in a Free Society*, S.C.M. Press, 1967, pp. 18–19.

morass of relativism? Is it worth all the trouble of examining the various theories of right and wrong if at the end of the exercise we have to admit that one man's view is as good as another's?

As a matter of fact we none of us do admit that one man's view is as good as another's. We argue fiercely for what we believe to be right, and against what we feel to be wrong. Is the argument merely about the difference in personal preferences? Sometimes, of course, it may be. A mother and daughter may have a furious dispute about the colour of a new hat. The daughter may say, 'It would be absolutely wrong of you to wear that dreadful object at the meeting tomorrow.' But this is an exaggerated use of language. What it really boils down to is that her mother likes purple and she detests it. It is difficult to imagine any situation in which the colour of a hat could be a grave moral question. But supposing the argument is about the colour of a man's skin, and the mother says to her daughter, 'You have no right to marry a coloured man; you know my views: coloured people are by nature inferior.' That is a very different issue, and the protagonists in the argument sound as if they are talking about something very much more than personal preferences. They seem to be appealing to some objective standard beyond themselves, to a body of knowledge which, though it cannot be established scientifically, is nevertheless real.

Can this belief be justified, and if so, how? What is the source of this authority whereby the grain of right is sifted from the chaff of wrong? Can we speak correctly of a 'knowledge of right and wrong', or must the word 'knowledge' be confined to what can be proved by science? The question of what we mean by knowledge is one that has engaged the minds of philosophers, and it will be instructive to see what they have had to say about it. We have already noticed that ethics cannot be entirely separated from other subjects. It certainly overlaps with the field of philosophy. Indeed, since philosophy is concerned with the whole area of life and with the meaning of reality, it could be said that ethics is a branch of philosophy.

The history of the various ideas which men have entertained about the origin and content of moral standards is long and complex. It will not be possible here to do more than refer sketchily to some of the main ethical theories. Again, however, the necessity for even so slight an enquiry into the history of moral ideas may be questioned by some Christians. Let us then allow the protesting Christian his say and indicate some of the answers which may be given.

Is the examination of ethical theories necessary?

P.C. I realize that the history of men's thoughts on ethical matters may be of interest to scholars, but for the Christian such study is unnecessary. Morality is fundamentally a matter of what God has revealed, not of what men happen to think.

A. Some Christians do seem to have a fatal tendency to over-simplify important issues. It is no good constantly going back to square one. We have already (in the introductory chapter) exposed the fallacy of thinking that moral behaviour consists of simple obedience to obvious rules laid down by the Almighty. Several points emerged from that earlier discussion. One was that such rules as there are do not cover all situations. Another was that apparently simple rules, when examined in the context of real life, turn out not to be so simple after all. The same rule may be variously interpreted, or one rule may conflict with another.

P.C. I do not deny this. It is not part of my case that the application of the rules is simple. We need intelligence if we are to understand God's revelation, and integrity if we are to apply it to life. But my main contention still stands: the divine revelation is the sole source of moral guidance, and for the Christian there cannot be any other.

A. Before either agreeing or disagreeing with you, I would like to explore this a little further. One of the questions tabled in the opening chapter was whether a thing is right because God commands it, or whether God commands it because it is right.

P.C. I should say that a thing is right because God commands it.

A. And how do you know what God commands?

P.C. You read the Bible which is the Word of God.

A. Surely you are not saying that a Christian must obey all the commandments attributed to God in the Bible? It would appear that God issued some very terrible commands, such as 'Thou shalt not suffer a witch to live'.[1]

P.C. Ah yes, but you have to read the Bible with intelligence and discrimination. In the Old Testament we trace the development

[1] Exodus 22:18.

of men's ideas about God, and at the beginning those ideas are very primitive. It isn't God that is wrong, but the understanding of God and what He was saying.

A. But if, as I understand you now to be saying, the revelation of God's truth in the Bible is all mixed up with falsehood, how do you distinguish the one from the other? Are you really saying that only the commandments which square with your idea of right and wrong can be attributed to God? If so, it looks very much as if you are judging God rather than that He is judging you.

P.C. No, that is not at all the position. Christianity teaches that the full and final revelation of God is our Lord Jesus Christ. Anything, therefore, that contradicts Christ, even if it is in the Bible, must be wrong.

A. How do you know that Christ is the ultimate standard by which all else is to be judged?

P.C. It is, of course, a matter of faith – of acceptance that He is God incarnate.

A. Does this mean that those who have no faith can have no sense of right and wrong, and no moral convictions? There are, after all, many good people who do not believe in God. Some of them revere Jesus as a great moral teacher, but they regard Him as just a good man, perhaps the best man who ever lived. How do they come by their morality?

P.C. This is a difficult question. I am inclined to say that God is the source of all good, including good ideas, whether men acknowledge this or not.

A. But could the truth be that God commands a thing because it is right? If we put it that way, it means that right is something which exists beyond God. He has a *reason* for commanding it, namely that it is right. In this case, the right would exist even if there were no God. Surely this could explain why moral ideas are universal, though belief in God is not.

P.C. I suspect that we are now just playing with words. My concept of God is of One whose Being is so great that it embraces all good. I can see, however, that moral ideas have flourished, and still do, outside the community of Christian people, though often influenced by Christian teaching. I admit, therefore, that it may be instructive to examine ethical theories which men have employed to account for this fact.

A. Very good. We will make that the subject of the next chapter. I myself share your belief that God is the source of all good. Certainly God commands a thing because it is right, but the rightness is inseparable from the fact that He has made the world. The marks of the Creator are on every part of the creation, and its divine origin determines the shape of things and the way life works out. It is therefore also true that if God commands a thing it must be right. This view is entirely compatible with the belief that the divine influence is to be seen in the ethical thinking of men and women who lived before Christ, as well as in more recent moral systems which lay no claim to be Christian. Whether there is a specifically Christian morality and, if so, in what sense it differs from other, non-Christian, moralities is a point we must look at later.

3 Non-christian ethics

IN EXAMINING some of the ethical beliefs that have derived from other than Christian sources, we must of necessity be severely selective. In this chapter we shall confine our attention to the Greeks, the developments which followed the Renaissance, and some of the more recent thinking in the modern period.

The thinkers of Greece

Among the writers of the ancient world within the field of speculative ethical thinking, our debt to the Greeks is incomparably the greatest.[1]

L. T. Hobhouse, in his lengthy study of morals in evolution, says:

> With the early thinkers, contemporaries or perhaps predecessors of Socrates, who propounded the question 'What is the Good, the end of human life, the aim which a thinking being should set before him as the goal of his existence?' there begins a new epoch in moral development, the epoch in which the ethical consciousness, long dominated by the forces which shape its conceptions unawares, begins to re-act upon them, to turn round upon the conditions that have hitherto determined its growth and inquire into their why and wherefore. This is part of a movement which extends far beyond the sphere of ethics and attacks the very foundations of knowledge and belief.[2]

[1] For an admirable summary of the work of the Greek philosophical moralists, see Pamela M. Huby, *Greek Ethics*, Macmillan, 1967.

[2] L. T. Hobhouse, *Morals in Evolution*, Chapman and Hall, 1951, pp. 544–5.

The word 'sophistry', as it has come to be used, describes reasoning which is specious but fallacious. This is probably unfair to the *Sophists* (450—400 B.C.), a group of teachers who were among the most enlightened men of their age. They were concerned with the training of the youth of Athens for the duties of citizenship. They may not have contributed anything much of worth to abstract philosophy, but they laid a valuable emphasis on the need to apply ideas about goodness to the practical affairs of life. The general criticism of the Sophists was that they tried to apply ideas which they did not properly understand.

One of the main motivations underlying the moral theorizing of the Greeks was the fact of the diversity of ethical judgements which men discovered when they travelled abroad. In his *Journey Round the World*, Hecataeus of Miletus described the differences in outlook and customs of many peoples from India to Spain. The sort of facts to which he referred inevitably raised the question mentioned earlier: are not all ethical judgements merely matters of convention?

The first really big argument about this question is associated chiefly, though not exclusively, with the Sophists. In view of the complexity of the issues raised by the question, it is not surprising that the Sophists came up with many different and conflicting ideas. On the whole their influence was unsettling. The quest for truth usually is.

The wisdom of *Socrates* (470–399 B.C.) is a byword. His main contention was that if we are to live the moral life, we must carefully define the meaning of the moral terms we use, and understand precisely the end at which we are aiming. So Socrates spent his life questioning human assumptions and assertions. Although he modestly described himself as only a midwife to other men's ideas, and said that his own wisdom consisted mainly in knowing how much he didn't know, he taught that right conduct could be achieved through knowledge – and only through knowledge. When, however, it comes to the key question about what the moral end of life really is, Socrates seems to have no certain view. From the circle which surrounded this great philosopher grew several schools which propounded different answers to that question.

Historically, it is difficult – if not impossible – to distinguish precisely the thinking of Socrates from that of *Plato* (427–347 B.C.) because in the famous dialogues of Plato it is not clear to what extent the writer is using Socrates as the mouthpiece for his own ideas. We are, however, more concerned with the ideas than with their precise authorship.

The *Gorgias* is one of the early Platonic dialogues. In the first section of the work Socrates discusses with Gorgias the use of rhetoric and the art of persuasion. Persuasion can be of two kinds; the case presented can be grounded in sound reasoning, or psychological pressure can be exerted to gain acceptance of a proposition for which no adequate basis in reason can be advanced. In the later sections, first in dialogue with Polus and then with Callicles, the question which is probed is, 'What does a good consist in?' The important point which emerges from this discussion is that if you are to be able to define what is good, you must be able to describe the kind of common life within which that good can be realized. The truth of this is illuminated by the fact that the bad man lacks the ability to share a common life with his fellows; he is one who has rejected the accepted rules of society.

In the *Republic* the question of the common life within which the good can be realized is further examined. Plato endeavours to show what justice is, first in the State, and then in the soul. If all the basic needs of men are to be met in the State, three classes of citizen are required; the artisan, the soldier, and the ruler. By a rather strange argument Plato presents the idea of a corresponding tripartite division in the human soul: there are the rational, the appetitive, and the spirited parts. The appetitive element refers to bodily desires, and the rational to that element which is in conflict with those desires. The spirited part is concerned with standards of honourable behaviour, and waxes angry when reason is overruled. Just as in the State justice is the right functioning of the various parts of the whole, so it is also with the soul. The just State and just men can only exist together. In asking how the just man is to be educated Plato introduces his ideal figure of the philosopher-king.

The philosopher is the person who possesses true knowledge, as distinct from mere belief. Plato taught that behind the use of such words as 'beautiful' there is an objective Form which is beauty.

An object which we perceive with our senses as beautiful derives its character from participation in this Form. The supreme Form is the Form of the good. This is something which transcends existence. When the word 'good' is used of anything it expresses the relation of that thing to the Form of the good. It is only the really intelligent who can aspire to the vision of the Forms. Plato recognizes that the philosophers will rarely have much opportunity to help to create the just State, but he believes it worthwhile to describe it so that it may be the standard by which the actual attainments of men are measured.

The question with which Plato struggled is one that constantly recurs throughout the history of ethical thought – what is it that makes an action just or good? Is the criterion a rule founded on socially-established practice, or is it a divine revelation? Plato's criterion of a knowledge of the Forms is rightly criticized by Alasdair MacIntyre:

> One root of Plato's mistake here is his confusion of the kind of justification which is in place in geometry with that which is in place in matters of conduct. To treat *justice* and *good* as the names of Forms is to miss at once one essential feature of justice and goodness – namely, that they characterize not what is, but what ought to be. Sometimes what ought to be is, but more often not. And it always makes sense to ask of any existing object or state whether it is as it ought to be. But justice and goodness could not be objects or states of affairs about which it would make sense to inquire in this way. Aristotle was to make very much this criticism of Plato; Plato's own blindness to it is one contributory factor to his curious combination of an apparent total certitude as to what goodness and justice are, and a willingness to impose his own certitudes upon others, with a use of profoundly unsatisfactory arguments to support his convictions.[1]

Aristotle (384–322 B.C.) was a member of Plato's Academy. After a period away from Athens during which he was for a time tutor to the future Alexander the Great, he returned to found his own school, the Lyceum. He begins his *Ethics* by defining the good as 'that at which everything aims'. He then proceeds to ask if there

---

[1] *A Short History of Ethics*, Routledge and Kegan Paul, 1967, pp. 49–50.

is one supreme good which we desire for its own sake and not as a means to something else. He attacks Plato's idea of the good as a single and unitary notion. In fact the word 'good' is used in a great variety of ways.

The name which Aristotle gives to the final end, *the* good, is happiness. This is something men choose for its own sake and not just as a means to something else. What does happiness consist in? The answer is that it consists in the right exercise of what is unique to man – his powers of reason.

This sounds like a very promising line of thinking, yet Aristotle's eventual conclusions are strangely disappointing. Although he starts by objecting to Plato's Form of the Good as an abstract notion unrelated to life, he ends up with an attitude which is very similar in its contempt for human experience. For the characteristic activity of reason, that which is best in us, is a speculative sort of contemplation of unchanging truth which has no practical outcome; it is an end in itself. In the nature of the case such contemplation requires leisure, and consequently is only for those with a reasonable income. Aristotle addresses himself to a select few and sets forth a view of timeless truth as detached from and superior to the ordinary world which is the arena of ordinary human life and struggle.

Inevitably, the way men think is greatly influenced by their environment. The differences between Greek ethical thinking and that of later moral philosophy reflect the differences between Greek society and the forms of society which succeeded it. The point is crystallized in MacIntyre's remark that 'In general, Greek ethics asks, "What am I to do if I am to fare well?" Modern ethics ask, "What ought I to do if I am to do right?" and it asks this question in such a way that doing right is made something quite independent of faring well.'[2] What in fact happened historically to the basic ethical term 'good' is that, whereas in Greek usage it was applied to role fulfilment (i.e. a man was judged good as a farmer or as a father), later it came to be used in asking the more general question, 'What is a good man?' The coming into being of the large-scale State and the impersonal life of vast cities has had a profound effect on moral philosophy. It confronts the individual with a new range of moral questions very different from those which faced the person living in a Greek city-state.

[1] ibid., p. 84.

The *Stoic* school of philosophy was founded by Zeno (probably 342–270 B.C.). The word 'stoic 'comes from the word *stoa* (porch) from which Zeno used to teach. By this time the Greek city-state was in process of decay. As a consequence the Stoics drew a sharper line of division between the contemplative life of the sage and that of the ordinary good citizen than Plato and Aristotle had done. Happiness and fulfilment are to be found in calm detachment from the world with all its transient pleasures. Our desire for wordly pleasure will bring us nothing but disappointment and ruin. So we must face the world with *apatheia*. Our English translation, 'apathy', scarcely conveys the proper meaning of this Greek word. In the original sense of the word, the apathetic man is not lazy, but resolute; determined to show a 'stoical disregard' for all that happens around him. Morality is concerned with the pursuit of virtue independently of pleasure.

The *Epicureans* were contemporaneous with the Stoics. In some ways their philosophy seems to be in marked contrast with that of the Stoics, yet there are remarkable similarities. Epicurus taught that pleasure (*hedone*) is the only thing worth seeking. But hedonism takes various forms. It can be thought of in terms of vulgar sensualism. Indeed, the common use today of the word 'epicure' suggests someone who indulges overmuch in rich food. The Epicureans, however, believed that the pleasures of the mind are far more important and lasting than those of the body. They, therefore, eschewed those momentary pleasures which so often lead to frustration and misery, and placed their emphasis on the long-term pleasure which is derived from intellectual and aesthetic pursuits. It will be seen, then, that in terms of detachment from society, the philosophy of the Epicureans pointed in much the same direction as that of the Stoics.

It is a fascinating exercise to look back over the records of the thought and argument of the great Greek philosophers. Often the language and the thought-forms are so different from ours that their work seems stilted and unreal. Yet a little effort will reveal the fact that they were wrestling with great questions which still exercise the minds of thoughtful people. How are we to live, and how is society to be organized? What meanings are we to attach to moral terms, and what is the source of morality? What form should moral education take, and what should be its aim?

In seeking to answer these and other questions the Greeks were the architects of traditions of thought which have come down to us through the centuries. As we trace the history of moral ideas, and as we do our own thinking, we note how old theories recur and also how they are modified. Christians will find some of the master concepts of Greek moral philosophy acceptable and others not. We shall not quarrel, for example, with the proposition that the essence of virtue, of that which is right, is knowledge of what constitutes man's true end; nor with the assertion that it is in pursuit of that end that human life will find its most harmonious expression. But if it be asked why men so often do wrong instead of right, bringing great misery on themselves and society, our answer is different from that of the Greeks. They said that it is because of lack of knowledge, for with them it was axiomatic that to know the right is to do it. Christians recognize, however, that men frequently reject the right knowingly and wilfully.[1]

The Renaissance and after

The development of ethical thinking in the centuries following the Greek period was greatly influenced by Christianity. But since in this chapter we are concerned with the non-Christian ethics, we must now take note of the fact that in the period of history known as the Renaissance there occurred a tremendous shift of emphasis away from God and religion to man and the philosophy of humanism. In art and literature, and in the rapidly developing world of science, man began to throw off the shackles which religious authoritarianism had put upon his thinking. Theology, so often referred to as 'the queen of the sciences', was dethroned. The idea that physics, for example, could only properly be taught by Christians, came in the course of time to be regarded as ridiculous. Today there is little difference between the modern redbrick university and the ancient seats of learning which were religious foundations, so far as the place of the Christian religion is concerned. It is given its place, but afforded no special privileges or protection.

[1] cf. St Paul: 'The good which I want to do, I fail to do; but what I do is the wrong which is against my will' (Romans 7:19).

All this, of course, has come about over a long period, but as we look back we can see that no field of human thinking remained uninfluenced by this vast upheaval in the traditional ways of looking at life and the world. Ethical thinking was no exception. From the seventeenth century onward men sought to find a system of ethics which was independent of religion and which could command the agreement of reasonable men everywhere.

The first of the great names in the history of this independent line of ethical thinking in England is *Hobbes* (1588–1679). In his judgement the great aim of human life is the attainment of power. The greatest human desire is the desire to dominate. When an Anglican clergyman saw him give alms to a beggar outside St Paul's Cathedral, he asked Hobbes if he would have done this had not Christ commanded it. Hobbes replied that he gave the man the money merely because it gave him (the donor) pleasure. In fact, however, we are able to observe within ourselves both self-regarding motives and alongside them that unselfish concern for others which seeks their happiness even at the expense of our own.

The rational school, represented by *Locke* (1632–1704), *Wollaston* (1659–1724), and others held that moral ideas are capable of demonstration rather as are mathematical propositions. The key terms in moral discussion are 'good' and 'evil', the former being that which causes pleasure or diminishes pain, and the latter that which has the opposite effects. Locke's political philosophy is particularly important. It begins with the assertion that man's most important right is that of property. The authority of the State in passing laws to protect this natural right derives from a corporate transfer of power from the individuals who are the possessors of property. This raises the awkward question, 'By what authority does the State govern those who are without property?' Locke's not very satisfactory answer is that such persons have, by their very membership of society, given their tacit consent to the actions of the government. This, of course, is something which modern governments assume, and modern citizens accept, with varying degrees of readiness. We are all compelled to recognize that there are limits to the application of the principles of democracy.

The Cambridge Platonists, led by *Cudworth* (1617–1688) shared Locke's view that moral judgements resemble mathematical propositions. This group included *Henry More* (1614–1687), who set down a list of twenty-three ethical principles which he held to be self-evident to the mind. When one examines them, however, it is clear that what More called a definition is often a substantial value judgement.

The *Earl of Shaftesbury* (1671–1713) argued that it is not by the exercise of reason that ethical judgements are made, but by the exercise of an inner moral sense – 'an inward eye' – which is able to distinguish naturally between the admirable and the despicable. He gave a social connotation to his moral vocabulary by asserting that it is what is harmful to society that we instinctively feel to be wrong. Shaftesbury's ideas were attacked by *Mandeville* (1670–1733). He contended that in fact men are self-interested rather than altruistic, and that it is this very fact that promotes the public good because it stimulates economic enterprise and leads to prosperity.

One of the great names among the eighteenth-century moralists is that of a Scotsman, *David Hume* (1711–1776). He rejected the fundamental contention of the rationalist school of thinkers. Reason by itself cannot move us to action. What moves us to action is not this particular fact or that, but the likely consequences in terms of pleasure or pain which will flow from a given situation. Right and wrong are matters of feeling rather than reasoning, of the passions rather than the mind. Factual statements are one thing; moral judgements are another – there is no bridge between 'is' and 'ought'. Yet, in fact, Hume does himself cross that bridge when he argues that the reason why we obey rules which it would often be in our interest to break is that we are aware of how much we are harmed by the fact that others infringe them. In this argument the 'ought' of a moral rule is derived from the 'is' of certain allegedly factual observations.

Immanuel Kant (1724–1804) was remarkable in what he took for granted. He argued that experience does not consist in passive reception of impressions; it would be meaningless unless we applied to our perception those concepts and categories which enable us to understand it. He applies this idea to morals, and claims that morals are independent of nature. Moral consciousness is taken for granted. It is a fact to be examined.

Kant begins his discussion of morality with the assertion that the only completely good thing is a good will. The motive, or intention, of a man is more important than his action. And the only motive of a good will is to do its duty. Duty is conceived of as obedience to a law which is binding on all men of reason. The test of universality which Kant applied to moral imperatives is discussed a little later in this chapter. Kant's approach to morality is open to the grave criticism that in making moral judgements independent of the social order it is apt to encourage a conformist attitude which allows social evils to go unchallenged, and this can lead to disaster.

Jeremy Bentham (1748–1832) is representative of the utilitarians. His central affirmation is that the only consistent criterion to guide our actions is an assessment of their consequences, pleasurable or painful. He believed the theory that there are such things as 'natural rights', or that there is a 'natural law' to be erroneous. If the protagonists of this theory are asked to make a list of those 'natural rights', they will all set down different items; from which fact Bentham deduces that the whole notion is 'nonsense on stilts'.

What happens when there is a clash between the interests of the individual and those of society? On this point Bentham is not entirely consistent. He seems to recognize that public and private interest may not always coincide, but in his *Deontology* (papers published after his death) he identifies the greatest happiness of the individual with the pursuit of the greatest happiness of the greatest number.

Later still, the form of ethical thinking was greatly influenced by the Darwinian theory of evolution. Attempts were made to draw parallels between biological evolution and the evolution of morals. In the work of the German philosopher *Arthur Schopenhauer* (1788–1860) we find a pessimistic rejection of the hopeful outlook associated with the idea of evolutionary progress. Since the striving of man's will is against what is defective in his present condition, his is bound to be a life full of misery. The only way of escape from that misery is by repression of the will – even of the will to live.

Professor A. G. N. Flew has written an interesting monograph[1] in which he argues against the idea that Darwin's theory contains a law of moral progress. He shows that many of the philosophical deductions made from the theory are due to a misunderstanding of the way natural selection works. 'The survival of the fittest' carries no moral overtones. The fit who survive are those that have what it takes to survive in the circumstances of the moment. Thus, a miserable microbe may survive in the body of the saint who is unable to withstand its attack.

Three types of ethical theory

Even in so brief an account of ethical theories as has been attempted in this chapter, we have glimpsed a variety of ideas about the nature of right and wrong. In spite of many differences in detail, however, it is possible to distinguish three main types of theory. Firstly, there are those ethical theorists who think of the supreme moral standard as a law which teaches us what it is right for us to do. Secondly, there are those who think in terms of a good (usually described as pleasure or happiness) at which we are to aim; the rightness or wrongness of our actions being determined by reference to that good. Thirdly, and closely connected to this idea, there are those for whom the supreme standard is the perfect development of personality, or self-realization. We shall now look at each of these theories in turn, though it is important to recognize that they overlap in the various ethical systems which men have devised.

1) *Law:* According to the first of the three theories just mentioned, morality consists of obedience to a law. This is sometimes described as an ethic of duty. The rightness or wrongness of an action does not depend upon its consequences; the moral quality is inherent in the act itself.

[1] *Evolutionary Ethics*, Macmillan, 1968.

It may be worth pausing a moment before going further to notice that confusion often arises in ethical discussion from the varied meanings which attach to the term 'law'. Some simple distinctions may be made. We often speak of the law of the land. The reference here is to legislation, to the rules laid down by the governing authority. That authority says to its citizens, 'These are the laws of this country and you must obey them.' A citizen can, of course, break the law of the land. It may even be his duty to do so if he believes that it conflicts with some higher law. Further, the law of the land may itself be changed, in the light of changed conditions, or because the general attitude of society has shifted in regard to the subject of the legislation. Next there are the laws of nature. These are really codified observations of what is. There are, for example, the laws of expansion and contraction. If I heat a certain metal to a specified temperature it will always expand by the same amount. These are the laws which say not 'it must', but 'it does'.

In what way does a moral law differ from a state law, or a natural law? The answer is that it lays down not what must happen, in the sense referred to above, not what necessarily does happen, but what *ought* to happen.

As we have already seen, the conception of morality as a law was given its strongest and most cogent expression by Immanuel Kant. For him the moral imperative of duty has no reference to any end at which I may be aiming. The only good thing is a good will. A good will is one that acts in accordance with reason. But what does it mean to act in accordance with reason? One of the things Kant believed about reason was that it is universal. If we all followed reason correctly we should all come up with the same answer to any particular moral problem. What it boils down to, therefore, is this: I am obeying the moral law if I am acting in the way that I would will everyone else to act.

There is obvious value in this concept of universality. When a mother says to her wayward child, 'What would happen, do you suppose, if everyone did what you are doing?' she is making (she hopes) an incontestable point. In the more formal language of ethics she is saying: 'We must judge our actions from the point of view of a universal self, not from a private standpoint of our own,' and 'We must act in a way that is consistent with the idea of this higher self.'[1] But if we try to extract from this principle of universality positive guidance about what we ought to do in all circumstances, its inadequacy becomes apparent. The fact is that the conditions of life vary enormously between one person and another. Often what appear to be identical acts performed in identical circumstances are not so; there are hidden differences which we cannot discern which alter the moral evaluation of the situation. There is, therefore, a fundamental weakness in any system of morality which is based exclusively on absolute laws which must be universally applied.

2) *Intrinsic good:* The theory of intrinsic good as the arbiter of right and wrong is the next to be examined. Again it will help if we try to clear up a certain confusion which can arise from the ambiguity which attaches to the word 'good'. At the beginning of the last chapter we looked at the connexion between the word 'good' and the ends or results of an action, and it is worth returning to the point again.

Usually, when we refer to a thing as 'good' we mean that it is good as a means of securing some end or result. If I say, 'That is a very good pen you gave me,' I do not mean that the pen is good in itself; I mean that it is a good instrument for my purpose, which is to write. We say, 'Our John is earning a good wage.' We do not mean that the money in his pay-packet is good in itself. We mean that it is sufficient to enable him to buy his clothes, pay for his lodgings and food, and various other items, with perhaps a margin left over for savings. But if we examine all these things which John's money will buy, we shall see that they, too, are not good in themselves, but only as means to an end. His clothes will keep him warm and maybe enhance his appearance; his lodgings will give him shelter and other advantages; his food will sustain his life and health; and his savings will bring him security and the avoidance of financial anxiety.

Is there anything which can be described as good in itself, worth having not because it leads to anything else but because it is the end to which all else leads? Most people would probably say yes to that. The implications of that answer can be brought out in an imaginary dialogue between A and B.

[1] J. S. Mackenzie, *Manual of Ethics*, University Tutorial Press, 1929, p. 164.

A. Obviously there is one thing which is good in itself, and that is pleasure or happiness. This surely is what everyone really desires. Many parents, for example, may have reservations about the marriage upon which their son is entering, but they will say, 'Well, as long as they are happy, that's all that matters.' It seems to me that the hedonistic philosophy is essentially sound.

B. You say that pleasure or happiness is what everyone really desires, but is this true? A man will say to his nagging wife, 'You are never happy unless you are miserable.' It surely is a fact that people do seem to find desirable all kinds of things which are not in the least pleasurable.

A. What I meant by saying that only pleasure is good in itself is that this is the one thing which we *ought* to aim at. Surely it goes without saying that pain and misery are evil and that we should, therefore, do everything we can to eliminate them, and everything possible to increase human happiness. What else is life about?

B. What you have just said raises a number of questions in my mind. Assuming that pleasure is the one intrinsic good, do you mean yours or somebody else's?

A. I really mean both. There is an old song which says, 'I want to be happy, but I can't be happy, till I've made you happy too.' We must, therefore, aim at both. In practice they amount to the same thing.

B. On the contrary, I suggest that very often the two conflict. If I am to seek the happiness of others, I must often deny myself. There is a further difficulty. Even if I say that my own happiness is the one thing which is good in itself, do I mean my immediate happiness, or my long-term, or ultimate happiness? Very often I must sacrifice immediate pleasure in the interests of long-term happiness. (In the event, of course, I may prove to have been mistaken; it might have been better to seize the momentary pleasure while it was available.)

A. On one point at any rate I think I am clear. The kind of hedonism I believe in is not egoistic, but universalistic. In other words, I believe that I am acting rightly when I seek 'the greatest happiness of the greatest number'.

B. I do not see that this phrase can have any very exact meaning; certainly it is too imprecise to use as a measuring-rod to determine right and wrong. How can you decide between the respective values of giving great pleasure to a few people and a little pleasure to a great number? Surely, if pleasure is the one thing good in itself then you must choose the former, since the few people will know an intensity of pleasure which is a greater good than the sum of all the more anaemic pleasures of the larger number. Jeremy Bentham devised what is called the 'hedonistic calculus'. This was supposed to be a method of calculating the amount of pleasure (or pain) that would result from one's actions. He used such criteria as intensity, duration, and purity. But it really is impossible to measure the amount of pleasure as if it were like water in a jar. We ought perhaps to make a distinction between these two words, 'pleasure' and 'happiness'. A man's happiness is more than the sum of all his pleasures. A man's life may be described as happy if he has achieved something of real value, even though he has known little of pleasure himself, and been unable to bring much pleasure to others. If that is true, then we have to ask what that end is which goes even beyond pleasure.

3) *Self-realization:* Can we say that the highest good (*summum bonum*), in the light of which all else is to be judged, is the realization of our human potential? As it stands, the suggestion is quite unacceptable, for human beings are capable of a great many things, good, bad, and indifferent. They are capable, like Captain Oates, of heroic deeds of self-sacrifice (good); of counting the number of buses passing their door (indifferent); and of killing little children by dropping napalm (bad).

The proposition looks more reasonable if we speak not just in terms of self-realization, but in terms of realizing our true selves. Most of us at some time or other have done something of which we were ashamed, and when apologizing have said, 'I'm sorry, I was not my true self when I did that.'

The use of this phrase 'my true self' is interesting. It seems to imply a deep belief in some quality of life which intuitively I recognize as right, as consistent with my human status. This is something which is very real, but also elusive: my 'reach is greater than my grasp'. In the highest expression of it the concept of self-realization is seen as the quest for perfection, and, since we are social beings, for a perfection which embraces all mankind.

Modern philosophy

The discussion of morality, and of the history and meaning of the terms employed, continues, for it is a subject of perennial importance and inexhaustible interest. There are three types of philosophy which have been dominant in the Western world since the 1920s, each of which in its way has contributed to the idea that all moral judgements are subjective and relative. We conclude this brief survey with a note on each of them.

1) *Logical positivism:* This is the name given to a philosophic theory which was popular in the 1920s and 1930s. The central assertion of this theory is that the only real knowledge is that which comes to us through our senses. This means, to give a negative example, that if I say, 'God is good', the logical positivist will say, 'Nonsense, you cannot see God, touch, hear, smell, or taste Him, therefore you can have no knowledge of Him.'

What about statements of ethical judgement? Are not these, too, devoid of meaning? 'No, not entirely,' replies the logical positivist, 'they are in fact expressions of emotional feeling. When a man says, "This is right; that is wrong," he is merely saying, "This I like; that I dislike." It follows, since we are all different, that there is and can be no uniformity about moral judgements. One man's meat is another man's poison, but to say that morally speaking meat is good and poison bad is to do no more than express your own personal view.'

This philosophical outlook is now outmoded. It will not stand up to close examination. It is perfectly true that very often our assertions about right and wrong are very much affected by our aesthetic feelings and emotions. This, however, is a matter which wise people know they must watch very carefully. A person may recoil emotionally from the whole idea of artificial human insemination. This does not mean that the use of the technique is necessarily wrong. If the husband be the donor, and if the circumstances warrant its use, the method may bring the joy of full family life to the childless couple. We often do things we dislike because we believe them to be right, and may abstain from something we like because we judge it to be wrong. We are left with the question 'Why?' and the logical positivist has no satisfactory answer.

2) *Linguistic analysis:* The linguistic analysis school of philosophy has rendered us a great service in drawing attention to the importance of language. Philosophers of this school are concerned not so much with the ultimate meaning of life as with the meaning of the words we use when talking about life. It is a fascinating subject – too fascinating in fact. Few things are more off-putting than the man who is so interested in the way he is speaking that he really does not care what he is actually saying. But it is a very useful exercise to sit down quietly and examine some of the statements we make. When we do this it will often become clear that our moral judgements are not made in a vacuum; they are connected with other beliefs which may not have been consciously in our minds when we stated our conclusion.

The truth of this contention can be demonstrated by analysing almost any specific comment we are likely to make on any of the great social problems of the day. If I say that gambling is wrong, I may be challenged by someone who maintains that it is a very good thing. My opponent may argue that it provides a great deal of amusement for large numbers of people. I shall then reply that there is another side of the matter to be considered. I am not opposed to innocent amusement but, quite apart from the very harmful consequences of individual excess, there is the principle that wealth ought not to be distributed on the basis of chance and in response to the claims of avarice. Before the argument has gone much further we shall be talking about the kind of society we want, and what we believe to be the ultimate purpose of life.

The linguistic analyst has helped us to understand how we arrive at moral judgements. But his usefulness evaporates at the very moment when our need is greatest. If we ask him what view we should take of the ultimate purpose of life, or what sort of society we should desire as the goal of all our striving, he will say that this is entirely for us to decide. He may advise us to accept the general attitudes of the society to which we belong. Very often, of course, this is a sensible thing to do because, although we are apt sometimes to speak disparagingly of 'conventional morality', there is much that is good in the accepted conventions. It does not follow, however, that what society thinks is always right.

If we accepted that thesis we should have to discard any belief in the possibility of progress. And few would deny that in some moral matters society has progressed. In Britain we no longer tolerate the exploitation of child labour, and the iniquitous notion that prostitution is a necessary bastion of 'respectability' has now been disowned. The movements for reform were pioneered by those who refused to accept conventional morality of their day. But if I may not assume that the general moral sense of the community is always to be trusted, to what other criterion of judgement can I appeal?

3) *Existentialism:* The existentialist philosophers of the Continent, like Heidegger and Sartre, put an enormous emphasis on freedom. For them this is the one absolutely essential fact about human existence: man, if he will, can repudiate all the restrictions placed upon him by his past, his nature, and the conditions of his existence. It is true, of course, that the concept of morality makes no sense unless we can believe in the reality of freedom. A man cannot be said to be acting morally unless he is freely choosing between right and wrong. But the existential view is different: it is not that we are free to choose between right and wrong, but that we are free to decide what is to be right and what is to be wrong. Man creates his own values from moment to moment.

It is not possible within the short span of this chapter to make more than this passing reference to the existentialists. They do not all adopt the extreme views expounded by Sartre. Many Christian writers have acknowledged their debt to philosophical ideas of existentialism, notably Rudolf Bultmann. He apparently believes that Christian ethics are 'situational' in the extreme sense that a right action is always one made within the context of the moment, and without reference to any moral rules, or principles, or traditional insights. We shall be considering situation ethics more carefully in Chapter 6.

There is obvious value in the existentialist emphasis on freedom, for far too often we allow ourselves to be shackled by outmoded ideas and pressurized by social conventions. We do not exercise the freedom we have because we are afraid, and find it easier to conform. But there is always the danger that in rebelling against one extreme we fall into an opposite error. This surely is what the existentialists have done. Freedom is not the casting off of all restraints; that is licence, and can lead to anarchy. If the Christian existentialist says, 'Ah, but we rely of course on our own inner conscience or intuition,' we have to ask what is the origin of the 'I ought' of conscience, and why we sometimes have to confess that what we conscientiously believed to be right was wrong.[1]

Concluding comments

At the conclusion of this rapid survey of some of the points that have emerged from centuries of ethical discussion, it is not difficult to imagine the following conversation between the patient reader and the author.

P.R. I appreciate that the present chapter contains only a very limited selection of the main ethical theories which have been advanced to explain the concepts of right and wrong. I must confess, however, that I find it all very inconclusive. It is rather depressing to find so many conflicting views. If the trumpet gives so uncertain a sound, it really is not to be wondered at that there are so many moral problems in the world.

A. I should be sorry if you were depressed. I do not think there is any need to be. It would in my opinion be a very salutary thing if all Christians realized that the art of moral judgement is complex. There is nothing very Christian about the pretence that we know all the answers. The man who insists on seeing everything in plain black and white terms tends to be harsh and unsympathetic, and these qualities are certainly not among the Christian virtues.

P.R. Nevertheless, surely the purpose of ethical discussion is to clarify and not to confuse.

A. That is true enough, though, in fact, the realization that a question is not as simple as was supposed can be very confusing. Those who set out to look for the truth must expect to encounter a certain amount of confusion in their own minds. Nevertheless, I think you have overlooked the fact that while none of the theories advanced have proved on examination to be wholly satisfactory, most of them have contributed something to our understanding. Neither separately nor taken together do they

[1] For a very thorough treatment of the various types of ethical theory mentioned in this chapter see John Hospers, *Human Conduct*, Rupert Hart-Davis, 1963, p. 600.

answer all our questions. But to expect that we can solve all the problems posed by the existence of the moral sense in man is as absurd as believing that the answer to the question 'What is the universe?' can be written on the back of a postage stamp.

P.R. There are, however, two questions which seem to me to demand an answer without further delay, and they are: 'In view of this universal sense of right and wrong, would it be correct to say that morality is natural to man?' and 'Is there a specifically Christian ethic?'

A. These are the questions which will be examined in the two chapters which follow.

4 Is morality natural?

ONE OF OUR more colourful politicians is said to have evolved a technique for dealing with awkward questions at public meetings. 'A very good question, my friend,' he says. 'Next please!' I am sorely tempted to wish that we could emulate the politician and by-pass the question with which this chapter is concerned. Those acquainted with the literature on the subject will know the reason why. Even the most lucid of the exponents of ethics is capable of becoming opaque when he turns to the subject of natural law. Yet the very words 'natural law' occupy a massive place in the history of ethical thought. If, on the one hand, their meaning seems to be as intangible as sea mists, on the other hand it appears to be as deeply embedded in the soil of life as the roots of those ancient trees which have stood sentinel over centuries of history.

Popular acceptance of the idea of natural law

I have already referred more than once to the fact that a sense of right and wrong seems to be a characteristic of the whole human race. Often in our common speech we imply the belief that this sense is natural to man as man. If we read of some particularly brutal and motiveless murder, we say, 'the man must be insane'. By this we mean that he is not a normal human being; if he were, he would not have done this terrible deed. It is not so much that we are trying to excuse the murderer; we are rather seeking to explain him. In doing so we assume that human beings don't act as he has done: such horrible behaviour is inhuman.

When dealing with a less spectacular type of rogue, most people are prepared to believe 'there's some good in him somewhere'. The moral sense may have atrophied, but it has not been completely destroyed. I recall a godly preacher of an earlier generation who often brought his sermon to a ringing climax with the verse:

> *Down in the human heart,*
> *Crushed by the Tempter,*
> *Feelings lie buried that grace can restore.*
> *Touched by a loving hand,*
> *Wakened by kindness,*
> *Chords that were broken will vibrate once more.*

It is interesting to observe that often when governments or individual politicians do what is wrong, they seek to justify their policies in moral terms. What government (even Adolf Hitler's) ever launched a war with the slogan 'Join up and fight for the triumph of evil over good; do the wrong thing, and support your country'? In fact, both sides in the conflict appeal to the rightness of their cause.

Perhaps the most significant expression in modern times of this conviction that morality is natural to man is to be found in the Universal Declaration of Human Rights, adopted and proclaimed by the General Assembly of the United Nations on the 10th December, 1948. Article I of that Declaration reads:

All human beings are born free and equal in dignity and rights. They are endowed with reason and conscience and should act towards one another in a spirit of brotherhood.

Behind this admirable document lies the belief that there are certain inalienable rights which belong to men by reason of their human status. It is further assumed that this is a self-evident truth which is universally valid. Is this assumption justified? We shall be in a better position to answer that question when we have examined the concept of natural law.

What is meant by nature?

As I have said before, a great deal of confusion can be caused in ethical discussion by failure to define the terms being used. The word 'nature' can be used in a number of different ways. The natural man can be contrasted with the spiritual man, usually to the detriment of the former. Yet we sometimes say of a person, 'He is naturally good.' Since goodness is a spiritual quality, the contrast between the natural and the spiritual seems to have disappeared in that sentence. 'Natural' is the word sometimes used to indicate the opposite of reserved or sophisticated: 'Such a natural girl Fred has got engaged to.' Often, when we speak of nature, we are thinking of the wide open spaces, the cattle in the fields, and the simplicities (real or imagined) of rural life. Yet again we may speak of man's true nature, meaning that which makes him really human. It is in this sense that the word 'nature' is customarily used in ethical discussions. We noticed in the last chapter that Socrates, Plato, and Aristotle defined the nature of man and of what is right for him in terms of his true end or potential. The idea of natural law goes right back to these ancient Greek philosophers. They found some moral laws and customs which seemed to be universal, and these, they concluded, must be implanted in men by nature itself. They were, as we might say, 'of the nature of things'. The Stoics taught that all men partake in the divine reason. By exercising this divinely-implanted gift of reason men can discern the true ends of life, and can know what is right and wrong. We are doing right when we obey this natural law.

In a moment we shall have to ask what is the content of the natural law, for there are some who doubt whether in fact there are any moral precepts which are accepted by all people in all places. But it is interesting to observe that it was precisely that kind of dubiety about the existence of any sort of universally agreed concensus which first gave rise to the doctrine of natural law. As we noted earlier, it was when the Greeks began to travel abroad and push out the frontiers of their knowledge that moral scepticism began to grow. They discovered that there are many ways of looking at life, and that human behaviour patterns vary considerably from place to place. They became aware of what today we call 'pluralism' in human society. It is not difficult to understand how some came to the conclusion that morality is merely a matter of local opinion and prevailing custom. This view was refuted by those philosophers who pointed to the one universal fact which is more important than all the differences – the fact that man is reasonable by his very nature, and so reflects that universal reason which binds the universe together as a national whole. If there were no reason in man, he would have no sense of right and wrong.

When we were distinguishing between the various usages of the word 'law' (p. 35), we noticed that a law of nature, as commonly understood, is not the same as a moral law. The former is descriptive, the latter is prescriptive. One deals with the 'is' and the other with the 'ought'. Often, however, these two meanings are confused. This appears to have happened in the familiar presentation of the Roman Catholic case against contraception. The discussion between a Roman Catholic and a non-Roman Catholic could proceed as follows:

An example of confusion

R.C. The Roman Catholic condemnation of contraception rests squarely on the doctrine of natural law. Our position can be stated briefly and simply. We hold the traditional view that men, by the exercise of right reason applied to the facts of any matter, can discern what is right and wrong. If you apply your reason to a consideration of human sexuality, it is obvious that the purpose of our sexual organs is procreation. Anything, therefore, that interferes with procreation is against nature; and what is against nature is against the God who made nature; and what is against God is sin. Since contraceptives are designed precisely to thwart the procreative intention of nature, it follows that contraceptive intercourse is sinful.

N.R.C. There are several points in this argument which require closer scrutiny. Take your phrase 'anything, therefore, that interferes with procreation is against nature'. Surely there are many things that interfere with procreation – things over which men and women have no control. There are, for example, the infertile days of each month, the 'safe period' which nature itself imposes. There is also the onset of old age, and the disappearance of fertility.

47

R.C. But these factors are part of nature, and nature cannot contradict itself. When I spoke of interference with procreation, I meant deliberate interference, the introduction of artificial means of preventing nature from doing what is obviously its proper work. You would surely agree that sexual intercourse leads naturally to conception.

N.R.C. I certainly agree that it is a physical fact that sexual intercourse and conception are linked together in the chain of cause and effect. But I do not see that this fact in itself imposes any moral requirement upon us.

R.C. But you can't break the law of nature and get away with it.

N.R.C. We shall not get much further forward with this discussion unless we realize that the term 'natural law' can mean two things. So far you have been using it to mean the physical law of cause and effect. This is different from the moral law. It really is meaningless to talk about obeying the physical laws of nature. We cannot either obey or disobey, because they tell us not what we ought to do, but what in fact will happen. We use language rather loosely. When an apple falls from a tree to the ground we say that it is obeying the law of gravity. It would perhaps be better to say that it is demonstrating the law of gravity. It is not obeying in the sense that we obey an order from some higher authority. Obedience implies the ability to disobey. This an apple cannot do.

R.C. Now you are getting off the track. Apples are one thing; people are another. Men and women are capable both of obeying and disobeying, and I say they must obey the law of nature.

N.R.C. But if by obeying you mean that we must accept all that 'naturally' happens, we don't do anything of the sort, and it would be disastrous if we did. If I am invaded by certain germs, and take no steps to arrest the disease, the natural consequence is that I shall die. Every day we thwart physical nature in one direction by co-operating with it in another. We exercise our freedom of choice. I cannot alter the natural fact that if I stay out all night in winter wearing no clothes I shall perish, nor the natural fact that if I remain indoors where the temperature is higher I shall stay healthy. I can, however, choose between these two sets of natural conditions. One of the results of scientific advance is that our range of choice is widened. An example of this is the use of contraceptives. It has now become possible with a fair degree of efficiency to decide whether an act of sexual intercourse shall be (at least potentially) procreative, or whether it shall not.

R.C. But surely contraceptive intercourse is unnatural, or artificial, compared with normal intercourse.

N.R.C. Well, there you have used three words – unnatural, artificial, and normal – all of which need to be defined. I should certainly want to query the implied judgement that contraceptive intercourse is abnormal. But let us concentrate on this word 'unnatural'. If you take the word 'natural' as indicating that which belongs to the physical world, then most certainly contraceptive intercourse is natural. The techniques of contraception demonstrate the laws of nature just as clearly as does an act of sexual intercourse which leads to conception. When you said just now, 'You can't break the law of nature,' presumably you meant that we ought not to choose to let one set of physical laws operate rather than another.

R.C. Yes, that is what I meant.

N.R.C. In that case you have made a moral judgement which must be further considered. But I must point out that whether it is valid or not, it does not follow from your opening argument. That argument began with the assertion, 'Anything, therefore, that interferes with procreation is against nature'. I have pointed out that contraceptive intercourse is just as much a demonstration of the law of nature as any other physical happening. As you yourself said, 'nature cannot contradict itself'.

R.C. Your argument is only valid if the term natural law is taken to be synonymous with what scientists call the law of nature. I admit that these two terms are not always carefully distinguished, and the present discussion is useful in that it has brought out the difference between the two ways of understanding natural law. No doubt I contributed to the confusion which often surrounds the debate on contraception by failing to define my terms. Now that the point has been cleared up, however, I think my case still stands. I am saying that the use of contraceptives is sinful because it is against the moral law of God.

N.R.C. On what ground do you say that?

R.C. I will try to explain. I am aware that moral philosophers have made great play of the fact that you cannot move simply from *is* to *ought*, but surely in making moral judgements we have to

look at the facts as they are. What *is* constitutes the raw material
out of which our moral judgements are made.

N.R.C. That, I think, is entirely right thinking.

R.C. Very well then. Surely it is reasonable to say that since so
obviously sexual intercourse *is* for procreation, then we *ought*
not to prevent it doing its work.

N.R.C. But the vast majority of people who use contraceptives
do not entirely prevent intercourse from leading to conception.
(For the sake of this discussion we will confine our thinking to
married couples. I am aware that contraceptives, like most other
things, can be misused, and it will only confuse the issue if we
debate the use of contraceptives by the unmarried, or for the
purpose of preventing altogether the birth of children to healthy
married people.) Married couples who use contraceptives would
contend that they do so to enhance the marriage relationship,
and to plan their family in the most responsible way they can.

R.C. They are nevertheless frustrating the primary purpose of
sexual intercourse, and in so doing are altering the nature of the
act.

N.R.C. I should contest both these points. What is meant by
'primary purpose'? The fact is, surely, that sexual intercourse
does not have just one purpose. It has a unitive, or relational, or
spiritual function. The Church has recognized this. A marriage,
however solemnly contracted, is no marriage unless it is consum-
mated. By the physical act of union man and wife are made 'one
flesh'. Now this mysterious one-ness, to which sexual intercourse
so richly contributes, alone creates the proper environment for a
child. There is a sense, therefore, in which sexual intercourse
ought not to be allowed to do its procreative work until it has
done its relational work. Perhaps it is significant that the first
reference to human sexuality in the Bible[1] is about relationship;
there is as yet no reference to babies. Often, when Roman Catholics speak of 'the primary purpose of sexual intercourse', they
seem to mean 'the only one that is of any importance'. They thus
reflect the lop-sidedness of a Christian tradition that has emphasized the procreational at the expense of the relational aspect
of human sexuality.

R.C. I think I should point out that the Roman Church does
recognize the truth of what you have been saying by allowing

[1] Genesis 1:27.

the use of the 'safe period' during which intercourse is unlikely to lead to conception. But we do hold that the use of contraceptives distorts or destroys the nature of the act itself. Surely that is obvious.

N.R.C. I do not think it is obvious at all. On the contrary, I think it is an academic notion which is belied by the actual experience of countless married couples. I would sum up my position by saying that when a Christian talks in terms of the natural law he must embrace within this term God's purpose for him not just as a physical being (as if he were merely an animal), but as a human being – body, mind, and soul.

The definition of Natural Law

One of the best definitions of Natural Law is that worked out by Cicero (c. 55 B.C.):

> True law is right reason in agreement with Nature; it is of universal application, unchanging and everlasting; it summons to duty by its commands, and averts from wrongdoing by its prohibitions. And it does not lay its commands or prohibitions upon good men in vain, though neither have any effect on the wicked. It is a sin to try to alter this law, nor is it allowable to attempt to repeal any part of it, and it is impossible to abolish it entirely. We cannot be freed from its obligations by Senate or People, and we need not look outside ourselves for an expounder or interpreter of it. And there will not be different laws at Rome and at Athens, or different laws now and in the future, but one eternal and unchangeable law will be valid for all nations and for all times, and there will be one master and one ruler, that is, God over us all, for he is Author of this law, its promulgator and its enforcing judge.[1]

In the next chapter we shall be examining the question whether there is a specifically Christian ethic. For the moment we take note of the fact that St Paul subscribed to the idea of Natural Law in a most significant sentence: 'When Gentiles who do not possess the law, carry out its precepts by the light of nature, then, although they have no law, they are their own law, for they display

---

[1] *De Republica*, III, xxii, 33, as translated in D'Entreves, *Natural Law*, pp. 20–21.

the effect of the law inscribed on their own hearts.'[1] What the apostle is saying, in effect, is this: 'The Gentiles do not have the advantage of the Jewish law to guide them, but nevertheless they do have a real moral sense, and they can, by the use of their reason, know what is right and what is wrong.' (In the Hebrew understanding, the 'heart' is the seat of reason rather than of emotion, as our use of the word implies.)

For the first thousand years of Christian history there was little to encourage Christians to look for natural virtue in this fallen world. But with the coming of the Middle Ages a more optimistic view of the natural order emerged, and with this a new emphasis on the doctrine of Natural Law. The fullest and clearest expression of this doctrine, from the Christian point of view, is to be found in the *Summa Theologica* of Thomas Aquinas.

What is the content of this Natural Law? St Thomas asserts that there are two fundamental principles which are the basis of all morality and which are self-evident and incontrovertible. These are that the good is to be done and the evil avoided; and that the good is that which all things seek after. The second of these implies that there is a natural moral bent in man. From these basic principles the detailed precepts of morality can be deduced.

Objections to the doctrine of Natural Law

There are several objections to the idea of Natural Law. The first is the one often expressed by those who for the first time stumble on the statement of its basic content given by Aquinas. Having fought through all the verbiage surrounding the doctrine, it is disconcerting to discover at the centre a principle at once so obvious and so vague that it seems to be quite useless as the basis for responsible living. It appears to beg all the questions.

This, however, is not quite fair to the protagonists of Natural Law. The primary significance of the doctrine is the assurance it gives us that morality is meaningful, that it is worthwhile talking about right and wrong because these are real terms. If the foundation fact of Natural Law is accepted, then on that can be built the structure of a detailed system of ethics. But if there is no foundation, there can be no building. That foundation is the

[1] Romans 2:14, 15.

assertion that the ultimate reality is good. The more real a thing is the more it participates in the goodness of being. On the other hand, we surrender to evil when we turn away from reality. For St Thomas there is no distinction between 'is' and 'ought'; our moral obligations spring out of the fact of our existence; they are part of the natural order which God has created.

A second objection to the doctrine of Natural Law is that, when we move from the theoretical discussion of it to the facts of life as they are, it becomes evident that there is no universally accepted body of self-evident ethical truth. If one ranges far enough in history, or widely enough in geography, one is bound to be impressed by the almost endless variety of moral beliefs and customs.

There can be no doubt that a very great variety of ethical beliefs and practices has existed and still does exist. Nevertheless, beneath the apparent differences there are striking similarities, as Professor Ginsberg brought out in his interesting book *On the Diversity of Morals*. 'There are,' he says, 'no societies without rules of conduct backed by the general approval of the members. There are none which do not regard that which contributes to the needs and survival of the group as good, none which do not condemn conduct interfering with the common needs and threatening the stability of human relations.'[1] J. H. Jacques concludes his examination of this particular objection to Natural Law by saying, 'The concept of Natural Law cannot be invalidated by an appeal to the field work of students of comparative ethics. There is, in fact, reason to suppose that their discoveries will, in the end, strengthen the arguments in favour of the concept of Natural Law rather than serve to refute them.'[2]

A third objection to Natural Law is that in the working out of its detailed precepts too much reliance is placed on human reason. According to Jeremy Taylor, the eighteenth-century Anglican theologian, 'reason is a box of quicksilver'. Luther believed that the world was like an inn, with the devil as its landlord. Protestants have always emphasized the pervasiveness of sin and the extent to which it has corrupted man's reason and his will. It is only by God's grace that we can know what is right, and be given the strength to do it.

[1] Heinemann, 1956, p. 110.
[2] *The Right and the Wrong*, S.P.C.K., 1965, p. 81.

Thomas Aquinas grapples with this objection, and his answer, in brief, is that though man has been corrupted by sin he is not totally depraved. Man is still able to choose. What would be the point in Jesus saying to sinful men 'Come, follow me' if their capacity to choose had been totally destroyed? The very fact that we are often hypocritical reflects the truth that we are sinners, but also the truth that we are not wholly depraved, otherwise why would we want to appear good when we are not? Hypocrisy, as has been truly said, is the homage which vice pays to virtue.

The conclusion to which this discussion of Natural Law leads is perhaps best expressed in the words of F. R. Barry when he suggests that 'the permanent value of the concept is not so much in yielding a moral code as in its insistence that morality is natural to man, not imposed upon him either by the *fiat* of a capricious deity or by priests, tyrants, or other kinds of "establishment". '[1]

Conscience

The assertion of Natural Law that the detailed precepts of morality can be deduced from basic principles implies in man a capacity to make these deductions. That capacity is known as conscience, and was defined by Joseph Butler in the following terms:

There is a principle of reflection in men, by which they distinguish between, approve, and disapprove their own actions. We are plainly constituted such sort of creatures as to reflect upon our own nature. The mind can take a view of what passes within itself, its propensions, aversions, passions, affections, as respecting such objects and in such degrees; and of the several actions consequent thereupon. In this survey it approves of one, disapproves of another, and towards a third is affected in neither of these ways but is quite indifferent. This principle in man, by which he approves or disapproves his heart, temper, and actions, is conscience; for this is the strict sense of the word, though sometimes it is used so as to take in more.[2]

---

[1] *Christian Ethics and Secular Society*, Hodder and Stoughton, 1966, p. 46.
[2] 'Upon Human Nature', *Fifteen Sermons*, Bell, London, 1952, para. 8.

We are bound to ask what is the nature of conscience, this strange voice which speaks within the mind and soul of every man. Although conscience is often referred to as if it were authoritative, rather like the judge in his court, it is nearer the truth to liken conscience to the advocate pleading a case. There is, in fact, no appeal against the judge: what he says goes, and we have no choice but to obey. As we all know, however, we may disobey our conscience. Not only that, but conscience may err. Men have done dreadful things quite 'conscientiously', so, although we may describe conscience as the capacity which enables us to hear the voice of God, we dare not identify the two.

The authority of conscience is recognized by moral theologians. A man must always follow his conscience. This conviction has been reasserted in the debate following the publication of the papal encyclical on the Regulation of Birth. But along with this has gone the emphasis on the need for conscience to be educated. Just as a man's musical taste may be improved by increasing his knowledge of music, and by mixing with those whose taste is 'good', so his moral sensitivity may be increased in a similar way.

The Christian Church is, among other things, a school for the education of conscience. It provides a fellowship of people who are, by the very terms of their membership and profession, pledged to do right and avoid wrong. That fellowship, and the individual members of it, are shaped and informed by the Bible, and by the traditional teachings of the Church. But because the fellowship is a living thing, and not insensitive to the Holy Spirit, the interpretation of the Bible and the understanding of Church traditions are also subject to the laws of growth and adaptation. It is within this context that the individual conscience is trained, and men and women enabled to 'perceive and know what things they ought to do'.

Even so, especially in so complex an age as this, there will be many occasions when severe doubts remain as to what is right. There is very great need for more opportunities for the discussion in depth of some of the moral perplexities of our time. Insufficient use is made of the kind of documentation provided in these days by the expert committees of the Churches. There is no escape from the burdensome obligation of casuistry, which is the attempt to work out the detailed answers to moral problems. (Something is said in the next chapter about casuistry as traditionally practised.)

It is impossible to discuss the education of conscience without referring, however briefly, to the question of authority. The humble Christian will be deeply aware of the fact that God has spoken through the corporate judgement of the Church. The teaching of the Church, centred on the Bible, will have great authority. Manifestly, however, no one can believe that the majority is always right, and, indeed, the Church has sometimes benefited from rebels who refused to 'toe the party line'.

There is no neat and easy answer to the questions about the nature and source of the teaching authority of the Church, and about the circumstances in which a man may rightly set aside an article of teaching in favour of some contrary judgement dictated by his own conscience. On this latter point we look to the practice of casuistry to guide us. On the former point, it is important to recognize the difference between two types of authority. One is the authority imposed by the despot; the other is the authority exercised by the father. The response to these two very different kinds of authority is submission on the one hand, and willing obedience on the other. Although the Church has sometimes acted despotically, it hardly needs to be stressed that the only authority which it can rightly claim to derive from the Scriptures is that of a father (or mother). That authority proceeds from the fulfilment of God's promise to guide His people into all the truth, and rests upon the acceptance of the articles of teaching by the whole body of the faithful. The individual Christian will only set aside the *consensus fidelium*, the gathered wisdom of the Church, for the gravest of reasons, and in obedience to a conscience that will not permit him to do otherwise.

5 Christian ethics

Is JOHN BROWN a Christian? It sounds a straightforward question, but it may be a very difficult one to answer. Patient readers will forgive me if I allow an impatient reader to interrupt.

I.R. I do hope we are not going to invent difficulties. I was happy to note the title of this chapter and think that you have taken far too long to get to the heart of the matter. General ethical discussion is bound to be rather vague and inconclusive. But when we come to the consideration of Christian ethics, then we are on firm ground at last; we really know what we are talking about. Why not then get straight on with the task, instead of introducing a tedious discussion about whether some character called John Brown is a Christian?

A. I am not at all anxious to be devious; on the contrary. But I do believe that if we stay a moment with the question whether John Brown is a Christian, we shall see that there is an initial difficulty about the discussion of Christian ethics which not all Christians appreciate.

I.R. Very well then, may I suggest that if you want to know if John Brown is a Christian, the simplest way is to ask him.

A. That may not help very much. Supposing he says, 'Of course I am, I go to church every Sunday.'

I.R. Going to church does not necessarily make a man a Christian.

A. I agree with you. John Brown may be an unprincipled rascal in spite of his church-going. On the other hand, he may be a very good man: honest, kind, and widely-respected for his unselfish service to the community. But in spite of this he may answer our question by saying, 'No, I'm not a Christian: I've never felt good enough to belong to any Church.'

I.R. I quite agree that there are such people. But we must remember that it takes more than good works to make a man a Christian. I'm afraid I should have to say that John Brown is not a Christian, but he exemplifies a high standard of Christian behaviour. It could be that he is a Christian without knowing it. Our Lord seems to have suggested that this is possible in that striking picture of the Judgement Day.[1] Those who had never consciously confessed Him were surprised when they discovered that they were accepted as righteous: 'Lord, when was it that we saw you hungry and fed you, or thirsty and gave you drink, a stranger and took you home, or naked and clothed you? When did we see you ill or in prison, and come to visit you?'[2]

A. You have brought out a point of great significance. You say that there is a Christian standard of behaviour, but that it is not confined to confessing Christians. That is a fact which I want to examine more closely in this chapter. You also seem quite clear in your mind about the existence of a specifically Christian ethic.

I.R. Most certainly. Indeed, this seems to me to be the one unchanging element in Christianity. Understandably, Christian theology has undergone many changes. Theology is the thinking of men about God. That thinking is bound to be affected by the cultural patterns and changing thought forms of successive ages. Even the highest human thoughts about God can never be more than poor and partial approximations to the truth about Him. But ethics is a different matter: the ethical demands of the Christian faith have never varied.

A. I must say that this seems to me to be a statement which does not bear scrutiny in the light of the historical evidence. Moreover, it seems to imply a degree of unanimity among Christians which a quick survey of the present situation will show to be manifestly lacking. I'm afraid, therefore, that it is with these awkward facts that we must now try to deal.

Is there a specifically Christian ethic?

The two facts which have been underlined in the above dialogue are that the moral convictions of Christians are also shared by (at least some) non-Christians; and that Christians are not

[1] Matthew 25: 31–46.
[2] *ad loc.*, vv. 37–39.

always agreed on the answer to ethical questions. In view of this we are compelled to ask whether the phrase 'the Christian ethic' has any meaning. The initial problem of Christian ethics is to discover precisely what it means.

The fact that as Christians we often find non-Christians sharing our moral convictions should occasion us no surprise. Many Christians would probably be astonished to find that vast volumes have been written on the subject of ethics with little or no reference to our Lord. It is no part of the Christian claim that the followers of Jesus have a monopoly of goodness. Those who make such a claim demonstrate not only a lack of charity, but a paucity both of knowledge and faith. The Bible itself bears ample testimony to the fact that ethics did not begin with the birth of Jesus. The prologue of St John's Gospel is full of suggestiveness here. 'When all things began, the Word already was. The Word dwelt with God, and what God was, the Word was . . . All that came to be was alive with his life, and that life was the light of men . . . The real light which enlightens every man . . . He was in the world; but the world, though it owed its being to him, did not recognize him.'[1]

The fact that during the centuries before Christ there were many teachers whose ethical ideas compare favourably with those of Jesus is sometimes used to try to discredit Christianity. But Christians interpret the evidence as indicating the eternal presence of God in His world.

Similarly, Christians gladly acknowledge (or ought to acknowledge) that there is a great deal of moral sensitivity in the teachings of the non-Christian religions. Karl Barth was misguided when he stigmatized such acknowledgment as 'howling with the wolves'. It is a strange myopia which prevents Christians from recognizing the omnipresence of God in the world which, though it 'owes its being to him' does not 'recognize him'. Jesus more than once pointed to the good in men whom the religious people of His day regarded as beyond the pale. He made a Samaritan the hero of one of His best known stories. He said of a pagan centurion: 'I tell you this: nowhere, even in Israel, have I found such faith.'[2] Again, even the 'bad' men are 'good'. 'If you, then, bad as you are, know how to give your children what

[1] *ad loc.*, 1:1, 3, 9, 10.
[2] Matthew 8:13.

is good for them . . .'[1] We have the best of scriptural warrants for looking with appreciation on all that is good in other religions, and it is right that this attitude should be part of the missionary outlook of the modern Church. We are encouraged by our Lord Himself to look for 'the incognito Christ' whose spirit 'bloweth where it listeth'.

All of this is merely to acknowledge from the Christian point of view the validity of the contention of the previous chapter that morality is natural to man. But when we speak of Christian ethics do we not mean much more than is implied in the doctrine of natural law, which, whilst it gives us a good start, certainly does not provide adequate guidance for the detailed complexities of daily life?

Obviously the term 'Christian ethics' does mean much more than the application of the rule that the good is to be done and the evil avoided. Christianity is a way of life: it claims to control and direct the Christian over the whole area of his daily existence. But how can that be squared with the second of the two facts brought out in the dialogue at the beginning of this chapter: that Christians often disagree on ethical questions? Many a citizen must be confused by the fact that the Churches often present a divided judgement on matters of moment. Is there a Christian consensus on apartheid, the use of nuclear weapons, hanging, contraception, abortion, and divorce? However desirable we believe it to be that all the Churches should speak on subjects of this sort with a united voice, we have to admit that they do not. In view of this, can we still speak meaningfully of a Christian ethic? If we are to find a satisfactory answer to that question, we must give some attention to the origins and history of Christian morals. The obvious starting-point is the Bible.

The Bible as a source of Christian moral judgement

We have already criticized the view that the Bible is a kind of handy reference book, and that moral questions can be settled by quoting texts. Some texts, of course, can be very helpful, but only if we pay due regard to their context. Those who really care about the Bible and reverence its authority will be on guard against its uncritical use. If a man insists always on taking the

[1] Matthew 6:11.

Bible literally, he will make it impossible for many people to take it seriously. More than that, the moral implications of some parts of the Old Testament must be rejected precisely because they contradict what is taught in other parts of the Bible. No fair-minded person, however devout, can deny that the prophet Elisha comes very badly out of the story of the children who cried, 'Go up, thou bald head'.[1] It seems a trifling offence compared with the comments on latter-day preachers sometimes made by youths in the back pew. Yet we read that Elisha 'turned back and looked on them, and cursed them in the name of the Lord. And there came forth two she bears out of the wood, and tare forty and two children of them.' I contrast that with the reaction of a negro bishop with whom I went walking through a small town in Germany. Some little children ran up to him shouting 'Nigger!' He turned, and with an engaging charm free of any hint of resentment said, 'I have not been called that for years.' No one will doubt which of these two preachers reflected the demands of true morality.

The Old Testament only becomes theologically or ethically meaningful if we see in it the story of the development of religious and moral consciousness in the life of the Hebrew people. The tracing of that story is not easy. To begin with, the material is not arranged in chronological order. Furthermore, the ethical teaching is not presented in any systematic form: most of it is incidental and arises out of the ongoing everyday life of the people. The Jews were pragmatic rather than philosophic in their outlook. The manner and circumstances of their life changed as the primitive nomadic tribes of Israel settled in pastoral communities, and afterwards, under the monarchy, developed the urban mode of existence.

Even a casual reading of Hebrew history is bound to reveal the reverence with which the Jews regarded the *Torah*, or *Law* of God. The Decalogue is an attempt to systematize and preserve the more important of the divine instructions about what ought and ought not to be done.

The great prophets of Israel were responsible for an immeasurable enlargement of religious understanding. God is seen now not merely as a local deity, but as King of the whole earth, Sovereign Ruler of all nations. He is righteous, and demands

[1] 2 Kings 2:23, 24.

righteousness in His people. The ethical demands of prophetic religion often find expression in haunting words of great nobility, such as those of Micah: 'He hath shewed thee, O man, what is good; and what doth the Lord require of thee, but to do justly, and to love mercy, and to walk humbly with thy God?'[1]

It is in the highest reaches of prophetic insight that we meet the idea that righteousness does not and cannot consist merely in obedience to an external law. What a man does is important, but so also is the reason why he does it. Motive is an essential element in morality. This emphasis is found in the noble Book of Deuteronomy, in Jeremiah's prophecy, and most clearly of all in the teaching of Ezekiel: 'A new heart also will I give you, and a new spirit will I put within you: and I will take away the stony heart out of your flesh, and I will give you a heart of flesh. And I will put my Spirit within you, and cause you to walk in my statutes, and ye shall keep my judgements, and do them.'[2] Ezekiel looks forward to the creation of a redeemed society in which the demands of the moral law can really be met. The name of this new Jerusalem is *Jehovah Shama* – 'the Lord is there'.

Although, as we have observed, the Hebrews were a practical people, not given to deep philosophizing, we find, in the period following the great prophets, a class of writing called the Wisdom Literature. This represents at any rate the beginning of an attempt to provide a rational foundation for the intuitional ethics of the prophets. In Proverbs, Job, and in some of the Psalms, we find reflections about the place of man in the scheme of things, and the nature of the ultimate good or end of man.[3] The general ethical theory is that of hedonism: the reward of virtue is happiness: 'By humility and the fear of the Lord are riches, and honour, and life.'[4] Although this notion is shattered by the hard facts of life, as Job makes clear through the dramatic story of his own suffering, the general conviction of the Old Testament is that the sanctions of morality are the rewards and punishments dispensed by God.

The New Testament is rooted in the Old. Our Lord shared the reverence of the Hebrew people for the Law. He unhesitatingly asserted:

[1] 6:8.
[2] 36:26, 27.
[3] Job 38.
[4] Proverbs 22:4.

Do not suppose that I have come to abolish the Law and the prophets; I did not come to abolish, but to complete. I tell you this: so long as heaven and earth endure, not a letter, not a stroke, will disappear from the Law until all that must happen has happened. If any man therefore sets aside even the least of the Law's demands, and teaches others to do the same, he will have the lowest place in the kingdom of Heaven, whereas anyone who keeps the Law and teaches others so will stand high in the kingdom of Heaven. I tell you, unless you show your-selves far better men than the Pharisees and the doctors of the law, you can never enter the kingdom of Heaven.[1]

A little later, in Chapter 6, we shall be discussing the tension between law and love. For the moment it is worth noting carefully that in the passage just quoted Jesus gives no encouragement to those who desire in the interests of Christian freedom to throw all rules out of the window. But neither do His words support those who hold that morality consists in mere obedience to a set of rules. The whole of the Sermon on the Mount is a summary – doubtless collected by the Evangelist from many different utterances of our Lord – indicating the connexion between Old and New Testament morality. What our Lord does is to complete the process begun by the great prophets: He presses through to the heart of the matter. True morality is not mechanical con-formity with outward law, it is an inward assent to what is right, a keeping of the spirit of the law. So to the old rule against adultery is added, 'What I tell you is this: If a man looks on a woman with a lustful eye he has already committed adultery with her in his heart.'[2] Quite evidently, the keeping of the spirit is an even more demanding matter than keeping the letter of the law.

This ethical emphasis runs right through the New Testament, but it is not the heart of the gospel. The New Testament is certainly concerned with what men ought to do, but its primary concern is with what God has done – or rather is doing, for the gospel is a revelation in time of the timeless activity of the Al-mighty. And in Christ that activity is seen as the self-giving love of God reaching out to man, bringing him into a new relationship

[1] Matthew 5:17–20.
[2] Matthew 5:27, 28.

with his Maker and his fellows. 'When anyone is united to Christ, there is a new world; the old order has gone, and a new order has already begun.'[1] Christian ethics flows out of this inner experience of redemption and transformation. One test of the reality of that experience, therefore, and indeed the only test which the New Testament acknowledges, is the ethical test. Thus the questions put to those gathered before the judgement seat in the graphic 25th Chapter of St Matthew's gospel are searching ethical questions about personal behaviour and civic duty. (The distinction sometimes made between personal and social ethics is misleading: we are all persons in relationship.)

If, however, we look in the New Testament for a code of ethics, a system of rules which can be used to determine the right course of action in all circumstances, we shall look in vain. Indeed, anyone who looked at the New Testament with this in mind could be excused if he came to the conclusion that it is largely irrelevant so far as many of our modern problems are concerned. Many of those problems had not even been dreamed of when Christ was alive.

There is also the fact that the New Testament writers, and our Lord Himself, believed in the imminence of the *parousia* – the end of the world which would be heralded by the Second Coming of the Lord. Some have claimed that the New Testament is concerned only with an 'interim ethic', and therefore has nothing to say to an age like ours in which to most people the whole idea of a speedy and apocalyptic winding up of history is entirely alien.

A closer look at the New Testament will reveal the fact that the earnest, though mistaken, belief in the early return of our Lord adds a certain sharpness of edge to its moral teaching. Whilst here and there, as in the Pauline teaching on marriage, the apocalyptic expectation seems to have resulted in the abandonment of those longer-term considerations which must help to dictate a sound moral judgement, for the most part this is not so. It is, of course, true that Jesus and the apostles spoke to particular individuals at a particular time. But particularity is a theological rather than an ethical 'scandal'. If moral teaching is to be valid and helpful it must be specific, and this is what the teaching of the New Testament is in the sense just indicated.

[1] 2 Corinthians 5:17

The objection that moral teaching which is addressed to a first-century situation is invalid for the twentieth century can only be sustained by positing a view of morality as something static, and by denying the possibility that timely truths may sometimes possess the quality of timelessness. Both these positions are unacceptable on the understanding of morality which informs this book. The fact that the New Testament addresses itself often to strictly personal problems of behaviour, and to social situations very different from our own, does indeed pose problems for Christians. But those problems are an ineluctable part of the art of moral judgement. The problems are not insoluble. Those who dismiss the Bible as irrelevant so far as ethics is concerned cannot have realized its immense influence on the course of moral discussion, and on the actual lives of men and society. The biblical approach to the problems of individuals and small communities has implications for the life of individuals living in the larger and more complex societies of today. The working out of those implications is an important part of the whole task of 'doing' Christian ethics which is laid upon us as it was on our fathers before us.

The image of Jesus as primarily a great law-giver, one who was always making rules, is very far from the truth about Him as we meet it in the gospels. Indeed, He sometimes refused to settle a moral question, preferring to see His questioner work out the answer for himself. This is, in part, the significance of the parabolic method which Jesus used to make men think. When a lawyer wanted to know what constituted neighbourly action, Jesus told him the story of the Good Samaritan,[1] and said, in effect, 'Work it out from that.' Professor C. H. Dodd has done much to rescue the parables from the misunderstanding which has seen them as artfully contrived tales designed to press home a moral. He says, 'These rapid sketches are drawn with an unerring instinct for the essential points, and the detail that enters in is due purely to the Narrator's interest in the human scene and not at all, as commentators still stubbornly try to persuade us, to the exigencies of allegory. Indeed, if we read these stories without prejudice we shall be startled to see how far the attitude of the Narrator is from any narrowly moralizing tendency.'[2] What in fact Jesus was doing

[1] Luke 10:25–37.
[2] *The Authority of the Bible*, Nisbet, Revised Edition, 1938.

was to hold up various aspects of ordinary life. 'See,' He said in effect, 'this is what is happening in the world. It is God's world, and therefore if you look carefully you will see Him at work and know what He wants you to do.' We are far more likely to know where we stand if we have thus worked out the answer for ourselves than if we merely had a rule imposed upon us.

Much of the ethical guidance contained in the New Testament comes, of course, in the Pauline Epistles. In these, the great founder of the early missionary Churches sets forth the message of the gospel, but deals also with a variety of day-to-day issues. There is nothing strikingly original in this ethical teaching. Understandably, the little Christian communities surrounded by all the corruption of a pagan world were instructed in such matters as the eating of meat offered to idols, temperance, stewardship, sexual behaviour, and relationships within the family. Paul had sharply to rebuke the antinomian tendencies of those who thought they had become so 'spiritual' that their material actions did not matter at all. '"We are free to do anything," you say. Yes, but is everything good for us?'[1]

The really impressive thing about the ethical teaching of the early Church, however, is once again not its verbal content, but the sense of the freedom and newness of the experience out of which it comes. And that experience is the sense of the Spirit of Christ dwelling in the individual heart and in the life of the Christian fellowship. Because of this the old Commandments seem to have a new depth and richness. To love one's neighbour is seen not as a routine response to a written rule, but as an endless adventure in which, driven on by the Spirit of Christ, we explore and discover the manifold meanings of neighbourliness.

That process of exploration and discovery calls forth all the resources of sanctified intelligence with which God has endowed us. It requires that we read what the Bible has to say within the historic context in which the words were spoken and written, and then apply the insights and truths which emerge from that scrutiny to the very different world in which we live. It means a willingness to bring all our formulations of moral judgement to the touchstone of Christ, and this will often mean putting ourselves under the correction of the fellowship of the Church within which the Spirit of Christ is active to guide and inspire our thinking.

[1] 1 Corinthians 10:23.

Because the Christian life is a process of exploration, of discovery, it means that we are always reaching out after something better. The Christian ethic is not a system complete in itself; rather, it is creative and dynamic. This surely is the meaning of the words of Jesus, 'You must therefore be all Goodness, just as your heavenly Father is all Good.'[1] The scriptural holiness which was one of the great themes in the preaching of John Wesley is the search for that 'perfect love' which is seen alone in the heart of God. The somewhat sterile discussions about the extent to which Christians can attain to that perfection seem rather pointless. The supreme value of the doctrine is that it sets before us a limitless ideal. The corrective to any exaggerated claims by Christians in pursuit of holiness is the knowledge that love is a gift of God and not a human achievement, and the paradoxical experience referred to by Henry Twells:

> *And they who fain would serve Thee best*
> *Are conscious most of wrong within.*

The development of Christian ethics

In the rapid sketch of the development of ethical thought presented in Chapter 2 we omitted any description of the contribution of Christianity. Following the section dealing with ethics in the Bible, we may now appropriately refer briefly to the course of Christian ethical thinking in the centuries which followed the birth of the Church.

So far I have said nothing about asceticism in Christian thought and practice. In spite of suggestions to the contrary, Jesus was no ascetic. Swinburne's famous words:

> *Thou hast conquered, O pale Galilean,*
> *The world has grown grey with Thy breath*

are a travesty of the facts. The complaint of the religious zealots of His day was that Jesus was 'a glutton and a drinker, a friend of tax-gatherers and sinners!'[2] Nevertheless, there is an element of renunciation in the call of Christ: 'Jesus then said to His disciples, "If anyone wishes to be a follower of mine, he must leave self

---

[1] Matthew 5:48.
[2] Matthew 11:19.

behind; he must take up his cross and come with me".'[1] Jesus Himself was no stranger to fasting, and Paul speaks about 'buffeting' his body to keep it in subjection.

At the beginning of his admirable study of monasticism, H. B. Workman says: 'In every human heart, except, possibly, the utterly depraved, we find a yearning for self-surrender rising at times to a passion . . . This imperial note of our higher natures can never wholly be silenced by the lower, and finds expression in every form of religion.'[2]

It certainly found expression in the Christian Church, and particularly during a thousand years of its history, in the various forms of monasticism. Whilst there is much to admire in some of the manifestations of asceticism, there is also much to deplore. Although the Church affirmed that the Word became flesh, and underlined the positive Hebrew naturalism which finds such graphic expression in the Genesis story of creation, the belief that matter is evil had a profound effect on Christian thinking. It led to the notion that the path of redemption is the road of escape from the trammels of this evil world. Virginity came to be prized as the supreme Christian virtue. Modern readers recoil from the distasteful fanaticism of Tertullian, and of Jerome who praised his mother Paula because 'She mourned and fasted, she was squalid with dirt and her eyes were dim with weeping. For whole nights she would pray to the Lord for mercy, and often the rising of the sun found her still at her prayers.'[3]

When, under Constantine, Christianity became the official religion of the Roman Empire, the Church increased both in numbers and in worldliness. In reaction against this many Christians retreated from the world in the hope that by mortifying the flesh the fine flowers of the spirit would grow. In Egypt the chief influences were St Anthony (d. 356), and Pachomius (d. *circa* 345). Some of these spiritual athletes were gentle souls, but others were far from humble men, seeking to outdo others by the most excessive self-immolation. They lived on the top of stone pillars eating a few dried dates each day, or they built themselves shacks on mosquito-infested swamps, and endured the torture of perpetual insect bites.

---

[1] Matthew 16:24.
[2] *The Evolution of the Monastic Ideal*, Epworth, 1913, p. 3.
[3] Epistle *XLV*.

The development of monasticism in the East was greatly influenced by St Benedict who made the monasteries centres of Christian education and useful work; and similarly in the West by St Augustine. The thirteenth century saw the rise of the great mendicant orders of Dominicans, Franciscans, and Carmelites.

One of the consequences of monasticism was the development of a double standard of morality very similar to the old pagan distinction between 'philosophic' and 'civic' excellence. Thus we read of ordinary Christian virtue and monastic virtue. The list of seven deadly sins originated in the cloister. These are: Pride, Avarice, Anger, Gluttony, Unchastity, and in addition two (sometimes three) from the following (varying according to the source being quoted): Envy, Vain-glory, Gloominess, and Languid Indifference.

In the ethical teaching of Augustine (354–430 A.D.), the so-called 'theological virtues' of faith, hope, and love are regarded as the essential elements of Christian virtue. To these are added the old cardinal virtues of prudence, temperance, courage, and justice, which were regarded by the Stoics as the natural basis of the moral life. This distinction between two types of virtue is misleading, however, for it obscures the fact that, for the Christian, Harriet Auber's words are true:

> *And every virtue we possess,*
> *And every conquest won,*
> *And every thought of holiness,*
> *Are His alone.*

The perpetual danger confronting the architects of our moral traditions has been the tendency to relapse into the kind of dead legalism which was rejected both by Jesus and St Paul. During the seventh and eighth centuries we find that the use of 'penitential books' was spreading. These were lists of sins with their appropriate ecclesiastical punishments. Later on they dealt with cases of conscience, and so laid the basis for the system of casuistry which was fully developed in the fourteenth and fifteenth centuries. Casuistry is the application of Christian principles to particular cases. It attempts to find the Christian 'answer' in cases where the right way forward is in doubt, either because it is not clear how far a given law is binding on an individual in a certain set of circumstances, or because two laws appear to be in direct conflict. A classic example of the kind of problem with which the casuist is concerned is that of the pacifist. He is torn between the Christian obligation to eschew violence, and allegiance to his country which demands that he fight.

Moral theology has employed various technical terms to describe the answers which can be given to moral problems. One of these is tutiorism, or rigorism. This really means that we must never allow ourselves the benefit of the doubt, but in every circumstance must stick uncompromisingly to the law. But this is an approach which begs most of the questions and does, in fact, break down in practice. If it is taken seriously it is apt to lead to an over-scrupulous and judgemental attitude which is itself an offence against moral sensitivity. If, then, we must sometimes give ourselves the benefit of the doubt, in what circumstances is it right to do so? Four answers have been given to this question, each with a technical name. The term 'probabiliorism' describes the view that, having weighed the various arguments in the case, I must decide my course of action according to those which seem weightiest. This, however, is not particularly helpful if the real crux of my difficulty is that I can't decide which arguments are weightiest. 'Aequiprobabilism' is no better, for this says that when the chances are even, I may properly disregard the law and take the side of liberty. But what if I can't decide whether or not the chances *are* even? The position most widely accepted by moral theologians is 'probabilism'. It says that when in doubt I may follow an opinion which is certainly and substantially probable; that is, one which has been put forward by some reputable authority. I am not to be held guilty if I adopt such an opinion even though it is contradicted by some other competent authority. 'Laxism' is the view that I may disregard the law if any sort of case at all can be made out for liberty. This position is indefensible, and amounts to little more than saying 'please yourself'.

If we stop to analyse our own methods of decision-making we shall probably find that in terms of the above descriptions we are probabiliorists most of the time, and probabilists on occasion. Because probabilism may lead to laxity, more recent casuistry has devised the term 'compensationism' to describe the method which pays very close attention to the circumstances of a particular case, and says that the more serious the law in question, the stronger must be the opinion in favour of abandoning it, if the benefit of the doubt is to be allowed. It seems a sensible and sound addendum to the traditional understanding of the means whereby moral decisions are made.

The present state of opinion in the Churches about the basis of moral judgement affords unprecedented opportunities for conversation of a sympathetic kind between Christians of different traditions. In particular, the closer relations between Protestants and Roman Catholics provide many occasions for fruitful dialogue. Protestants should be able to learn much from the past history and present-day discussions of moral questions in the Roman Church. The methods of detailed analysis employed by Roman Catholics have much to commend them but, as the past shows, the pitfalls of legalism abound. There is no escape for any of us from the necessity of casuistry defined as 'the application of the principles of moral theology to individual cases'. We are more likely to avoid mistakes in the present if we are well-informed about the errors of the past.

The Reformers protested wholeheartedly against the notion of salvation by works which was implicit in the casuistry of the medieval Church. Casuistry itself came to have a bad name (the word still has an unfortunate sound). It led eventually to the whole business of purchasing merit, the sale of indulgences, and the other corrupt practices against which Martin Luther took his stand. Man is justified by faith alone through the grace of Christ. But in the matter of morality the Reformers made little essential change. The concept of Christian morality was still that of an absolute law, though the authority behind it was that of the Bible rather than of the Church.

During the seventeenth century, as we saw earlier, men turned their minds once again to the search for a philosophical basis for morality independent of religion.

Concluding comments

It needs little imagination to picture at this point the discontented reader looking over my shoulder and saying something like this:

D.R. I am bound to say that I find this chapter unsatisfactory and inconclusive.

A. Well, I am certainly dissatisfied with it myself. Quite apart from the fact that it might have been done much better, I have had to leave out a vast amount. But even if I had developed all the points more fully, and devoted much more space to historical description, I think you might still have found it inconclusive. What exactly do you mean by the word?

D.R. It seems to me that your whole treatment of the subject is vague and woolly. In these days people need clear answers to straight questions. But what you have done is to reveal a great deal of confusion. You have exposed the disagreements among Christians. You have virtually said that the Bible gives us no clear guidance. You asked the question whether there is such a thing as a Christian ethic, but you do not seem to have given a clear answer.

A. That certainly is a strong criticism, and I must make an equally blunt reply. We would surely agree that we have a fundamental duty as Christians to face the truth. This is what I have tried to do in this chapter. And I do not see how anyone can deny the truth that Christian ethics are complex. I hope we might also agree that a Christian must not deceive himself by supposing there are simple answers to difficult questions when, in fact, there aren't. I did not say, and I do not believe, that 'the Bible gives us no clear guidance'. On the contrary, I believe that it is 'a lamp unto my feet, and a light unto my path'.[1] But I believe that the light is often diffused, and that it must be focused on to the actualities of concrete situations through the burning-glass of intelligent scrutiny. In endeavouring to do this I shall be assisted by the traditions of the Church. I shall also value the work of moral philosophers who force us to look at the meaning of the words and phrases we use. I shall be encouraged by the knowledge that the moral sense which prompts me to search for answers is natural to man, and that there is common ground between me and many others over a whole range of ethical questions. I shall lean heavily on the help and support of the Christian fellowship. And above all, I shall rely on the continuing work of the Holy Spirit active within that fellowship. That constitutes a short summary of what I have been saying in this

[1] Psalm 119:105.

chapter, and if anyone asks me for a brief description of what I mean by Christian ethics, this is what I shall say. In a word, the unique thing about the Christian ethic is not its text but its context.

D.R. Are you really saying, then, that there is no such thing as the Christian answer to all the problems of the day, and that it is wrong to look for an agreed Christian solution?

A. Let me take those two points separately. On the first of them I would like to quote the measured judgement of Dr F. R. Barry:

> We must never claim to know all the answers. We can do much harm by giving the impression that there is some ready-made 'Christian answer'. All of us, Christians and Humanists alike, are in the same predicament together. We are all alike being carried along by forces which nobody yet fully understands, and none of the questions arising can be answered simply by quoting texts from the Bible or looking up the rules in the book of words. Christian faith in the Lordship of Christ does not imply that we know 'the Christian answer' to the complex ethical issues of our time. There is no ready-made Christian ethic which can just be 'applied' – as though it were paint or wall paper. Moral decisions have always to be made inside an actual, concrete situation – all ethics are 'situational' in that sense – and no authority, human or divine, could say just what Christians ought to do in circumstances that had not yet arisen.[1]

D.R. What about my second point: are we wrong to seek for a Christian consensus?

A. No, I do not think we are. We must remember, for our encouragement, that there are some matters on which Christians once disagreed upon which they now have reached agreement. Slavery is an important example. Moreover, on many questions of personal behaviour you will find Christians (and many non-Christians, too) acting in the same way because they are in no doubt about what is right. Christians agree that in most, if not all situations it is right to tell the truth, to care for their children, to respect their neighbours property, and so on. There is a recognized pattern of Christian behaviour, and when a Christian breaks out of that pattern, when, say, a vicar elopes with the

[1] F. R. Barry, *Christian Ethics and Secular Society*, Hodder and Stoughton, 1966, p. 31.

church warden's wife, he is the exception which proves the rule. But, of course, there are questions of both personal and social morality on which Christians disagree to a notable extent. On some of these matters – like the best approach to the population problem – concerted action is needed. It is, therefore, right to seek to extend the area of agreement, and it is not the least of the values of the ecumenical movement that it is enhancing the prospects of achieving this.

D.R. Do you think we shall ever reach complete agreement among Christians on all ethical questions?

A. It seems most unlikely. And I wonder whether in any case it is desirable to think in these terms. Is it not rather presumptuous to suppose that we could ever know all the answers? Ethics is concerned with the ultimate purpose of life. The more one probes and explores the subject, the more one realizes how much there is to learn. And that is a very humbling experience. Perhaps the best thing we can hope for is that we may know enough to know a little of how much we do not know.

D.R. Christian ethics, then, is not so much a set of conclusions as a continuing debate.

A. I think it is both. Some points are clear, others are not. A moral judgement which is valid in one generation, or which seems so, may not be in the next, either because the situation has radically altered, or because our understanding of the facts of the situation has been revised, or because our moral assessment of those facts has changed. So the debate must continue. There is no escape from that.

D.R. What is the state of the ethical debate today?

A. It is a very interesting one. It could be summed up in the phrase 'the new morality debate', and this is the subject of the next chapter.

6 The new morality debate

THERE ARE TWO false attitudes towards the subject of this chapter which call for immediate comment. One of these was expressed recently by a man at a meeting who, when I let fall the phrase 'the new morality debate', rose to say, 'There is no debate: all that was settled when our Lord Jesus Christ rose from the dead.'

It is extremely difficult to know how to reply to an intervention of this sort. My interrupter was, as Mark Twain would have put it, 'a good man in the worst sense of the word'. Like the old lady who, on being told there was a lion approaching from the rear, replied, 'Oh, thank you, please pass the cucumber sandwiches,' some Christians seem to be unaware of the ferment around them. Long acquaintance with the practices of traditional religion has provided a mental insulation which is quite deadly in its effectiveness. Nevertheless there is a debate, and Christians who care about the Christian faith, and believe in its relevance, can ill afford to be ignorant of what the argument is about.

The other attitude is amply illustrated by Sir Arnold Lunn and Mr Garth Lean in their little book *The New Morality*.[1] This is a knockabout piece in which we are told that Britain faces 'a moral Dunkirk'.[2] This is partly the responsibility of the New Moralists whose 'clotted confusion'[3] is described as the advocacy of 'a morality so diluted and ill-defined that the power of God is virtually unnecessary in order to keep it'.[4]

[1] Blandford Press, 1964.
[2] op cit., p. 151.
[3] ibid., p. 5.
[4] ibid., p. 96.

The chapter on 'Some South Bank Theologians' makes the familiar mistake of supposing that you can dispose of serious arguments by tying a label round the necks of those who seek to expound them. No sensible Christian believes in the infallibility of the Bishop of Woolwich, but it is a strange blindness which prevents his critics from recognizing that he has raised inescapable issues which are of fundamental importance both within the field of theology and of ethics. By all means let his writings be subjected to critical scrutiny, but to dismiss them merely as 'the offer of an emasculated Christianity'[1] is to betray a shallowness which is much more reprehensible than any errors of judgement or confusions of thought with which Dr Robinson may be charged.

The background to the debate

The fact is that we live in a world which is in revolt against authoritarianism and paternalism of every sort. People are less and less disposed to accept what somebody says merely because of the position he holds. Any attempt to reimpose the old establishment pattern in which the many do what the few command is bound to provoke the strongest reaction. Rebellion and protest are key words in any honest assessment of what is happening in our homes, in politics and industry, and in the Church. The cracks in the monolithic structure of even the Roman Church are now too wide to be ignored. We must resist the temptations already described, either to try to ignore the evidence, or to ridicule sincere attempts at Christian analysis of what is happening. It will be far more profitable to attempt to understand the reasons for the moral confusion of our time and to assess its significance.

One obvious reason for moral perplexity is the speed of scientific advance. This has affected the situation in a variety of ways. It has altered fundamentally our mode of thinking. Our educational system encourages an enquiring, sceptical attitude rather than the docile acceptance of opinions pressed on us 'from above'. Any attempt to impose traditional beliefs unsupported by intelligible arguments is apt to elicit the response, 'Who says so?'

Moreover, because of the speed and range of scientific and technological achievement, old situations are being transformed

[1] ibid., p. 98.

and new ones created. An obvious example of the transformation of an old situation is the population problem. If once it could be argued that it was a moral duty to have as many children as possible in order to people the earth, what is the shape of moral obligation in a world suddenly threatened by over-population? It is science, very largely, which has brought about that transformation. (And, incidentally, it is science which will provide us with the most effective means of coping with it.)

As for new situations, these confront us almost daily. The discovery of nuclear energy has given a new dimension to the debate about the rights and wrongs of warfare. Many who once knew where they stood are now uncertain, and some who were uncertain about their Christian obligation are now quite sure that there can be no moral defence of the use of nuclear weapons of mass destruction.

We have already noted how, parallel with the effects of science, developments in the field of philosophy have resulted in a critical attitude towards moral statements. Psychology, too, has had an unsettling influence. It has challenged the notion of personal, moral responsibility, as we shall see in the next chapter.

Many social factors have combined to undermine the sanctions of the old morality. A couple of generations ago a young man could grow up in a remote village and know little about the world outside. But today the television masts sprout from the roof-tops of the thatched cottages that remain, and through the window of the box in the corner come sights and sounds from the ends of the earth. Even the monks in a remote Scottish monastery, lacking either radio or newspaper, seem nevertheless to be invaded by the restless, questing, uncertain spirit of the age. As Malcolm Muggeridge said in a wry comment during a visit there, 'The Bishop of Woolwich seems to have got into the woodwork of the place.' And the young folk who live in what were the closed communities of the past are more mobile than ever before. Any attempt at giving them a sheltered upbringing is doomed to failure, and even if it succeeded, it would be a poor preparation for life in the kind of world we know today. Many young couples set up their homes in some place far removed from the kind of parental oversight that continued over a long period of years when the family was a closely-knit kinship group, and married children settled down under or near the family roof-tree. They discover that there are other philosophies of life than the one with which they were reared. They are forced to evolve their own patterns and values, and in the process, perhaps, to question some of the things they were brought up to believe.

Theology does not – or should not try to – exist in a cultural vacuum. It is inevitably affected by what goes on in the world about it. But it has also had to take account of developments within its own special field of study. There has been a new emphasis on incarnational theology, leading to the rejection of a false dualism which denigrates the material. The general trend of biblical scholarship during this century has been to discredit the idea of code-morality, and to challenge the view of Jesus as a moral legislator.

In view of all these factors, it is not surprising that there is a big debate going on about morality. But Christians enter into that debate ill-equipped to deal with the issues which it raises if they have already reached the depressing conclusion that things are bad and getting rapidly worse. Moral confusion is not necessarily to be equated with moral recession. Some Christians seem almost eager to believe the worst, and in some perverted fashion are positively disappointed if it can be shown that the situation is rather better than they had supposed. What, for example, is one to make of the minister who asked me to supply him over the telephone with the divorce statistics for the past twenty years because he intended 'to preach next Sunday on the moral decadence of the British people'? Half-way through the recital of the statistics, the divorce rate began to fall. 'Oh, what a pity,' he interjected, 'that will completely spoil my argument.' Facile optimism is indeed a sin, but even worse is the sort of pessimism which refuses to see that God is at work in His world. The number of resolutions passed by Church bodies deploring this and that is really quite deplorable. A moralistic and judgemental attitude towards our fellows will get us nowhere. Many of the sweeping generalizations about 'moral decay' proceed from ignorance rather than knowledge. Attempts at moral comparisons between one age and another are perilous, and the misuse of social statistics can very successfully stand the truth on its head.

If my experience of many discussions on this subject is anything to go by, it is only fair at this point to allow a protesting reader to enter the discussion for a brief exchange of views.

Are morals in decay?

P.R. I am all for taking a balanced view of things, and dealing responsibly with serious issues, but it does seem to me you are falling over backwards. Some of those who speak about moral decay may be superficial in their judgements, but you seem to be suggesting that there's nothing much wrong with the world.

A. I certainly do not hold that view. I believe the world is full of wickedness. The obscenity of war still brings misery to many. There is a great deal of dishonesty and meanness in the community. I am aware of the illegitimacy and crime statistics, and know that many people are promiscuous.

P.R. How then can you pretend that we are not witnessing a moral landslide?

A. I am not really much interested in trying to prove this one way or the other. In fact, I do not see how it can be proved. What I am sure about is that the popular attempts to do so are misguided and inconclusive. As I have suggested, social statistics are slippery things to handle. I tremble to think of the way they are often used by preachers and amateur moralists.

P.R. But surely facts are facts. You referred critically to a minister who wanted the divorce returns. But, although they have fluctuated, you would agree that the trend for some years past has been upward. Is this not plain evidence of the decay of morals?

A. I do not dispute the facts, of course. But I am concerned at the deductions. The incidence of divorce has been affected by a number of factors, such as changes in the law, the granting of legal aid, earlier marriages, and increased longevity. It is difficult to imagine that these factors in themselves reflect a downward trend in morals.

P.R. Why then is it that so many Christians are convinced that the world is getting more wicked?

A. I'm afraid that it has always been true that one of the dangers of religion is that it makes some people take a jaundiced view of life. I must point out, however, that there are many Christians who are not convinced that the world is getting more wicked. It may be that the view of some is distorted by the fact that, on the whole, it's the bad things that get the big headlines; and this is an age of high-pressure news and rapid communication. But if you have a mind to look for them, there are plenty of items to enter

79

on the credit side of the account. Was there ever a time when society was so opposed to cruelty to children? And though war and racism divide the world, there is a growing horror of both, so that it is even possible to cherish the hope that the conscience of mankind might reject them.

P.R. Is it possible that in some things we are getting worse, and in other things better?

A. It is certainly possible. My main concern, however, is to move away from this somewhat sterile attempt to sit in judgement on a whole generation. Understanding and sympathy seem to me to be much more important than generalized judgements and moralistic posturings. I am anxious to get on with the attempt to discover what the new morality debate is about.

The starting point

When we were discussing Christian ethics in the previous chapter, we saw that the heart of the matter was our loving response to the love of God. Jesus did not teach a new code of ethics; indeed, He accepted and reinforced the old Jewish law. But He transformed it by showing its inner meaning, and by giving to His followers, in relationship with Himself, a new power to live the good life.

It is evident, then, that law and love both have a place in the understanding of Christian ethics. But what is their place, and how are they related? Here is the nub of the problem.

The trouble with both these words 'law' and 'love' is that the protagonists in the new morality debate can easily take one or other of them as a horse might take the bit between its teeth. Those who believe that love is the key word stress that the essence of love is spontaneity, its freedom from fixed rules and all the crippling paraphanalia of unalterable codes. Even though the Bible says 'Thou shalt love the Lord Thy God', love cannot be commanded. We are not capable of loving to order. One of the characteristics of love is that it jumps over the fences men erect to restrict it or keep it out, and it will find a way through every kind of limitation.

A weighty case can be made out against a legalistic concept of morality. Rules can only be applied to the externals of human behaviour; they cannot take any account of motive. Inevitably they tend to be mainly negative. If, for example, we attempt to define chastity in terms of rules, we shall probably say that it means 'no intercourse outside marriage', and this indeed is how many people regard it. But that is a very poor definition. It tells us what we shouldn't do, but not what we should. It is very difficult to commend virtues which are set forth in merely negative or prohibitory terms. Moreover, if a man keeps the rule for the wrong reason, he cannot be held to be acting morally. Again, a legalistic approach to morals tends to produce a self-centred scrupulosity. The man with the rule book bulging out of his pocket can be a very unpleasant person, displaying the kind of judgemental attitude which is a positive incitement even to the righteous to kick over the traces. A preoccupation with rule-keeping can lead to a distorted sense of proportion. Pettifogging matters are treated with a solemnity they do not deserve. To all this must be added the fact to which we have referred more than once, that in many situations we are faced with unprecedented factors to which none of the old rules seem to apply. And for that matter, even long-established situations sometimes leave even the most articulate moralist wondering what he ought to say. It may be observed that in the long debate in the British Council of Churches on the *Sex and Morality* report, whilst one speaker after another stressed the clear and unquestionable nature of the Christian rule against premarital sexual intercourse, when a question was asked about the rules on petting, no one seemed to know what to say. One could almost have believed that no one had heard of the practice. Certainly it was very evident that the whole question of the kinds and degrees of physical expression of affection which are proper before marriage was not one on which churchmen found it easy to produce the rule-book.

If, however, those who see love as the key to the meaning of morality can make out a strong case against the legalists, those who see law as the essential foundation are also able to present a strong defence of their viewpoint. They would probably argue that much of what has just been said is a caricature of their position. Much of the talk about love is sloppy and unscriptural. If love is the headstrong, spontaneous quality which the anti-legalists suggest, then all the more reason why it should be controlled by obedience to law. Conformity with the rule of law is the essential foundation of all civilized living. This is a hard world: not all people are loving, and no one is loving all the time.

Morality, therefore, must be based on something more stable than love. It may be that some mature persons who have become very wise and morally sensitive can afford to sit lightly to the established rules of behaviour. But most people are not like that. The young especially need guidance. They expect to have the law laid down, and if older people don't do this, or leave them to work out the answers on their own, they are failing in the discharge of a vital responsibility. The 'permissive society' has already gone much too far in the direction of casting off rules and restraints. All of this is not to deny that love is the greatest of virtues, but love must be disciplined.

Those who argue thus turn to the Bible for support. They not only point to the constant emphasis of the New Testament. Jesus Himself said, 'Do not suppose that I have come to abolish the Law and the prophets; I did not come to abolish, but to complete. I tell you this: so long as heaven and earth endure, not a letter, not a stroke, will disappear from the Law until all that must happen has happened.'[1] St Paul writes about 'the law of Christ'. He says, 'Help one another to carry these heavy loads, and in this way you will fulfil the law of Christ.'[2] The Apostle, for all his talk about being free from the law, was himself always laying down the law, and who can deny that Jesus issued at least some rules for His followers?

Repeatedly we have observed the need for clear definition of the terms used in ethical discussion. So often the waters of discussion are muddied by the sediment of words and phrases loosely and variously construed. Frequently the truth will be found somewhere in between opposing statements which at first sight appear to be contradictory and irreconcilable. Is this the case in the argument we have just been examining? We shall now take a closer look at what several of the responsible participants in the new morality debate are saying to see if we can define the issues more clearly.

Situation ethics

One of the best-known exponents of the 'situation ethics' with which the new morality is associated is the American Professor, Dr Joseph Fletcher. In his book on the subject he says, 'The

[1] Matthew 5:17, 18.
[2] Galatians 6:2.

reader will find a method here, but no system. It is a method of "situational" or "contextual" decision-making, but system-building has no part in it.'[1] The purpose of that assertion is conveyed in an anecdote: 'A friend of mine arrived in St Louis just as a presidential campaign was ending, and the cab driver, not being above the battle, volunteered his testimony. "I and my father and grandfather before me, and their fathers, have always been straight-ticket Republicans." "Ah," said my friend, who is himself a Republican, "I take it that means you will vote for Senator So-and-So." "No," said the driver, "there are times when a man has to push his principles aside and do the right thing." That St Louis cabbie is this book's hero.'[2]

It is quite clear that Dr Fletcher is trying to steer a course between two extremes which have made their appearance again and again in the history of ethical thought. On the one hand there is the legalism to which we have already referred. The danger here is that rule is piled upon rule until in the end all the spontaneity which makes love powerful and attractive is choked. On the other hand there is antinomianism (the word means 'against law'). This has taken various forms including the libertinism which Paul had to rebuke when he found it among some of those newly converted to the faith: 'What then? Are we to sin, because we are not under law but under grace? Of course not.'[3]

Situationism is in between legalism and antinomianism. 'The situationist enters into every decision-making situation fully armed with the ethical maxims of his community and its heritage, and he treats them with respect as illuminators of his problems. Just the same he is prepared in any situation to compromise them or set them aside *in the situation* if love seems better served by doing so.'[4]

The question immediately arises: 'How can we know when it is right to set aside any particular rule? What is the final court of appeal? Are there no rules of absolute validity?' The situationist answer to this is that there are no absolutely invariable rules, but there is one law or principle which is absolute, and which can

[1] *Situation Ethics*, S.C.M. Press, 1966, p. 11.
[2] ibid., p. 13.
[3] Romans 6:15.
[4] *Situation Ethics*, p. 26.

never be denied by those who want to do the right, and that is the law or principle of love. Because love is indeed a 'swampy' word, and can mean all kinds of things to all sorts of people, the Greek word *agape* is used. *Agape* is Christian love as revealed and expounded in the New Testament.

The six propositions which Dr Fletcher describes as the fundamentals of Christian conscience can be summarized as follows:

1) Only one thing is intrinsically good, namely love.
2) The ultimate norm of Christian decisions is love.
3) Love and justice are the same, for justice is love distributed.
4) Love wills the neighbour's good, whether we like him or not.
5) Only the end justifies the means: nothing else.
6) Decisions ought to be made situationally, not prescriptively.

The key to the understanding of situation ethics is in the first of the above-mentioned propositions. It answers the question with which all ethical discussion must start, namely whether value is intrinsic or extrinsic. Nothing can of itself always be labelled either right or wrong, asserts the situationist, for right and wrong depend upon the situation. The only thing that is necessarily and invariably good is love, because love alone is good in itself. Conversely, the only thing that is necessarily and invariably evil is lack of love.

In a more recent book, Dr Fletcher sets forth succinctly what he regards as 'the four pillars of the method of Christian ethics': (1) a prayerful reliance on God's grace, (2) the law of love as the norm, (3) knowledge of the facts, of the empirical situation in all its variety and relativity, and (4) judgement – i.e. decision – which is responsibility in humility.[1]

These references to the work of Dr Fletcher, brief as they are, will perhaps be sufficient to indicate the general drift of his thinking. In this country popular attention was first directed to his work in Bishop Robinson's *Honest to God*, in the chapter entitled 'The New Morality'. (The phrase, incidentally, did not originate with Dr Robinson, but was used in 1956 in a document issued by the Supreme Sacred Congregation of the Holy Office in Rome.) Much of the critical reaction to the publication of

[1] *Moral Responsibility*, S.C.M. Press, 1967, p. 28.

Honest to God concentrated on the chapter on 'The New Morality'. Some of the criticism was wildly irresponsible, and indicated just how much pent-up frustration lurks behind many a respectable waistcoat. Some critics, however, were seriously disturbed by the assertion that nothing of itself can always be labelled wrong. They asked, 'What about rape, or cruelty to a child? Surely it can be said without any doubt that such things are always wrong? Pre-varication on simple matters of this kind can only spread confusion and undermine all respect for morality.'

The situationist would admit straight away that no responsible Christian would want for one moment to defend rape or cruelty, or to pretend that such gross behaviour could ever be right. What the situationist seeks to emphasize is the reason for the wrongness of such actions. They are wrong in all circumstances for the same reason that other things are wrong in some circumstances – namely, that they are the denial of love. It is inconceivable that rape could ever be the expression of love. There are, then, some unbreakable rules. A lie, however, whilst wrong in most cases, could be right on occasion just because it is the expression of love.

At the end of *Moral Responsibility*, Dr Fletcher invites his readers to test whether they are situationists or not:

Let me close with a little embroidery on the story of Solomon and the two harlots who claimed the same baby (1 Kings 3:16–28). He ordered the child cut in half, divided between them, and just as the soldier's sword was about to descend one woman (the true mother) cried, 'No, let the child be given to my antagonist!' That was loving concern of a sacrificial order. But now, let us suppose that Solomon had insisted that since each women *claimed* to be the mother each should have at least part of the child. This poses another issue than sacrificial love, as in the story. It raises the issue of the claim of a moral principle, about truth telling. And suppose that she then said, telling an outright lie: 'Oh, no. I confess that I have falsely testified. The child is really hers, not mine.' Would she be doing *right*? Do you, gentle reader, want to know whether you are or are not really a situationist? Do you want to know whether your sense of responsibility is agapeic or forensic? Then answer: Would she have done right?[1]

[1] ibid., pp. 240, 241.

Morality old and new

In *Christian Morals Today*[1] the Bishop of Woolwich attempts with great skill to reconcile the old and new concepts of morality by suggesting that they 'correspond with two starting-points, two approaches to certain perennial polarities in Christian ethics, which are not antithetical but complementary.'[2] These he expounds under the three headings: 'Fixity and Freedom', 'Law and Love', 'Authority and Experience'. This thesis is critically examined by Paul Ramsey in *Deeds and Rules in Christian Ethics*.[3] He asserts that the argument is based on a fallacy because, in fact, it is not true that the antinomy of Law and Love can be identified with the other antinomies of Fixity and Freedom, and Authority and Experience. The conclusion that love in its freedom cannot ever bind itself in unalterable rules is dictated by the form in which the argument is presented. That form tends to exclude from the start any possibility that love can be expressed in unalterable rules. Ramsey adopts, for the purposes of his own treatment, the rather ugly terminology of Professor William K. Frankena. There are, according to this, two views of how Christian love best exhibits itself in practice. These are described as *act-agapism* and *rule-agapism*. The former holds that we are never to appeal to rules. We enter into every situation, and ask what is the best response that love can make to it. The latter does not ask what *act* most fully expresses love, but which *rules of action* are most love-embodying.

Using this terminology, Ramsey accuses Robinson of ambivalence between the two views. The Bishop's general outlook is that of act-agapism, but now and then he opens the door to rule-agapism, as when he says: 'I would, of course, be the first to agree that there are a whole class of actions – like stealing, lying, committing adultery – which are so fundamentally destructive of human relationships that no differences of century or society can change their character.'[4]

That sounds very much as if there are indeed at least some unbreakable rules which always embody love, and never vary. Yet Robinson proceeds, 'But this does not, of course, mean that

[1] S.C.M. Press, 1964.
[2] op. cit., p. 10.
[3] Oliver and Boyd, 1965.
[4] *Christian Morals Today*, p. 16.

86

stealing or lying can in certain circumstances never be right.'[1]
In denying that Christians can allow that lying or stealing can
ever be right, Ramsey argues that what in fact Christians have
done is to clarify the meaning of the words 'lying' and 'stealing':

> The work of Christian ethics in clarifying the categories –
> truth-telling, promise-keeping, theft, lying, murder – is not
> ordinarily a matter of love allowing an exception to a fixed
> definition of these terms but a matter of love illuminating the
> meaning of them. What looks like a right to deviate from the
> rule is really love's duty to do so because of the love-full
> meaning of the 'natural justice' summarized in these classes of
> actions or because of an expansion or deepening of the meaning
> of these rules of conduct. This is the way love sensitizes and
> instructs conscience.[2]

What the author is doing in the passage just quoted is to ask us
to re-examine our concepts, the meaning of the terms we use.
Later in the same book he examines the ethical teaching of Paul
Lehmann and criticizes him strongly for the way he discusses
truth-telling as 'optimum verbal veracity'.[3] No one who has
thought deeply about the matter would regard this as a satisfactory definition of truth-telling, Ramsey argues. Obviously,
telling the truth is often a very complex matter, as we noticed
during the dialogue on pp. 12–14. One has to ask what is the
nature of the truth demanded by the particular occasion. 'To
tell the truth requires, it would seem, both a certain correspondence and integrity between thought and speech and a co-
respondence and integrity between the speaker and other
persons.'[4]

I have endeavoured by quoting from several of the protagonists
in the new morality debate to indicate the nature of the discussion
and the main issues which are being considered. The reader may
feel at the end of the exercise that there is much of value to be
gained by cool and dispassionate study of those issues. Certainly
any fair examination of the arguments is bound to lead to the

[1] ibid., p. 16.
[2] op. cit., p. 30.
[3] ibid., p. 68.
[4] ibid., p. 70,

conclusion that there is no excuse for the abusive criticisms that Christians sometimes hurl at one another because they have not really understood what is being said.

On the vexed question whether there are any invariable rules, the differences between the protagonists seem to approach vanishing point. One speaks about the occasional theft as being a justified exception, and the other says that to take someone else's property may be right if the structure of society is such that the owner's possession of it is unjust. In other words, when Robin Hood took a purse of gold from a rich man and distributed it among the poor, he was not really stealing at all (which is why even Church deacons applaud his exploits with a good conscience). He was only doing what Her Majesty's Tax Collector does today: he soaks the rich to provide public assistance and other amenities for the poor.

A valuable point is being driven home both by those who say there are justified exceptions to the rules and by those who say that on closer examination the exceptions are really not exceptions at all – and even by those pure act-agapists who find no place for rules. They are all directing our attention to the inwardness of morals. This is what Jesus did. He set His face against the ever-present danger of the kind of morality that hardens into a harsh inflexibility which is the denial of the love it ought to express. The road which runs between Pharisaism and libertinism is a razor's edge: the straight and narrow way which Jesus called us to tread.

At its best, the new morality debate challenges us to participate in the endless search after a greater moral sensitivity. The attempt to clarify our concepts, the striving for a more precise use of language, are parts of an essential discipline. The debate must go on. Christians must not be afraid of the clash of conflicting views. The time to worry is when everybody agrees, or when the whole subject seems to have been tied up neatly with no question left to ask. For ethics, like theology, deals with eternal verities set in the midst of changing times. Stagnation means death. Too much certainty is not good for us: it robs us of the humility which is proper to our lowly station and our fallible minds. The man who sees everything in black and white is morally colour blind.

Let the final word on this subject be supplied by Professor T. W. Manson:

If the Christian ethic is anything at all it is a living, growing thing. 'Love as I have loved you' is not to be construed solely in the past; if there is anything in the Christian religion 'I have loved you' is true of the past, the present, and the future. 'I *have* loved,' in the perfect tense, means that it is a past thing which continues into the present until the end of time. Further, just as the power and inspiration of the Christian ethic is represented in a living person and a living body, so the achievement of Christian ethics is always something new and original. Christian ethics is certainly not a slavish obedience to rules and regulations. It is active living, and therefore it has the power to go to the heart of every ethical situation as it arises. It has the power to see what response is called for in terms of feeling, word and act, and the power to make that response, and make it creatively and effectively. In short, Christian ethics is a work of art.[1]

---

[1] *Ethics and the Gospel*, S.C.M. Press, 1960, pp. 102–103.

7 Morality and the law

IN THIS CHAPTER I shall be using the word 'law' as shorthand for 'the law of the land', and the issue I want to discuss can be introduced by contrasting two personal experiences.

I recall attending a conference at which representatives from Eastern and Western Europe met together. In the group to which I was allocated there was a leading Christian from one of the countries of Eastern Europe. I asked him if he felt able to give us some account of the conditions under which he had to work, and in particular what sort of limitations the State imposed upon that work. A shadow passed over his face, and after prolonged hesitation he said, 'I will say nothing till every notebook is closed and every pen is in the pocket.' He then told us haltingly of the restrictions placed upon freedom of speech and movement in his country. He had not known until two days before our conference was due to begin whether he would be allowed to attend. Those of us from the West listened in sympathetic silence, fretting inwardly at the thought of such intolerable interference with personal liberty.

Motoring through Birmingham one day, I wanted to telephone my wife in London. I stopped at six kiosks before I found one instrument which would work. All the others had been wrecked by vandals. I felt a very strong desire to interfere quite drastically with the personal liberty of the hooligans who had caused such intolerable inconvenience.

The two incidents raise a number of important questions. What is the proper balance between law and liberty? What constitutes the authority which lies behind the law? Is the law co-extensive with morality and, if not, what is the relationship between them? To what extent should the law seek to enforce morality?

These questions admit of no brief and simple answers. Few would quarrel with the assertion that you cannot enforce morality, in that a moral action must be the voluntary response of a free person. It is not mere conformity with a rule; it is action which flows from right motive. Nevertheless, there is, and must be, a close connexion between law and morality. The theory known as legal positivism denies this connexion and posits the view that the law is merely what the State determines. According to this account, the State does not serve the ends of justice. It does, in fact, create justice. This, of course, is a disastrous theory. It is the philosophy underlying the police state. It robs the term 'human rights' of any meaning. The common man has no right of appeal against what the State lays down: he is not to reason why, for the legal is what can be enforced, and what can be enforced is right.

It does not follow, however, that morality and law are co-terminous. A large number of our laws reflect the general moral sense of the community. The laws relating to road safety, for example, indicate our general concern for the welfare of those who use the roads. It might be right for me to break the letter of the law by driving above the speed limit, as I once did, to save the life of a sick woman who had to be got to hospital within minutes, but that is an exceptional case. But if we look back over history it is quite evident that many laws have been indisputably bad. The law of England once permitted the hanging of a thief for stealing a sheep. Some of the ancient, though as yet unrescinded, laws on Sunday observance are absurd, and reflect neither morality nor common-sense.

A further point to notice is that while the law punishes some forms of immoral behaviour, it takes no notice of others. Thus incest is a crime, but fornication and adultery are not. Solicitation for purposes of prostitution is an offence punishable at law, though prostitution itself is not. Obviously there is a line which separates one kind of offence from another, but that line is not clearly drawn between private and public actions. Moreover, the line is not always drawn in the same place and, in fact, in recent times several acts which were criminal offences have ceased to be so. Suicide has been removed from the orbit of the criminal law, and so have private homosexual acts between consenting adults.

The last-mentioned amendment of the law came about in response to the recommendations of the Report of the Committee on Homosexual Offences and Prostitution (The Wolfenden Report).[1] This Report was a social document of considerable importance. Before proceeding to an examination of the matters on which it was required to make recommendations, it explored the question of the scope and function of the criminal law in respect of those matters. What it said was set forth with admirable clarity, and has a relevance beyond the immediate concern of the Committee with sexual offences. The basic propositions propounded by Sir John Wolfenden and his colleagues have stimulated some very useful discussion of the issues with which this chapter is concerned. It will, therefore, be helpful to examine what the Report has to say, and then to look at the views of several distinguished writers who have more recently contributed to the debate.

The Wolfenden Report

In the second chapter of the Report, Sir John Wolfenden and his Committee discuss what are the essential elements of a criminal offence:

> There appears to be no unquestioned definition of what constitutes or ought to constitute a crime. To define it as 'an act which is punished by the State' does not answer the question: What acts ought to be punished by the State? We have therefore worked with our own formulation of the function of the criminal law so far as it concerns the subjects of this enquiry. In this field, its function, as we see it, is to preserve public order and decency, to protect the citizen from what is offensive or injurious, and to provide sufficient safeguards against exploitation and corruption of others, particularly those who are specially vulnerable because they are young, weak in body or mind, inexperienced, or in a state of special physical, official or economic dependence.[2]

[1] H.M.S.O. 1957, Cmnd. 247.
[2] op. cit., pp. 9–10.

The limitations of the law are also important:

> It is not, in our view, the function of the law to intervene in the private lives of citizens, or to seek to enforce any particular pattern of behaviour, further than is necessary to carry out the purposes we have outlined. It follows that we do not believe it to be a function of the law to attempt to cover all the fields of sexual behaviour. Certain forms of sexual behaviour are regarded by many as sinful, morally wrong, or objectionable for reasons of conscience, or of religious or cultural tradition; and such actions may be reprobated on these grounds. But the criminal law does not cover all such actions at the present time; for instance, adultery and fornication are not offences for which a person can be punished by the criminal law. Nor indeed is prostitution as such.[1]

The point expounded in this paragraph is underlined later in the Report where the arguments against a change in the law are being countered:

> There remains one additional counter-argument which we believe to be decisive, namely, the importance which society and the law ought to give to individual freedom of choice and action in matters of private morality. Unless a deliberate attempt is to be made by society, acting through the agency of the law, to equate the sphere of crime with that of sin, there must remain a realm of private morality and immorality which is, in brief and crude terms, not the law's business. To say this is not to condone or encourage private immorality. On the contrary, to emphasize the personal and private nature of moral or immoral conduct is to emphasize the personal and private responsibility of the individual for his own actions and that is a responsibility which a mature agent can properly be expected to carry for himself without the threat of punishment from the law.[2]

The Wolfenden proposition examined

The basic position of the Wolfenden Committee as described above is subjected to critical examination by Lord Devlin in an

[1] ibid., p. 10.
[2] ibid., p. 24.

essay entitled *The Enforcement of Morals*.[1] He notes the point to which I have already drawn attention that the law does not in all cases confine its attention to questions of public order and decency. It does claim jurisdiction over acts done in private, such as euthanasia and abortion. This, he claims, it has every right to do, because a recognized morality is the absolutely essential cement of society without which it would disintegrate. 'If society has a right to make a judgement, and has it on the basis that a recognized morality is as necessary to society as, say, a recognized government, then society may use the law to preserve morality in the same way as it uses it to safeguard anything else that is essential to its existence.'[2] The point is stated unequivocally in a sentence which has been widely quoted: 'The suppression of vice is as much the law's business as the suppression of subversive activities; it is no more possible to define a sphere of private morality than it is to define one of private subversive activity.'[3]

How do we ascertain what is the recognized moral judgement of society, which, on this view, it is the law's business to enforce? The answer which Lord Devlin gives is that we use the standard of the ordinary reasonable citizen – the 'man on the Clapham omnibus' who may, in fact, be called to serve on a jury and thus play a distinct part in the dispensing of justice. Lord Devlin lays down four general principles which should determine where the line is drawn by the law in safeguarding the rights and interests of society on the one hand and those of the individual on the other. These are:

1) Nothing should be punished by the law that does not lie beyond the limits of tolerance.
2) The limits of tolerance shift, and this fact must be taken into account.
3) As far as possible, privacy should be respected.
4) The law is concerned with a minimum standard of behaviour and therefore does not represent the full standards of behaviour which any society sets for its members.

[1] Oxford University Press, 1959.
[2] op. cit., p. 11.
[3] ibid., p. 14.

94

The judgement on which these principles are founded is that the criminal law exists for the protection of society and not – as the Wolfenden Committee argues – for the protection of the individual.

A further contribution to the discussion is made by Professor H. L. A. Hart in *Law, Liberty and Morality*.[1] He begins by noting that the principles enunciated by the Wolfenden Committee are much the same as those of J. S. Mill who in his famous *Essay on Liberty* said, 'The only purpose for which power can rightly be exercised over any member of a civilized community against his will is to prevent harm to others. His own good either physical or moral is not a sufficient warrant. He cannot rightfully be compelled to do or forbear because it will be better for him to do so, because it will make him happier, because in the opinion of others to do so would be wise or even right.'[2]

Professor Hart takes his stand with Mill. He admits that English law does in some instances seek to enforce morality and would seek in those cases to reform the law. But he argues that some of the examples of this quoted by supporters of the legal enforcement of morals are not real examples; they are subject to a different explanation. He takes Lord Devlin to task for interpreting the fact that the criminal law does not usually admit the consent of the victim as a defence to mean that there are certain moral standards which society requires to be observed. Hart asserts that the rules excluding the victim's consent as a defence 'may perfectly well be explained as a piece of paternalism, designed to protect individuals against themselves'.[3] It is not entirely clear in every case, however, which of the two explanations, enforcement or paternalism, is to be regarded as the appropriate one.

In the final part of his book Hart criticizes Lord Devlin's contention that the preservation of a society's morality is essential to its continued existence. Of this utilitarian argument he says, 'The objection to it is that his crucial statement of fact is unsupported by evidence; it is Utilitarianism without benefit of facts.'[4] And:

[1] Oxford University Press, 1963.
[2] Everyman Edition, p. 73.
[3] *Law, Liberty and Morality*, p. 31.
[4] ibid., p. 55.

No evidence is produced to show that deviation, from accepted sexual morality, even by adults in private, is something which, like treason, threatens the existence of society. No reputable historian maintained this thesis, and there is indeed much evidence against it. As a proposition of fact it is entitled to no more respect than the Emperor Justinian's statement that homosexuality was the cause of earthquakes. Lord Devlin's belief in it, and his apparent indifference to the question of evidence, are at points traceable to an undiscussed assumption. This is that all morality – sexual morality together with the morality that forbids acts injurious to others such as killing, stealing and dishonesty – forms a single seamless web, so that those who deviate from any part are likely or perhaps bound to deviate from the whole. It is of course clear (and one of the oldest insights of political theory) that society could not exist without a morality which mirrored and supplemented the law's proscription of conduct injurious to others. But there is again no evidence to support, and much to refute, the theory that those who deviate from conventional sexual morality are in other ways hostile to society.[1]

It is interesting to note Hart's acceptance of the fact that 'society could not exist without a morality which mirrored and supplemented the law's proscription of conduct injurious to others'. Basil Mitchell takes up this point in a very competent examination of the case put by the two protagonists in the debate, and comments: 'It looks as if Lord Devlin's argument might, even on Professor Hart's premises, sanction enforcement of *some* morality, though perhaps not "private morality" (however that phrase is to be interpreted).'[2] At the end of his closely-knit discussion of the main issues which Devlin and Hart have explored, he reaches a conclusion which mediates between their two positions. It seems to me an admirably reasonable conclusion, and I quote it in full:

1. The function of the law is not only to protect individuals from harm, but to protect the essential institutions of a society. These functions overlap, since the sorts of harm an individual

[1] ibid., pp. 50–51.
[2] *Law, Morality and Religion in a Secular Society*, Oxford University Press, 1967, pp. 16–17.

may suffer are to some extent determined by the institutions he lives under.

2. The law should not punish behaviour on the sole ground that it is, or is generally thought to be, immoral; but it cannot be, in all respects, morally neutral. Not only does it presuppose certain 'universal values' whose scope and relative importance it has sometimes to determine, but its commitment to 'paternalism' requires it to adopt some conception of what tends seriously to corrupt the ethos of society, whether in the form of cruelty, unwarranted violence, race hatred, or 'commercialized vice'.

3. The morality which the law presupposes is not beyond criticism and ought to be open to informed discussion and debate together with the fullest use of social research where this is relevant.

4. The protection of institutions, and legitimate concern for the ethos of society, may sometimes justify what I have called 'the reinforcement of morality'. This applies as much to a morality that is plainly utilitarian as to any other. But the onus ought to lie heavily upon those who would interfere in private behaviour, even though a clear line cannot be drawn between public and private morality.

The refusal to draw such a line is often taken as the mark of an illiberal attitude. It is necessary, therefore, to indicate what are the considerations which legislators should bear in mind. They include these principles:

a. So far as possible, privacy should be respected.
b. It is, as a rule, bad to pass laws which are difficult to enforce and whose enforcement tends, therefore, to be patchy and inequitable.
c. It is bad to pass laws which do not command the respect of most reasonable people who are subject to them.
d. One should not pass laws which are likely to fail in their object or produce a great deal of suffering, or other evils such as blackmail.
e. Legislation should be avoided which involves punishing people for what they very largely cannot help.[1]

[1] ibid., pp. 134–135.

Instead of attempting a neat summary of the main points which emerge from the testimony of the various experts whom we have called to give evidence, it may sharpen some of the issues if we imagine a dialogue between two interested readers, A and B:

A. The key question seems to be the distinction between private and public acts. On this point the experts seem unable to come to a clear conclusion. This is not perhaps a very satisfactory state of affairs, and is bound to lead to confusion in the discussion about the sort of legislation we ought to have.

B. I take it that you are arguing from the position that the law ought not to interfere at all with purely private acts. The difficulty in distinguishing what such acts are would cause no confusion if it were accepted that the law has a right and a duty to govern the whole of life, private and public.

A. Yes, I hold very strongly to the view that the less the law interferes the better. Freedom is very precious, even freedom to go to the devil, if a man so pleases. There is the other side of the coin, too: since, as has been pointed out earlier in this chapter, a moral action is the voluntary response of a free person, the law should leave as large an area as possible within which men and women are free to act as they will. In short the best way in which the law can safeguard morality is to leave well alone: the fewer laws we have, the better.

B. I agree that there is a danger in the multiplication of laws, and I am all for respecting privacy. But I return to the difficult question: is there really such a thing as a purely private action? It seems to me that there is not. For good or ill the individual is one of the cells in the body politic. Moral infection can spread from cell to cell, so that even the most private acts can have public consequences.

A. As a theory your argument is incontestable. The law, however, must deal with practical realities. Let us consider fornication. Christians, at any rate, and doubtless many others who are not Christians, would say that fornication is immoral, but is not illegal. Would you make it so on the ground that, though it is a private act, it affects the whole of society?

B. No, I would not do so for several reasons. One is that though I am disposed to believe that fornication is bad for individuals and bad for society, this is difficult to prove. For example, the argument that it undermines the institution of marriage is difficult to maintain in the light of the undoubted strength of that institution today. Again, I realize that in a democracy the laws are made by the people, and I doubt whether there is any deep moral conviction among the majority of people on this particular point. Even if I thought it desirable to have a law against fornication, it would be idle to expect the nation to agree to enforce a moral conviction it hadn't got. Then finally, I don't see how such a law could be enforced. It would certainly lead to blackmail, and perhaps to other consequences worse than the evil it sought to avoid.

A. You have, I think, analysed correctly the position about fornication. But what you have said has also served to illustrate some of the points made by the learned witnesses who have testified in the earlier part of this chapter. There are, for example, b), c) and d) of the considerations which Mr Basil Mitchell stated should be borne in mind by our legislators (see p. 97). I think that what you have said also leads clearly to the third of his main conclusions (see p. 97). It must never be assumed that social legislation is permanent and beyond criticism. It must, for good or ill (sometimes for the one and sometimes the other), take account of changes in the moral outlook of the nation. It must also take account of fuller understanding of the nature and effects of various types of behaviour.

B. Does this, in fact, happen?

A. Yes. The introduction of breathalyser tests to determine the alcohol content of a motorist's blood was opposed by some as an unwarranted interference with personal liberty. The change in the law was brought about by scientifically established facts about the effects of the consumption of alcohol on driving skills, and a consequent deepening of moral concern in the nation about the tragically high accident rate. I think the removal of private homosexual acts from the list of criminal offences was also partly due to the revision of an exaggerated estimate of their personal and social harmfulness which could not be substantiated by factual evidence.

B. But, given the lack of precision in the attempt to determine the exact function of the law and its right to interfere with what many regard as purely private behaviour; given also the variety of moral views found within the community – is there not bound to be a good deal of untidiness in our law?

A. Of course there is, for life is a very untidy business. This is bound to be so because new facts are constantly being unearthed to upset our neat calculations. A certain untidiness, too, is inseparable from the freedom which Christians stand for. This is the point brought out in a passage in Professor Herbert Butterfield's *History and Human Relations*: 'A Christian civilization, precisely because it must embrace so high a conception of personality, must move towards what Christians themselves must regard as its own undoing – towards freedom of conscience instead of greater solidarity of faith. A world in which personality and conscience are respected, so that men may choose the God they will worship and the moral end they will serve – this and this only is a Christian civilization when human development has reached a certain point.'[1] That being so, Christian citizens who carry their moral convictions into the important arena where laws are made and amended must expect to have a difficult time.

[1] Collins, 1951, p. 132.

THE NEWSPAPER on my desk contains a pathetic little paragraph. It tells the story of a hard-working young couple shortly to be married. For months they have been busy preparing the house which is to be their home. Paint and paper, love and skill had transformed it and they had just installed the furniture purchased with their hard-earned savings. Then vandals broke in and wrecked the whole place from floor to ceiling. As far as they know, the couple haven't an enemy in the world: it must have been the utterly senseless action of persons bent on destruction. The couple will, of course, start all over again, and the neighbours in their little street are taking up a collection, as nothing was insured.

Faced with this kind of thing many people in these days will probably want to ask what are the causes of such delinquency. Behind this desire to establish causes lie several interesting assumptions. One is that if we are able to understand why some people behave in this way, it may be easier to correct their anti-social attitudes and so prevent their disruptive activities. Another is that there must be reasons why people act unreasonably. The second of these assumptions is absolutely fundamental to the whole business of living as persons. It also reasserts that close connexion between reason and morality which has been evident in our study of the subject in earlier chapters. Some animals can talk, but no animal can tell a lie, or tell the truth. If Fanny Craddock's pet parrot says 'You're a rotten cook', the statement is untrue, but the bird is not lying, it's just making a noise. The words may sound exactly the same as those spoken by a person, but they are not the same at all. A person can express an opinion; a parrot has no opinions. The difference between a person and a parrot is that the former has the power of reason and the latter has not. Because of this we say that a person is responsible for his actions and a parrot is not.

Unhappily, however, the first part of this statement cannot stand as it is; it must be qualified in a number of ways. How far is responsibility limited by circumstances? And supposing a man says, 'Why should I have a reason for doing things?' The only answer to that is that any sentence which begins with 'Why' is asking for a reason, and yet the questioner is denying the need to give any reasons. This, therefore, reduces language to meaning-lessness and robs conversation of any further point. Such a man is really contracting out of being a person.

Before we get too far away from the vandals who destroyed the patient work of our young couple, we had better note that the simple reaction of some people to this kind of behaviour is: 'Its a pity we abolished the cat; a good flogging is what they need.' The question of penal policy will be considered in Chapter 12 but here we are concerned with the attempt to see more clearly what is meant by personal moral responsibility, and how far we can in truth be held to be responsible for our actions.

Responsibility and intention

A point of fundamental importance in determining the morality or otherwise of an action is the question of the intention of the person who performed it. A man must be held responsible for any consequences of his action which he could have reasonably foreseen. If, for example, I put down a front garden path and leave one of the stones two inches higher than the rest so that my neighbour trips and breaks a limb, then I must accept a real degree of blame. But it cannot with fairness be said that I am as much to blame as if I stretched a string across the path with the deliberate intention of making my neighbour fall. Sometimes the consequences of an action are entirely different both from my intention and from anything I could have foreseen. I may stoop to pick up a ticket for a man who has dropped it on a railway platform. He may lean over at precisely the same moment, our heads may collide, and he may fall off the edge of the platform and sprain his ankle. Neither of us is really to blame: it is just an unfortunate accident. Here, then, is one quite simple and basic way in which we must often qualify the assertion that a man is responsible for his actions.

Responsibility and environment

We are all influenced enormously by our environment. Very often a successful business man who has become a highly-respected citizen and a member of the local council will say, perhaps at a dinner in his honour, 'I owe more than I can ever say to the home in which I was reared; my mother and father made me what I am.' It is odd, however, that sometimes the man who has said that seems unwilling to accept the testimony of a criminal who asserts, 'I never had a chance; I owe my downfall to the home in which I was dragged up, and the parents who made my life a hell.'

The social sciences are beginning to clear a few paths through the jungles of conjecture which surround the whole subject of the effects of environment on human behaviour patterns; but progress is slow. Certain broad generalizations are commonly made, such as that many criminals come from disturbed or broken homes. Such statements certainly substantiate the thesis that we are all influenced by environmental factors, but they do not take us very far along the road of detailed understanding. Referring to sociological research into the causes of crime, Josephine Bell says, 'The subject matter is of vast proportions and by its nature necessarily extremely complex. There will never, probably, be a simple scientific law governing the appearance, incidence and nature of crime.'[1]

The same point is made by Barbara Wootton at the end of her lengthy book *Social Science and Social Pathology*:

It is clear from what has been said that few generalizations can be made with confidence about those whose behaviour is socially unacceptable, and that not many are applicable even to any one group of these. For the popular theories about the

[1] *Crime in our Time*, Nicholas Vane, 1962, p. 215.

delinquency of latchkey children, about social failure repeating itself generation after generation, about the beneficial effects of boys' clubs or the disastrous consequences of illegitimacy – for these and similar generalizations we have, as yet at any rate, little solid factual evidence. Perhaps we can go so far as to say that the lack of secure affection in infancy is likely to create difficulties in after-life, and that one possible manifestation of these difficulties is a reluctance to conform to what society expects. But that those who are not loved are likely themselves to hate rather than to love is hardly a discovery for which modern science can take the credit. Man has known this truth in theory for as long as he has disregarded it in practice.[1]

Responsibility and heredity

The same kind of imprecise conclusion in matters of detail is registered by those who have studied the bearing of hereditary factors on human character and behaviour. Before I sat on a Home Office Committee on Juvenile Delinquency I thought I knew one or two things about the causes of anti-social behaviour. My certainties receded rapidly, however, after I had listened for a while to the experts. You may make what seems to you to be the most obvious general statement, and they will insist either that it is wrong or that it must be severely qualified – and they will produce facts and figures to prove their point. To quote Lady Wootton again:

> In general, therefore, it may be said that ecological studies have succeeded in establishing that things are very much what one would expect them to be: birds of a feather flock, or at any rate are found, together. But it is the interpretation of these findings which is the critical issue; and this remains a matter for speculation. If it is true that criminality, or, more precisely, some types of criminality, are highly concentrated in particular areas, or associated with slum conditions, then three crucial questions arise. First, is this concentration due to the fact that the slums are tenanted by the dregs of the population who would perpetuate their deplorable habits wherever they lived? Second,

[1] Allen and Unwin, 1959, p. 301.

if this is the case, is the transmission biological or merely cultural? Or, third, are slum habits the direct products of the corruption of slum life, destined to disappear in a more favourable environment?[1]

Commenting on these different theories, the same author makes the point that social policy must depend to a considerable extent on the relative importance which may be attached to them:

> From the angle of policy, it clearly makes a great difference which of these hypotheses is nearest the truth. If sordid areas are tenanted by families whose biological inheritance must be reckoned, in terms of current social values, as at the least unfortunate, then the advocates of sterilization can raise their voices. But if, on the other hand, the perpetuation of unacceptable ways of life in these areas is a cultural rather than a biological process, then the outlook for children who are removed to a more favourable environment (as the children of criminal or exceptionally difficult parents not infrequently are) should be about as good as for anybody else. And if the localized incidence of certain forms of criminality is due merely to the direct impact of slum conditions upon slum-dwellers, then the obvious course is to pull down the slums; and that should be the end of the trouble.[2]

Studies in the aetiology of particular human afflictions reveal the same uncertainty, or rather the way in which a theory accepted one day can be discarded, or at any rate partially overthrown, the next. Homosexuality is a case in point. If we begin with the simple question, 'Are homosexuals born or made?' we shall soon find ourselves looking at rival theories and conflicting evidence. At the end of the last century Richard von Krafft-Ebing advanced the view that the cerebrum contains male and female centres, and that homosexuality results from the dominance of the wrong centre. This theory has, however, been exploded by subsequent biological investigations. Havelock Ellis believed that

[1] op. cit., pp. 70–71.
[2] ibid., p. 71.

the homosexual condition was due to hormonal unbalance, but more recent research has failed to substantiate this, and the view most frequently expressed today is that the causes of homosexuality are psychological rather than genetic.

Responsibility and mental sickness

Most people will probably feel that the clearest ground for accepting diminished responsibility as a fact is the existence of mental sickness. It is interesting that whereas once we treated lunatics as criminals, now we often seem to treat criminals as lunatics. We often hear it said that an offender is 'unfit' to plead, by which is meant that he is so deranged in mind that he would not be able to make any sense of the court proceedings. If that is the case it seems only just to recognize that he cannot be held fully responsible for the offence with which he is charged. The explanation we are able to give of the man's behaviour has turned into exculpation. The verdict is that he is guilty – that is, the fact that he committed an offence is not in dispute – but he is not blameworthy (or not fully so) as he would be if he had been in his right mind.

There is, of course, great truth in this as a general position, and we may rightly feel that the acceptance of this approach to the treatment of some offenders has brought us closer to justice. The difficulties start when we try to define more exactly the degree of culpability in particular cases. Unless the distinction between sickness and criminality is entirely obliterated, a line must somewhere be drawn. But where? The most famous answer to this question, so far as English law is concerned, is that embodied in the McNaghten rules, laid down in 1843. Under these rules a man is held to be responsible for his actions unless he is 'labouring under such a defect of reason, from disease of the mind, as not to know the nature and quality of the act he was doing, or, if he did know it, that he did not know he was doing what was wrong'.[1]

The McNaghten Rules have been strongly criticized because of their intellectualism and their entire disregard of emotional factors. The Rules are based on a concept similar to that of *mens rea*. This is the doctrine which says that a child under the

[1] Report of the Royal Commission on Capital Punishment, 1953, p. 79.

age of eight is incapable of committing a crime because he is not yet able to understand the difference between right and wrong. The emphasis, it will be seen, is on the ability to understand. Certainly one value of this approach to the determination of degrees of responsibility is that it is comparatively simple to check the state of the mind of the accused by reference to matters other than the crime he is alleged to have committed. Obviously, the argument becomes circular if it is said that he must have been mad to commit such an act and therefore he must be excused on the ground of his madness. But if it can be shown that the accused frequently posts his letters by putting them down the drain, and waits for the bus by the pillar box, then it is a fair deduction that he is not fully responsible for his actions and lacks the measure of understanding that would make him so.

Nevertheless, there is truth in the contention that irresponsibility and insanity are often associated not so much with defects in the powers of reasoning as with disordered emotions. An accused person might have known what he was doing, and might have known that it was wrong, but it might also be shown that he acted under an irresistible impulse.

The idea of irresistible impulse as a valid plea in favour of a judgement of diminished responsibility has often been criticized on the grounds that it involves us again in a circular definition: an irresistible impulse is merely an impulse that was not resisted. But there may be more to it than that.

To say that the impulse was irresistible is to claim more than just that it was not resisted. Over and above the fact that the urge was not resisted, other evidence can be given to show that the accused lacked the ability to resist it. Such evidence might consist in the fact that he had very good reasons for not acting as he did, e.g. because a policeman was standing beside him; that he had no good reason for acting as he did, e.g. he was already plentifully supplied with articles like the one he stole; that in the past he had in similar circumstances given way to the impulse; that before committing the crime in question he had said that he felt such an impulse and could not resist it.[1]

[1] P. G. Fitzgerald, *Criminal Law and Punishment*, Clarendon Press, 1962, pp. 135 and 136.

A movement in the direction of extending the McNaghten formula was made in 1957 when the following provision was introduced into the Homicide Act:

Where a person kills or is party to the killing of another, he shall not be convicted of murder if he was suffering from such abnormality of mind (whether arising from a condition of arrested or retarded development of mind or any inherent causes or induced by disease or injury) as substantially impaired his mental responsibility for his acts and omissions in doing or being a party to the killing.[1]

Whilst most people with any knowledge of mental illness would agree that it can involve both intellect and emotions, the fact must frankly be faced that it is almost impossible to define either mental health or mental disorder with anything like scientific precision. If the reader doubts this, let him try to produce adequate definitions. Health and sickness are easier to recognize than define, and there are infinite gradations of meaning within both categories. In the literature on mental health the sort of word which frequently occurs is 'adjustment'. The mentally healthy person is the one who is adjusted harmoniously to his environment. But supposing his environment is a sick society, will not adjustment to it mean partaking of its sickness, and could it not be said that the really healthy person is one who, far from being in harmony with his environment, is in rebellion against it? To ask the question is perhaps sufficient to show that concepts of mental health and sickness are inevitably bound up with value-judgements. It is impossible to measure a man's state of mental health with a thermometer or any other scientific gauge.

As long as the understanding of the nature of mental sickness remains so imprecise, it is obviously difficult to formulate the legal criteria which determine the degree of responsibility. The recognition that mental illness may have an emotional as well as an intellectual component does not diminish the difficulty. On the contrary, for this reason some of the more advanced penologists advocate ignoring the question of responsibility. They urge that we should recognize that crime is a disease, and therefore the criminal should be treated as a sick person. It is possible to

[1] Section 2(i).

argue for and against this point of view, but surely at the end of the day the crucial question must be which of the two methods – punishment or treatment – produces the best results in terms of the reduction of crime and the reformation of the criminal. We shall have to return to this aspect of the matter in Chapter 12. In the meantime the reader may want to express anxiety about the conclusion to which the argument seems to have led.

Responsibility, sickness and sin

R. Yes, I certainly am disturbed by the trend of the argument. It seems to me that much of the valuable work being done by Churches, youth centres and educational establishments of every sort is being undermined by psychologists who say that we are not responsible for our actions. What is the good of our urging people to act responsibly if they are encouraged by the alleged experts in human motivation to believe that we are all puppets on a string manipulated by powers over which we have no control?

A. You have, of course, overstated the position. No reputable psychologist would say that the term 'human responsibility' is devoid of all meaning. The old debate between determinism and free will is necessarily inconclusive. What the psychologists and others have been able to do is to shed a little more light on the territory that lies between the two poles of that discussion. We may want to say that men are free to choose between good and evil, but we know that some are freer than others. New knowledge helps us to distinguish a little more accurately and fairly between the more free and the less free.

R. It does seem, however, that once you begin to qualify the concept of personal moral responsibility and hedge it about with all sorts of ifs and buts, you are faced with tremendous difficulties. Surely it is simpler to say that every man is responsible for his own actions: as the Bible puts it, 'The soul that sinneth, it shall die.'[1]

A. It certainly would be simpler, but surely we must concern ourselves not with what is simple, but with what is true. The truth is often far from simple. Furthermore, we really ought not to quote the Bible in support of our views unless we look carefully at the whole of what it says. The remainder of the verse from which you read runs: 'The son shall not bear the iniquity of the

[1] Ezekiel 18:20.

father, neither shall the father bear the iniquity of the son: the righteousness of the righteous shall be upon him, and the wickedness of the wicked shall be upon him.' Now this verse does not contain the whole truth, but I suggest that it indicates a movement away from the over-simple suggestion that a man is necessarily to be blamed for everything that happens about him. There is no sophistication or refinement of argument here, but at least it is recognized that it is unfair to blame the son for the wrongs done by his father. Although Ezekiel puts the blame squarely on each individual, there is surely here the first glimmering of a doctrine of diminished responsibility.

R. I think that may be straining the meaning of the text a little. But what really concerns me is the way in which the argument of this chapter seems to be undermining the idea of sin. Now here, surely, there can be no room for doubt. The Bible teaches the reality of sin, and says that we are all sinners. It does not say we are sick and in need of treatment; it says we are sinners in need of forgiveness. If we are going to lend ourselves to the notion that sin is really sickness, then surely we have destroyed the meaning of the gospel: it becomes an anachronism, and the best thing we can do is to close all the churches and open more hospitals.

A. I think you have fallen into a very common error by making a rigid distinction between sickness and sin which is, in fact, foreign to the spirit and teaching of the New Testament. Jesus Himself linked the two together. He said to one man whom He had healed, 'Now that you are well again, leave your sinful ways, or you may suffer something worse.'[1]

R. But here Jesus is pointing to the fact that often sickness is the result of sin, not that the two things are the same.

A. But on other occasions He suggests that the connexion between sin and sickness is closer than that between cause and effect. On one occasion the Pharisees said to Jesus' disciples, 'Why is it that your master eats with tax-gatherers and sinners?' Jesus heard them and said, 'It is not the healthy that need a doctor, but the sick.'[2] Our Lord is accusing the self-righteous Pharisees of hypocrisy: they think they are all right, but they are sinners like the rest. But those sinners are referred to as 'the sick'. And

[1] John 5:14.
[2] Matthew 9:11, 12.

this is not just a figure of speech: it is entirely consistent with His total attitude to men and women.

R. Surely you are not suggesting that Jesus excused sin, and led people to accept the idea that they were not to be held responsible for their actions?

A. No, I am not saying that, though He did say to the adulteress who was brought to Him that He did not condemn her.

R. That is in the passage[1] which is omitted from many of the ancient manuscripts and is, therefore, of doubtful authenticity.

A. I am aware of that, but it seems to me to convey very accurately the spirit of the Master as it is reflected in the gospels generally. But my main point is that the close connexion in the New Testament between sin and sickness does not lead to a less serious view of sin, but rather to a deeper understanding of its terrible power. Charles Wesley refers to 'the depths of in-bred sin'. It is a very limited view of sin which sees it merely as those thoughts or actions which express deliberate wickedness. Often we sin in ignorance, and our ignorance is itself part of our sinful condition. Sometimes we will to do evil; at other times we sin against our own wills; as St Paul graphically puts it: 'I do not even acknowledge my own actions as mine, for what I do is not what I want to do, but what I detest. But if what I do is against my will, it means that I agree with the law and hold it to be admirable. But as things are, it is no longer I who perform the action, but sin that lodges in me. For I know that nothing good lodges in me – in my unspiritual nature, I mean – for though the will to do good is there, the deed is not. The good which I want to do, I fail to do; but what I do is the wrong which is against my will; and if what I do is against my will, clearly it is no longer I who am the agent, but sin that has its lodging in me.'[2] The Apostle goes on from this to speak about salvation. Jesus Christ is able to take the whole man and transform even the unconscious depths of his being. Here, I think, we come up against one of the paradoxes of the Christian faith, that it is the slaves of Christ who are truly free, and as free men they are able to accept responsibility for their actions.

R. Since most of us fall short of that state of wholeness which Christians describe as full salvation, it would seem that it is very

[1] John 8:1–11.
[2] Romans 7:15–20.

difficult to judge other people (and even to judge ourselves, sometimes) with complete fairness.

A. Not merely very difficult, but impossible, I would say. Isn't that why Jesus said, 'Pass no judgement, and you will not be judged'?[1] Most of us are far too ready to pass judgement on others, but understanding and sympathy will usually carry us much farther than denunciation. Perhaps the greatest benefit conferred on religious counsellors by the psychiatrists is what they have taught us about the value of the non-judgemental approach to others in need. This is admirably summed up in two paragraphs which deal with ways in which the psychiatrist can help the priest:

1. By providing new understanding concerning human behaviour. The unconscious is the most important concept in psychiatry. It has been likened to a repository in which we deposit pleasant and unpleasant experiences. In normal life they remain undisturbed, but when associated with an unusual force of emotion they are apt to upset the balance of the mind. It therefore becomes difficult sometimes to determine when our behaviour is purely the result of conscious decisions, or determined by deep, inner psychic motivations of which we are unaware.

2. By helping the priest re-learn methods which have always belonged to the cure of souls, but have become forgotten and neglected. For example, the art of listening – one of the finest qualifications of a good priest is to know how to listen, and listen intelligently. We have been trained to be talkers, and are therefore more prone to moralize, to give out 'pious platitudes', or 'sermonettes'.[2]

---

[1] Matthew 7:1.
[2] Norman Autton, *The Pastoral Care of the Mentally Ill*, S.P.C.K., 1963, p. 150.

9 From theory to practice

So FAR WE HAVE been largely concerned with theory, with important but abstract questions about the concepts of morality. The time has come when we must look at some of the concrete situations which have kept edging their way into our discussions, but which now must be squarely faced. The Christian is both a person and a member of society. He is required to make personal decisions and to share in those decision-making processes which determine the shape of society. Both aspects of his moral obligation are closely related, and no attempt has been made in this book carefully to distinguish between personal and social ethics. Both as a person and as a member of society the Christian lives his life in a world which is full of alien influences. It is within and as a part of this demanding situation that he must work out the nature of his vocation.

The perennial temptation for the Christian is to turn his back upon the world, and even to quote texts like 'Do not touch what is unclean',[1] as a justification for non-involvement. But the general teaching of the New Testament is clear. The people of God are not called to enter an ark of safety, but to be the leaven in the midst of the lump. 'Not everyone who calls me "Lord, Lord" will enter into the Kingdom of Heaven, but only those who do the will of my heavenly Father.'[2] We need to equip ourselves with a theology of Christian social action.

If we are to do the will of God, theory must be turned into practice. Enough has been said already in this book to make it

[1] 2 Corinthians 6:17.
[2] Matthew 7:21.

abundantly clear that Christians have no neat and tidy answers to complex problems, neither will they always agree about what ought to be done. Happily, however, not only is there in these days wide agreement that ethics must be 'done' and not just debated, but also, as I shall show in a moment, increasing Christian co-operation in the doing of them. It is out of this situation that I venture later in this chapter to set down certain propositions about how the transition from theory to practice may be made more effective. These propositions will, I hope, be planks of a bridge joining the first half of the book to the second. But before coming to the bridge it may be useful to give a brief summary of the ground so far covered in the previous chapters.

Recapitulation

We began with a number of questions thrown up in the course of a spirited discussion of the basis of Christian moral judgement. These questions were seen to be of far-reaching significance, involving us in an examination of the nature and scope of ethical enquiry. After some enquiry into the meaning of basic terms, and an argument about ancient and non-Christian ideas, we attempted a brief survey of the history of ethical thought. We noted the universality of a sense of right and wrong. This led us to ask whether it can be said that morality is natural to man, and to an exposition of the doctrine of natural law. Our conclusion was that morality is indeed a fact written into the structure of things by the Creator: a sense of right and wrong is a human attribute. But this being so, we had to go on to ask in what sense we may speak of *Christian* ethics. Here we saw the need to guard against the kind of arrogance which assumes that Christians know all the answers. The New Testament is full of ethical emphases; it leaves us in no doubt that Christianity is a way of life, but its main emphasis is on the freedom, depth, and sensitivity which the indwelling Christ brings into the life of the believer.

In Chapter 6 we faced some of the reasons for the moral confusion of our times, and the fact that Christians are not exempt. We gave reasons why the more alarmist assessments of the situation should be countered by a reasoned optimism, and expressed the judgement that the great value of the situational approach to ethics is its emphasis on the inwardness of morals.

Next came an investigation of the relationship between morality and the law of the land; and the various views about the extent to which the law should invade the sphere of 'private morals'.

Finally, an account of a particularly reprehensible piece of vandalism launched us into a consideration of personal moral responsibility, and the ways in which it must often be qualified. The trend of the argument led us to see the need for caution when judging others, and to a recognition of the significance of the new emphasis on the treatment, not merely the punishment, of offenders.

Six practical propositions

The extent to which the Churches have accepted the responsibility of 'doing' as well as debating ethics is to be seen in the creation of boards and departments of social responsibility. Increasingly in Britain these boards are able to co-operate. The Social Responsibility, Christian Aid, and Joint International Departments of the British Council of Churches, its Advisory Group on Sex, Marriage and the Family, as well as *ad hoc* working-parties set up by the Council, afford valuable opportunities for joint thought and action on a variety of social and international questions. The active participation of the Roman Catholic Church in the various sections of the Council's work has further enhanced the usefulness of this co-operation.

At this level much of the energy of the Churches is consumed in the effort to influence government policy and the course of parliamentary debate and decision on moral issues of one kind and another. Although, in the nature of the case, interviews with government officials can only be undertaken by a few selected people representing the responsible departments or boards of the Churches, it is important that the lines of communication with all the other levels of the Church should be kept open. A Church judgement will count for little unless it is backed by an informed opinion throughout the Church. More and more the denominational boards are trying to share their thinking with local Church groups, just as the British Council of Churches is seeking to strengthen its relations with local Councils of Churches. Sometimes a group of keen Christians in a locality undertake the study of some particular issue and feed back to the headquarters department the fruit of their research.

It is out of this ongoing activity that certain insights emerge. I set them down boldly in the form of six practical propositions.

1. To be effective we must be specific

In his book *A Pattern of Rulers* Lord Francis Williams has this to say about Stanley Baldwin: 'He moved easiest among large generalities and found it pleasanter to enunciate ideals than to apply them in detail.'[1] If that is true, one can only say that Mr Baldwin would have been a great success in many a Church meeting. So often Christian statements or resolutions about contemporary problems fail to come to terms with the actualities of a hard world. They do not make the essential leap from theory to practice. Sometimes even the theory is muddled. Many a Church resolution amounts to little more than saying, 'If only we were all Christians, things would in general be very much better', or, 'We don't like the way you are going about things and hope you will stop it at once.'

This kind of utterance is no good at all. It may do real harm to the image of the Church. We can't expect to be listened to if we make it clear that we don't know what we are talking about. This applies whether we are thinking in terms of pastoral counselling or in terms of resolutions dealing with public questions. The needy individual is likely to turn away in disgust or despair if we show by word or attitude that we really have no understanding of his situation. And if we say to the Christian politician, 'I believe Jesus Christ is the answer to the race problem,' he will be entirely within his rights to say, 'Then tell me what the government should now do about the Rhodesian situation.' As I have said earlier, Christians do not know all the answers. Their faith provides no easy or automatic answers to difficult problems. But this should not deter them from providing the best answers that faith and knowledge can devise.

2. To be specific we must enter into dialogue

The word 'dialogue' is an overworked item in the Christian vocabulary, but that is in itself a significant and encouraging fact. It betokens a humility and a readiness to co-operate which have not always been evident in the Christian approach to social problems. I give two illustrations of the way in which dialogue

[1] Longmans, 1965, p. 33.

is important if our witness as Christians is to be pointed and relevant.

First, it is essential to a full understanding of the facts about many of the problems with which we have to deal. Take drug addiction as an example. At one session of a working party on this subject to which I belonged we called a witness whom we thought would be able to help us. She had mixed a great deal with drug addicts, and knew the problem from the inside. Taking her seat among a group of churchmen, she began, 'I must frankly confess that I am an atheist and have never been inside a church.' She seemed a little surprised when we assured her that for the purposes of our enquiry *at that point*, the question of her faith or lack of it was neither here nor there. What was important was the fact that she had a great deal of information which we needed to possess. It goes without saying – though it is worth saying, nonetheless – that there is no such thing as a Christian judgement which is based on the fallacy that the facts don't matter. The effective presentation of the Christian social witness requires a willingness on the part of Christians to enter into conversation with all kinds of people, many of them non-believers, and the humility to learn from them.

Second, there is need for a similar approach when the Church, through its appointed representatives, speaks to the government and others in authority. Harshly critical resolutions may sound dramatic and encourage the faithful to believe they are doing something important, but quiet conversation with those responsible for making decisions is often more helpful. This is not to say that there is no place for straight criticism and even, on rare occasions, for denunciation. For the most part, however, we need to remember that those who represent us in Parliament are responsible men and women. They are more likely to listen to us if we show our willingness to listen to them. Where there is a difference of judgement, the right is rarely all on one side. Dialogue, therefore, can be constructive, and lead to fuller and quite specific understandings of what should be done.

3. When we enter into dialogue we must be prepared to compromise

Compromise is regarded as a dirty word, and there are, of course, forms of compromise which must be condemned. If I know a thing to be right, and for purely selfish reasons refuse to do it, I have compromised my conscience and have no defence. But so very often we do not find ourselves facing a clear choice between that which is wholly good and that which is wholly evil. Some poor fellow comes to us to lay before us the sorry, tangled tale of a life that has not worked out. Having honoured us with his confidence, he asks for our advice. Now if the situation were other than it is we might know exactly what to say. But the facts are as they are – hard and relentless. There is no road out which our conscience would wholly approve, yet it is intolerable that the man should stay where he is; impossible, too. So painfully we choose the best compromise we can discover. And, remembering the insights of the situationists, we give our advice with a measure of confidence, believing that Christian ethics has something to say not just to ideal circumstances but to those caught up in situations very far from ideal, and for whom the 'right' way falls short of the best we could desire.

When we consider our Christian duty in respect of social legislation it is very clear that there is no escape from compromise. How can there be if politics is 'the art of the possible'? On matters such as the law on Sunday or the law controlling gambling, Christians are apt to hold views different from those of other sections of the community. If the government introduces a measure of which Christians do not approve or cannot wholly support, they can indicate their outright opposition. There may be occasions when this is the only proper course to take. More often, however, the Churches will enter into discussions designed to secure such amendments as may improve the Bill if only to the extent of modifying its more objectionable clauses. If this is thought of in terms of compromise, then it must be said that it is the sort of compromise which Christians must be prepared to accept as necessary to the exercise of responsible citizenship.

4. We must accept the necessity for united action

All I need to do under this heading is to underline what I have said earlier in this chapter about effective co-operation between the denominations. Whatever other reasons there may be for giving ourselves, mind and soul, to the ecumenical movement, its importance is demonstrated beyond any possibility of doubt in the field of social action. Some of the most perceptive thinking on the frontiers between the Church and the world is being done in groups where the resources of all the Churches are being pooled. I cite as one conspicuous example the remarkable Report on *Human Reproduction* which is referred to more fully on p. 156. The great enterprise known as Christian Aid is the outstanding demonstration of the way in which the Churches can at least begin to make some sort of valid response to the ethical demand of the gospel to 'feed the hungry'.

As long as the Churches keep talking, there will no doubt be some who can discover justifications for denominationalism. When the Churches start doing, their denominationalism is recognized as the appalling impediment it has in fact become. The palsy of parochialism cripples the Church, and disables it from running effectively on God's errands of mercy to a needy world.

Both for the effective thinking and doing of ethics the unity of the Churches is essential.

5. We must establish our priorities

One of the least pleasant aspects of Church life is our ability to get worked up about the wrong things. There are, after all, greater sins and lesser sins, and to wax eloquent about the latter and say nothing about the former is surely a very great sin indeed. Colin Morris is a master of overstatement (perhaps that is the only way to get some truths across), but we certainly need to listen to him when he declares his burning conviction about the real meaning of 'obscenity'. His words are prompted by a Zambian who died of hunger not a hundred yards from his front door. The pathologist stated that his stomach contained a few leaves and what appeared to be a ball of grass.

> We are those who rise in wrath at the prevalent use of four-letter words that are at worst mere evidence of tastelessness or verbal ineptitude. The real obscenity, which should stick in our throats and choke us, is what we have done in Christ's name to degrade that little man with the shrunken stomach ... Obscenity is a strong word, but I know no other so apt ... Obscenity is the cardinal who cries 'Murder!' when a woman aborts a piece of bloody tissue but keeps silence or indeed gives his blessing whilst thousands of fully formed sons and daughters of women are incinerated in Viet Nam.[1]

[1] Colin Morris, *Include Me Out!* Epworth, 1968, pp. 43–44.

It is a word in season, after the manner of our Lord, who castigated the lawyers and Pharisees: 'Hypocrites! you pay tithes of mint and dill and cummin: but you have overlooked the weightier demands of the Law, justice, mercy, and good faith.'[1] Of all the matters we shall consider in the second half of this book none exceeds in importance the vast problem of how to deal with the growing menace of world hunger.

6. We must recognize the relationship between Christian Social Witness and Evangelism

Both of these are integral to the total mission of the Church. A man said to me, 'Is Martin Luther King a minister of the gospel?' When I replied in the affirmative he asked, 'Then why doesn't he get on with his proper work instead of getting mixed up in politics and freedom marches?' This comment overlooks an important fact. In this age the struggle for human rights is being waged with increasing intensity. Coloured people the world over are in revolt. Unless the Christian Church is on the right side in that struggle, and manifestly so, then it is idle to hope that the coloured majority of the human race will give the gospel a serious hearing in the days ahead. Why should they – if our talk about freedom and justice is mere talk? The word of the gospel must become incarnate in practical identification with those who are underprivileged and exploited. And this is where theology passes into ethics, and where social witness and evangelism join hands. Moreover, the gospel is never preached effectively in a cultural and social vacuum. We need to understand the world within which the message of the gospel is set forth. There is a sociological dimension to evangelism. The attempt to unravel the ethical dilemmas of our time must accompany the preaching of the Evangel. The so-called ethical implications of the gospel are, in fact, part of the message: they give shape and content to the discipleship to which salvation is the entrance.

---

[1] Matthew 23:23.

PART TWO

10 Chastity, marriage, and divorce

'SEX IS DEAD.' Such is the provocative title of an intriguing paper-back by Earl H. Brill,[1] who proceeds to demonstrate that he has his tongue in his cheek by writing some lively chapters on a subject that is of perennial interest, pious protestations to the contrary notwithstanding. And since such protestations are one of the least pleasant elements in our ecclesiastical tradition, we may as well begin with the resounding assertion that no Christian has any right not to be interested in the subject. The Bible is itself so concerned to come to grips with it that before we have reached the end of the opening chapter we have come upon what are perhaps the most profound words ever written about human sexuality.[2]

The Bible then must be our starting-point. Having looked at what it has to say about the significance of sexual polarity, we shall consider in this and the following chapter some of the matters which arise because of this fundamental structuring of the human race. Since we shall be moving in the most emotive area of ethical enquiry, we must try to be mindful of that all-important Christian responsibility which the song-writer Sydney Carter once described as 'a care for truth'.

Sex: a biblical perspective

'In the beginning God'. With these majestic words the Bible launches us upon the noble narratives of the creation. If what then

[1] S.C.M. Press; Heinemann, 1967.
[2] Genesis 1:27.

follows makes sense it does so only because it follows from that opening assertion. What follows is not, of course, a scientific account of the origin of the universe. To ask whether the early chapters of Genesis support the theory of evolution is as meaningless as asking whether John Wesley's sermons prove Einstein's theory of relativity. There are various kinds of truth, and different sorts of knowledge. Some readers of Genesis may be likened to the man who goes to the ironmongers to buy a loaf of bread.

If the Genesis story of creation is not scientific, neither is it historic. It is, therefore, foolish to challenge its veracity by saying, 'How could the writer know what happened at the dawn of history since he certainly was not there to see for himself, and neither was anyone else?'

The value of the creation narratives – apart from their very considerable literary worth – lies in the clues they provide to the ultimate meaning and significance of human life and the universe which we inhabit. There is one word which occurs six times in the first chapter of Genesis: it is the word 'good', which is to be found at the heart of all ethical discussion. Five times the author says about the things which God has made: 'and God saw everything that he had made, and, behold, it was very good.' Here there is no suspicion of dualism, of rival gods responsible for good and evil, no hint of a morbid dislike of the physical world: all is of God, and all is good. Including, be it noted, man's sexuality.

In Genesis 2:18 we are told of one thing which God regarded as not good: 'And the Lord God said, It is not good that the man should be alone.' It is surely significant and suggestive that the first references in the Bible to human sexuality are concerned not with its procreative function but with its power to create and sustain relationship. This is the more remarkable in view of the stress on procreation in the Old Testament. Failure to bear a child was regarded as a shameful thing. So Rachel when she eventually conceives says, 'God hath taken away my reproach.'[1] In the second account of creation contained in the second chapter of Genesis the woman is made out of a rib taken from the man's side, thus symbolizing the fact that they belong together. The fundamental nature of this partnership is stressed in the words which Jesus quoted: 'Therefore shall a man leave his father and

[1] Genesis 30:23.

his mother, and shall cleave unto his wife: and they shall be one flesh.'[1]

This duality of man, this fact that he is a 'being-in-relationship', is a reflection of the image of God. 'So God created man in his own image, in the image of God created he him; male and female created he them.'[2] Nothing in man's experience is more humbling than the contemplation of the mystery of the Being of God. We know so little that it's a wonder we dare to claim that we know anything at all. Yet what we know is what God Himself has graciously revealed, and so we are bold to state that He has made Himself known as a 'Being-in-relationship'. The one God whom Christians worship is Father, Son, and Holy Spirit. And what He is determines how He works and the shape of His design for us whom He loves. That design is to make us truly human. The essence of what that means is contained in the term 'right relationship'. All the happiness and fulfilment we can ever know flow directly from right relationship; the worst misery we suffer is the consequence of wrong relationship. Right relationship with neighbour and right relationship with God are not to be thought of as entirely separate and unconnected. On the contrary, they depend absolutely upon each other. Love of God and love of neighbour are inextricably joined.[3] The matter is stated with the utmost bluntness: 'If a man says "I love God", while hating his brother, he is a liar.'[4]

To accept this is to accept the necessity of coming to terms with sex, for quite plainly the sexual duality of man is central in the purpose of God. There are many kinds and degrees of human relationship but they are all in some sense sexual, and the most intense and potentially creative is that between man and wife. The Declaration of the Methodist Church on the Christian View of Marriage and the Family says in its opening paragraph, 'Since (sex) exists by Divine intention and is part of the Divine order of nature, Christians should regard it with reverence and joy.'[5]

This, however, Christians have never found consistently easy. Indeed, many have found it quite impossible. In spite of all our emancipation, for countless Christians sex is a subject they never

[1] Genesis 2:24 (quoted in Matthew 19:5 and Mark 10:7).
[2] Genesis 1:27.
[3] See Mark 12:29–32.
[4] I John 4:20.
[5] *Declarations of Conference on Social Questions*, Epworth, 1959, p. 96.

discuss. Even so devout a Christian as Bishop Barry, whose scholarly book on ethics I have already quoted with appreciation, betrays an odd reluctance when he comes to the discussion of sex. He introduces a paragraph with the words: 'Glad though I should be to avoid mention of a topic which is now becoming obsessional.'[1] But why 'glad'? The only proper Christian response to the vast spate of idle clap-trap on the subject is to set forth a calm and reasonable exposition of it (which, to be fair to Dr Barry, having overcome his reluctance, he proceeds to do). But is it not time that Christians learned to enjoy talking about sex? It is, after all, much more interesting than the weather, which we discuss interminably, and vastly more important.

Any such discussion, if it is honest, must enquire into the reasons for the sense of shame that for great numbers of people surrounds the whole subject. The reasons, of course, are rooted in the long experience of the race. I have attempted elsewhere to summarize the history of the two disastrously negative and corrupting ideas that have haunted the minds of men and helped to distort the positive and accepting attitude towards human sexuality which characterizes the opening chapters of the Bible.[2] These were the oriental-Greek dualism which regarded matter as evil and cast a particular slur on sex; and the arrogant domination of the male over the female which during the greater part of history has robbed the man-woman relationship of its full mutuality. To these may be added the fear which springs from an awareness of the enormous power of the sexual instinct and its consequent potential for evil as well as good.

The corrective of all false emphases, and the only possible starting point for any Christian consideration of the subjects dealt with in this chapter, is the biblical assertion that sex is good.

Chastity

But if sex is good, what is it good for? And how can we so use and control it as to ensure that it achieves its proper ends? The Christian answer to this question is for many people summed up in the word 'chastity'. There are, however, many different views as to what chastity is. We must try, therefore, to clear our minds on the matter.

[1] *Christian Ethics and Secular Society*, p. 157.
[2] See *The Mutual Society*, Epworth, 1962.

No doubt chastity is commonly regarded as meaning 'no sexual intercourse outside marriage'. A few minutes with the dictionary will prove instructive on this point. One dictionary definition of chastity is 'virginity'. If we look up virginity we shall find that it applies to people (usually, though not always, women) who have had no sexual intercourse. Another word which is equated with chastity is 'continent', and continence is further described as 'restraint in sexual indulgence, often absolute'.

Now if chastity is to be regarded as the word which best expresses the correct Christian view of how sex should be used and controlled, it is, to say the least of it, highly unfortunate that the word has such a depressingly negative connotation. The rule of chastity, in the sense in which it is popularly understood, tells us what we ought not to do, but nothing about what we ought to do. Moreover, it would appear to become obsolete when we marry. No wonder it is so difficult to commend so negative and truncated a virtue.

One aspect of the Christian task in respect of sex education is to re-define chastity so that it has a more positive content. Those who may be eager to attempt this reconstruction had better be warned that it is a hazardous and explosive business. They are likely to be accused of undermining morality, and 'leading young people astray'. Christians have often talked as if there were some strange magic about the marriage ceremony resulting in the rule: 'Sex before marriage is wrong; sex after marriage is all right.' Any attempt to challenge this rule as inadequate or unconvincing is frowned upon by those whose favourite dictum is 'our young people need guidance'.

The need for guidance is not in dispute. The question is, what kind of guidance, and how shall it be given? I do not deny for one moment the part which rules play in the daily life of the responsible person. They must, however, be the right rules. More important than that, they must be rules which are accepted as reasonable. This means that the authoritarian approach is useless. Any Christian teacher knows that at any rate among young Christians there is no doubt about what is the Church's rule. It is 'no sex before marriage'. But there is very widespread doubt about the reasons for the rule, and whether it is in fact valid. The conclusion is inescapable: the Church has been very successful in laying down the law, and singularly unsuccessful in making clear why the law makes sense. It is, therefore, to this latter task that it needs to turn its attention.

A good starting-point would be a critical examination of the rule of chastity as it is popularly understood, or perhaps we should say, misunderstood. In fact, the Church does not hold that sex before marriage is wrong. Sex, as we have seen, is good – before or after marriage. Sex is that ineluctable fact of maleness or femaleness which is given to us from the first moment of our genesis in the womb, and which remains with us till we die. I am, of course, using the word in its proper sense, and in the process rescuing it from the restrictions of the limited venereal, or physical, sense in which it is commonly used. As with ethical discussion generally, so particularly in sex education, half the battle is to sort out our vocabulary and give the full and proper meaning to the words we use.

If sex then in itself is good, it cannot be bad or wrong. When indignant Christians say about some piece of shoddy literature: 'It's disgraceful, it's too sexy,' they might stop to look at their use of language. If sex is good, how can a thing be 'too sexy'? Can a lily be too fragrant?

Of course, the rules we make about sex, however loose the language in which we express them, spring from an understanding that it can be used rightly and wrongly. It would, therefore, be much closer to the Church's true idea of chastity to say that it teaches that sexual intercourse, not sex, is wrong before marriage. Even that, however, is a very poor way of describing what chastity really means. What about sexual intercourse between married people? Is that made right simply because they are married? Certainly not. A man (or woman) can be selfish, exorbitant, insensitive, and cruel, so that married intercourse becomes a nightmare for the long-suffering partner whose dignity is so outraged that love turns to hatred.

The fact that this is so brings out a very important point about sexual intercourse. What makes it right is the quality of the relationship it expresses. But sexual intercourse does not only express a relationship; in a mysterious way it assists powerfully in the creation of a relationship. Before we can be sure that we are making the right rules about it, we must perforce enquire into the nature of the act and what it does to those who engage in it.

Now here we have to be very honest about the facts. One fact undoubtedly is that some acts of intercourse performed by some people have very little effect upon them. They would probably describe them as 'good fun', an 'enjoyable game'. Some moralists argue as if every unmarried person who had sexual intercourse ruined his chance of a happy marriage. We should be profoundly thankful that this is not so. Nevertheless, there is more to be said on the matter. If what I have just written is one of the facts of life, another is that sexual intercourse can turn life upside down for a person. It belongs to the nature of the act that it can produce in the heart of the participant an intense and real feeling of belonging to the other – so great that life will not seem complete without him. I am not arguing that it always has this effect, but that it can have. Moreover, in the nature of the case, you cannot be sure that it will not have this effect upon you. Since the experience of deep sexual union is one of the greatest of which we are capable, it would be foolish not to want it to have this effect. The power to love, to give oneself wholly to another, and in a reciprocal relationship to know the joy of possessing that other, is an experience so profound that no words can adequately describe it.

The Christian case for chastity rests upon an understanding of these facts. As we have already noted, the Bible speaks of man and wife, linked together in sexual union, as constituting a *henosis*: a one-flesh unity.[1] It is the intention of the Creator that sexual intercourse should be both the symbol of that unity and the mysterious means of securing it. If we are dealing with an act which has such vast potential, obviously we must take care how we approach it. The real folly of trivializing any of the great creative experiences of life is that we run the risk of becoming trivial and shallow persons, incapable of exploring the real depths of those experiences. The promiscuous sexual adventurer may remark cynically that 'sex is an overrated pastime'. Those who are fortunate enough to know better can only pity him.

In the past the defenders of chastity have relied very much on the threat of the unwanted pregnancy and of venereal disease as the price which might have to be paid by those who transgressed. Neither of these factors has been eliminated. But even if they could be, there must always remain the awful possibility of

[1] Matthew 19:5.

127

exposing another to the experience of rejection. Such a risk is always inherent in the kind of sexual intercourse which is not intended to be the expression of an irrevocable love. Actions speak louder than words. A woman is not being unreal or unreasonable if she says to a man who has promised to marry her but has now spurned her, 'You have broken my heart.' But even more real is the desolation of one who has experienced that act which is designed to be the expression of love's fullest commitment.

It will, of course, be argued against this view, that in fact sexual intercourse means just as much or as little as the participants intend it to mean, and that the attempt to invest it with some objective significance is a moralistic device. But there is no escape from the fact that very often the effects of sexual intercourse are quite other that the partners intended. They discover to their dismay that intercourse has done its 'real' work; that which, on the Christian view, it is designed to do.

The attempt to see sexual intercourse in terms of its relational end clearly rules out merely casual or promiscuous relationships as wrong. But what kind of relationship between a man and woman can make sexual intercourse between them right? The logic of the argument leads clearly to the judgement that it must be a relationship of mutual love. More than that, the partners must have accepted the absolutely binding nature of the commitment which the act symbolizes, and the obligations which go with it. To have sexual intercourse without that commitment and without the intention to fulfil those obligations is to act a lie. The person who gives himself (or herself) to another in this way is vulnerable as perhaps in no other experience of which we are capable. It is not merely the body which is naked and unprotected, it is the soul, the inner citadel of feeling. It would be wrong to approach so potentially sensitive an area of experience solemnly, for it ought to be full of fun and laughter, but it would be the greatest folly not to take it seriously.

Sexual intercourse is not an isolated act, it is the climax of a whole series of acts expressive of affection and desire. The commonest question among responsible young people when they talk about sex and love is how far it is right to go in the physical expression of the feelings they have for another. Here, if anywhere, we face the inadequacy, indeed the impossibility, of hard and fast rules imposed by a higher authority. The question asked is real and urgent. To regard it as in any sense improper is itself highly improper. The answer can only be in terms of a full understanding of chastity, which we might now perhaps define as 'responsible sexual behaviour'. The surest guide is love informed by knowledge, by understanding of ourselves and of each other. Chastity thus understood, far from being the antithesis of charity, is the very expression of it. This is the love which 'is patient . . . kind . . . never boastful, nor conceited, nor rude; never selfish, not quick to take offence'.[1]

Marriage and family

The discussion of chastity led to the conclusion that what makes sexual intercourse right is the complete mutual commitment of man and woman to each other and the acceptance of the obligations which are involved in this. Can such a relationship exist outside marriage? The very form of the enquiry really begs the question, 'What is marriage?' There can be no doubt that the very heart and essence of marriage is the mutual consent of the partners, the offering of their spiritual vows to each other, and enactment of those vows in all the physical expressions of a shared life. No amount of form-signing, no recital of solemn prayers and phrases over them, can make a couple one unless the consent and intention be present. It certainly does not follow from this, however, that the institutional aspects of marriage are superfluous. They are, in fact, a most important means of bolstering the intentions and promises of frail men and women such as we are. They are also a recognition that no man is an island, and that the marriage of two people is not a private affair, but has vital implications for society.

The law of England and Scotland defines marriage as 'the voluntary union for life of one man and one woman to the exclusion of all others', and in the Western world it has long been recognized that the elements of monogamy and permanence are in the best interest of all concerned. Behind this conception of marriage there lies a long and varied history. Marriage has taken various forms, but these have always been regulated by society. The very earliest type of human family was probably that of mother and offspring. Groups of families formed together for mutual help and protection in clans. Later there developed the

[1] 1 Corinthians 13:4,5.

patriarchal form of family life which we find in the Bible and through the centuries of our own more recent history. Whatever the form of marriage and family, the relationship of man and wife has never been regarded as a purely private affair. The processes of change have been dictated by the social and economic needs of the clan or community.

The Christian teaching accepts and reinforces the view that monogamous permanent marriage is the form best suited to the development of the highest and most stable kind of society. The phrase 'Christian marriage' is often used, especially by those who are anxious to preserve and defend the highest ideal of marriage. But what is the difference between Christian marriage and secular marriage? Christians should be very happy that so much of what we believe about this great institution is accepted also by non-Christians. The desire to draw clear lines of distinction may have the opposite effect from the one we desire. Surely what distinguishes any particular Christian marriage from the rest is the quality of faith, insight, compassion, and devotion which the couple under God bring to their shared life. Such quality is very real, but hard to define, and it will vary greatly from one Christian to another.

The two-fold purpose of marriage is set forth in the noble words of the Christian Order of Service for Marriage: 'Matrimony was ordained . . . for the mutual society, help, and comfort that the one ought to have of the other both in prosperity and adversity. It was also ordained that children might be brought up in the knowledge of God and to the praise of His Holy Name.' The linking together of the fellowship of man and wife, and the bringing up of children, is a reminder of the importance of environment in the development of a child towards maturity. The real tragedy of illegitimacy is that so often the child is robbed of that essential security without which an ordered and stable existence is excessively hard to achieve. It is part of the divine economy that the physical act which leads to conception – the uniting of sperm and ovum – also unites the partners in the act. This unity-in-love is the ideal environment for the child, and children are able to sense its reality long before they can understand its nature.

Since the forms of marriage and family have undergone many changes in the past, it is sometimes suggested that there is nothing sacrosanct about these institutions in their present forms; we may expect further changes as the race revolves. In one sense this is certainly true. The rapid spread of the idea of sex equality has had an enormous effect upon marriage and family relationships. It has meant the emergence of a new pattern of domesticity. Husband and wife now share the household chores to a degree which would have been unthinkable at the turn of the century. The marriage manuals lay great stress on the importance of sexual adjustment between husband and wife. This emphasis—which is perhaps rather excessive in some books – is evidence of the extent to which the sexual needs and feelings of women are now recognized and acknowledged. Since history has been largely the story of men written by men it is not surprising that 'the woman's angle' on most matters has been largely overlooked, and not least on sexual questions. The carrying of the principles of democracy into the home has undermined the old patriarchal pattern of authority, and led to a new kind of relationship not only between husband and wife, but between parents and children.

Other factors precipitating change include the earlier age at which young people reach physical maturity and at which they marry; the increased longevity of men and women; the mobility of large sections of the population; the reduction in the average size of the family and the consequent freeing of married women for employment outside the home; and a vast extension of popular education.

The consequences of these and other developments affecting marriage and the family are far-reaching. Inevitably, some of those consequences are not good. Marriage itself is subject to intense strains partly because so much is expected of it. Where more agreement is required between the partners, as is the case in these egalitarian days, more disagreement is likely. But if the whole situation is reviewed without prejudice there is no need to take the jaundiced view that some amateur moralists appear to do that the whole basis of society is in jeopardy. In fact there is much to encourage. Marriage is not only popular, but is demonstrating its immense toughness as an institution. In all kinds of ways the patterns of marriage and family relationship will continue to change. The Christian should accept the inevitability of change, and that not grudgingly but gladly, because of the opportunities it affords for progress and improvement. So far as the basic elements of monogamy and permanence are concerned, in spite of the prophecies of some *avant-garde* protagonists of so-called freedom, there is no indication of any serious challenge to the contention that these are essential to the best interests both of individuals and society.

Because marriage is seen as a demanding as well as an infinitely rewarding relationship, the need for sound training and preparation is increasingly recognized. No amount of sexual experimentation before marriage can prove compatability. Indeed, it may 'prove' the wrong thing. Sexual intercourse may be found to be difficult or disappointing, and the couple may decide that they are therefore not meant for each other. One or both of them may in actual fact be so constituted that they would find intercourse initially difficult with anyone. There is no substitute for comprehensive training covering the various aspects of marriage and designed to help men and women to understand themselves and their partners. The Churches are happily becoming more aware of their responsibilities in this field.

Divorce

What is meant by 'the indissolubility of marriage'? Behind that deceptively simple question lies one of the most divisive debates that has ever troubled the Christian conscience. Does it mean that marriages *ought not* to be dissolved; or does it mean that marriages *cannot* be dissolved?

There exists in this country an arrangement of co-operation and reciprocity between Church and State. The State recognizes the legality of marriages conducted in church according to the prescribed formularies, and the Church can recognize and bless a marriage entered into before the civil authority. This works very well. But the State has also taken to itself the power to dissolve the legal contract of marriage. What ought to be the attitude of Christians to this fact? There is no agreed answer. The Roman Catholic Church does not admit divorce, though it does make considerable use of the law of nullity. The Church of England recognizes the fact of divorce, but refuses to remarry divorced persons in church. The Greek Orthodox and Reformed Churches recognize divorce for certain grave causes.

What is the mind of our Lord on this matter? When He was questioned about it He replied, "'What did Moses command you?" They answered, "Moses permitted a man to divorce his wife by note of dismissal." Jesus said to them, "It was because you were so unteachable that he made this rule for you; but in the beginning, at the creation, God made them male and females. What God has joined together, man must not separate."[1] Matthew's account differs from that of Mark in one important respect: he includes the so-called 'exceptive clause'; 'If a man divorces his wife for any cause other than unchastity, and marries another, he commits adultery.'[2] St Paul appears to have known nothing of this exceptive clause. On the other hand, he seems to make an exception of his own when he says, in regard to a Christian married to a heathen: 'If the heathen partner wishes for a separation, let him have it.'[3] Some scholars believe that Matthew's clause of exception is a later addition, and not part of the original teaching of Jesus.

The biblical evidence, then, is inconclusive. If Matthew's gospel has reported Jesus correctly, it is still not clear from the text whether the wronged partner was free to remarry. The Roman Catholic Church has said 'No', while Luther and Calvin held that an adulterous spouse severed the bond of marriage and thus set the innocent partner free.

All Christians will accept the ideal of marriage as a lifelong union in which by love and fidelity the partners seek to do the will of God. When marriages are threatened they will do their utmost to heal them. By every possible means Christians will endeavour to strengthen the institution of marriage, recognizing its inestimable value. But when marriages die, what then? The word 'indissolubility' has a hollow ring when one is confronted with a couple who have lost all feeling for one another and have actually lived apart for perhaps as long as twenty years. Some Christians argue that the Church cannot uphold the highest standards of marriage if it is willing to countenance the breaking of vows solemnly made. There are Christians who have themselves experienced the pain of a broken marriage but who, for conscience's sake, have refused to seek the remedy of divorce. Their convictions can only be respected. But this is not the only tenable Christian view. Many would accept the official view of the

---

[1] Mark 10:4–9, with parallels in Matthew 19:1–9 and Luke 16:18.
[2] Matthew 19:9.
[3] 1 Corinthians 7:15.

Methodist Church that 'there are courses of conduct which so violate the pledges and obligations of marriage that of themselves, and in fact, they destroy it as a union of heart and soul . . . In regard to divorce, the Christian judgement will ask that the law of the State shall be so framed as to do honour to the ideal of permanent union and to promote the greatest possible number of stable marriages. Divorce, where there are children of the union, should be granted only after the gravest consideration of their interest, and, whether the marriage is childless or not, should be possible only when the marriage has broken down beyond the power of restoration.'[1]

There has been a growing dissatisfaction with the divorce laws of England. They tend to favour the least scrupulous members of society, they inhibit attempts at reconciliation, and there is often something unreal and even unjust about the verdicts of 'guilty' and 'innocent' which the courts are required to deliver. An Anglican Report published in 1966[2] proposed that in place of the present law there should be a new law which would make the irretrievable breakdown of marriage the sole ground for divorce. This principle was written into the Divorce Law Reform Bill which was given a favourable reception by the House of Commons on Second Reading on the 9th February, 1968.

There is, and there must continue to be, deep concern at the number of divorces in this country – more than 30,000 per year. No one can measure the amount of suffering undergone by the men, women, and children involved in the breakdown of so many marriages. No effort is too great to try to prevent the causes of that suffering. But as long as there is divorce, it is right that we should frame the kind of law which will avoid, so far as it can, the unnecessary cruelties and painful indignities which a bad law makes inevitable.

Footnote about homosexuality

There is a greater public awareness of the problem of homosexuality than there was even ten years ago. This is partly because our society has become accustomed to a greater freedom in the discussion of human sexuality in general, but also because of the pressure for amendment of the law on the subject.

[1] *Declarations of Conference on Social Questions*, Epworth, 1959, p. 123.
[2] *Putting Asunder*, S.P.C.K.

When the Wolfenden Recommendations were published in 1957 they created a storm of controversy. The Report on which those Recommendations were based helped to bring about a shift in public attitudes which made possible the passing by Parliament of the Sexual Offences Act 1967. This Act removed private homosexual acts between consenting adults from the orbit of the criminal law.

To what extent do the changes in the law reflect a fundamental alteration in the attitude to homosexuality of society in general, and the Church in particular? Without any doubt much of the heat has gone out of the discussion, and the more rational atmosphere is to be welcomed. Many misunderstandings have been removed, and the harsh attitudes of the past are giving way to a more sympathetic approach. The Wolfenden Report itself urged the need for more research into the aetiology of homosexuality. It would be generally agreed that the condition is the result of psychological conditioning rather than of genetic inheritance. Psychological prognostications about the possibility of cure vary according to the expert consulted. Within the Churches there are those who take seriously the pastoral care of the homosexual.

Most of the Christian spokesmen who argued in favour of the amendment of the law referred to above were careful to point out that though they approved of a law under which private homosexual acts between consenting adults would no longer be a crime, such acts were nonetheless sinful. There has been some evidence in recent writing of a desire to re-examine the basis of that judgement. For example, H. Kimball-Jones says,

We suggest that the Church must be willing to make the difficult, but necessary, step of recognizing the validity of mature homosexual relationships, encouraging the absolute invert to maintain a fidelity to one partner when his only other choice would be to lead a promiscuous life filled with guilt and fear. This would by no means be an endorsement of homosexuality by the Church. Rather it would simply be a realistic, and thus responsible, solution to an otherwise insoluble problem, for there is really no other practicable answer for those homosexuals who cannot change.[1]

[1] *Toward a Christian Understanding of the Homosexual*, S.C.M. Press, 1967, p. 108.

Before the Church can be certain about the kind of judgement it should make on a suggestion of this sort, and the attitude it reflects, it needs to be better informed about human sexuality in general and homosexuality in particular. In the end, the one thing that matters is the truth, for only as we know the truth about ourselves and each other can we fulfil the responsibilities of love.

11 Concerning conception

IT IS IN the train of events which run from conception, through gestation, to birth that we are most conscious of sharing in the mysterious ongoing creative activity of God. In one of the greatest of the Psalms the writer ponders the facts about our origin in words which move us by their sense of wonder: 'For thou hast possessed my reins: thou hast covered me in my mother's womb. I will praise thee, for I am fearfully and wonderfully made . . . My substance was not hid from thee, when I was made in secret . . . Thine eyes did see my substance, yet being unperfect; and in thy book all my members were written, which in continuance were fashioned, when as yet there was none of them.'[1]

It is not surprising that so fundamental an experience, affecting both the happiness and fulfilment of men and women, and the welfare of the race, should be the subject of intense ethical discussion. A new urgency is given to the question of conception control by the vast dimensions of the population problem. The main facts are becoming better known, and can be simply stated. Down the centuries the population has slowly increased, but in recent times the rate of increase has accelerated fantastically, due mainly to our ability to keep people (of all ages) alive who formerly would have died. From 2,500 millions in 1950, world population leapt to 3,000 millions within a decade, and this number will double by the end of the century.

These bare facts take on a sombre appearance when other factors are taken into account. The increase tends to be greatest in the already hungry countries. The population of India was

[1] Psalm 139:13-16.

250 millions in 1911, 351 millions in 1951, and 438 millions in 1961. The situation would be less serious if we could be sure that every child when it grows up would be able to work, and so help to renew the supplies on the world's pantry shelves. But far too many of them will be weak and ailing; or even if they are strong, they will find themselves in a situation where there is mass unemployment. Either way the result is the same: mouths to be fed, but no hands to help produce the food that is necessary. Whichever way we look at them the figures are frightening, and call to mind G. K. Chesterton's words:

> *I tell you naught for your comfort,*
> *Yea, naught for your desire*
> *Save that the sky grows darker yet,*
> *And the sea rises higher.*

The Paddock brothers may not be right in every detail of their dismal forecast in a book entitled *Famine 1975!*, but their general thesis is incontestable: 'the stork has passed the plough.'[1]

We shall return to the related problems of poverty and hunger when we discuss international questions in Chapter 14. For the moment we shall examine three areas of intense debate, each of which involves ethical questions of considerable complexity.

Contraception

Even if the principle of contraception is accepted without qualification, any particular method which causes damage to health is ruled out. In the case of the widely-used mechanical and chemical methods, it has been alleged by some who are opposed in principle to contraception that such methods may be a contributory factor in causing cancerous growths, sterility, and even lunacy. But the Biological and Medical Committee of the Royal Commission on Population found no evidence to support these charges.[2] It is to be hoped that the fears about oral methods will be found to be equally without foundation.

But there are, of course, wide differences of judgement among Christians on the principle of contraception. I shall confine my

[1] Weidenfeld & Nicolson, 1968, p. 44.
[2] Papers of the Royal Commission on Population, Vol. IV, paras. 46 & 52 (1950).

comments to the Roman Catholic and Protestant Churches, though it should be recognized that views similar to those described are held by Christians who belong to neither of these traditions.

The first thing to note is that the divisions between Christians on this issue can be over-simplified, and consequently distorted. It is sometimes said that Protestants favour planned parenthood while Roman Catholics oppose it. Such a statement, however, gives a quite false impression of the real situation. To begin with, the Roman Catholic Church advocates responsible parenthood, and recognizes that this may involve the deliberate limitation of the number of children. Pope Pius XII, in an address to the Italian Catholic Union of Midwives in 1951, said that such limitation is permissible 'if there are serious reasons, such as those often provided in the so-called "indications" of the medical, eugenical, economical, and social order'. Expounding this in *The Catholic Marriage Manual*, the Rev. George A. Kelly says, 'The obligation of parenthood does not require a couple to have as many children as is humanly possible.'[1]

The over-simplified distinction between the Roman Catholic and Protestant positions also overlooks the fact that on many of the aspects of the problem of population explosion there is no officially formulated view on either side. Some on both sides emphasize the importance of improving food supplies, while others lay stress on limiting population. It would, however, probably be generally agreed by Roman Catholics and Protestants that there is no one answer to the problems created by population pressures. Up till now the need to limit the size of families has received greater emphasis by Protestant writers than by Roman Catholics. Indeed, the Rev. George A. Kelly strongly urges the desirability of large families, and goes so far as to say, 'The control of births, therefore, should always be the exceptional situation in marriage, never the normal.'[2] There is evidence, however, of a growing appreciation among Roman Catholic writers of the demographic aspects of parenthood, and of the need to consider these when deciding the proper size for the family.

Once again, too simple a statement of the difference between Protestants and Roman Catholics may obscure the fact that there

---

[1] Robert Hale, 1960, p. 62.
[2] op. cit., p. 52.

have been considerable shifts in emphasis on both sides. Official Protestant concern about planned parenthood is of comparatively recent origin, and certainly the wide acceptance of contraception by Protestants is in marked contrast to their opposition to the first attempts to popularize it. On the Roman Catholic side, whilst the official teaching of the Church still condemns contraception, a large number of Roman Catholics practise it, and doubts about the validity of the arguments used in support of the established position are frequently expressed at various levels of responsible opinion within that Church.

Whilst, however, on many of the issues touching the population question the Roman Catholic Church and the Protestant Churches are closer together than is sometimes suggested, the extent of official disagreement on contraception can be seen by comparing and contrasting two pronouncements. The first is taken from the Declaration of the Methodist Conference on the subject of planned parenthood. This is chosen as being one of the clearest official statements of what may be regarded as a widely held consensus of Protestant judgement:

> Some Christians believe that the only legitimate means of conception-control is abstinence from intercourse when a child is not desired. The Methodist Church, however, believes that there are other permissible ways of preventing conception. Provided that the means employed are acceptable to both husband and wife, and that, on the best evidence available, they do neither physical nor emotional harm, for the purpose of conception-control there is no moral distinction between the practice of continence and the use of estimated periods of infertility, or of artificial barriers to the meeting of sperm and ovum, or indeed, of drugs which would, if made effective and safe, inhibit or control ovulation in a calculable way. The Conference declares that for Christian people the determining issues (in this as in all else) are moral and spiritual.[1]

The authoritative judgement of the Roman Catholic Church on contraception is set forth with equal clarity. Pope Pius XI, in his 1930 encyclical on Christian Marriage put the matter thus:

[1] *Declarations*, pp. 114–115.

'Since therefore the conjugal act is designed primarily by nature for the begetting of children, those who in exercising it deliberately frustrate its natural effect and purpose, sin against nature and commit a deed which is shameful and intrinsically vicious.'

This categorical condemnation, couched in the strongest terms, is a restatement of the traditional position adopted by St Augustine and elaborated by St Thomas Aquinas. St Augustine declared that 'intercourse even with one's legitimate wife is unlawful and wicked where the conception of the offspring is prevented. Onan, the Son of Juda, did this and the Lord killed him for it'.[1] About this teaching *The Catholic Marriage Manual* says, 'Many people like to believe that the Catholic teaching on birth prevention can be changed,' but 'a thousand years from now . . . murder, adultery, and contraception will still be sins.'[2]

Those who are unfamiliar with the methods of Roman Catholic reasoning, including, it would appear, some Roman Catholics, cannot understand how it is possible to hold so inflexible a position on such a matter. They point out that not even the use of nuclear weapons has been described by the Pope as 'shameful and intrinsically vicious'. How, then, can such words be used to describe behaviour accepted as right and proper by millions of good Christians?

The Roman Catholic condemnation of contraception is a simple deduction, based on the natural law. As the quotation from Pope Pius XI's encyclical shows, it is regarded as self-evident that the primary purpose of sexual intercourse is procreation. This is what our sexual parts are for. The act of coitus is for the giving and receiving of seed. If, therefore, the possibility of conception is deliberately excluded, the act becomes unnatural. It is not denied that the intercourse of married people also serves to deepen and enrich their mutual love, but this is a secondary end, not to be pursued at the expense of the primary end of

[1] The reference to Onan's sin, described in Genesis 38: 8–10 is still used by some Roman Catholic writers to support the case against contraception. Quite apart from the fact that the act referred to was *coitus interruptus* and not the use of contraceptives, it seems most likely that Onan was punished for breaking the leverite law which required a man to raise children to his brother's widow. In any case, many intelligent Christians would feel uneasy about the use of such a passage, culled from the narratives of antiquity, to enforce a judgement about the right course for a Christian in the twentieth century.

[2] op. cit., pp. 54–5.

procreation. Indeed, any artificial interference with the act so alters its nature as to injure its efficacy as a means of strengthening conjugal love. 'One wonders,' says the author of *The Catholic Marriage Manual*, 'how many husband-wife conflicts have their roots in contraceptive love.'[1]

It is no secret that great numbers of Roman Catholics, as well as sympathetic non-Roman observers, have looked to the Vatican Council for some modification of the existing view. Is there any real hope of such modification taking place? Would not any alteration in official teaching call in question the infallibility of the Pope?

It is important here to take note of the fact that the ordinary teaching of the Holy See, as found in papal encyclicals, though possessing very great authority and calling for the obedience of the faithful, is not to be regarded as infallible. Gregory Baum, citing the First Vatican Council, describes the two ways in which the infallible expression of Christian teaching is given. These are: 'a) through the solemn definitions (the extraordinary magisterium) of Councils and Popes speaking *ex cathedra*, and b) through the ordinary magisterium of the universal Church.'[2] (This latter is the unanimous Christian teaching of all the Roman Catholic bishops to which they have come not as the result of external conformity to papal pronouncements, but by their own individual and corporate reflections on the meaning of the gospel.)

The condemnation of contraception is contained in the ordinary teaching of successive Popes. A member of the Roman Catholic Church is, therefore, bound in obedience to submit to that teaching, but this does not preclude his calling for a re-examination of the matter by the ecclesiastical magisterium, nor his submitting the reasons why he believes such fresh consideration to be necessary.

In Chapter 4, as an illustration of the kind of confusion which the use of the word 'natural' often introduces into ethical discussion, I indicated some of the arguments which are advanced against the Roman Catholic position. There is no need to repeat those arguments here, but I do want to look in rather more detail at the distinction so often made between 'natural' and 'artificial'. As we have noted, the Roman Catholic Church is not

[1] ibid., p. 55.
[2] *Contraception and Holiness*, Fontana Books, 1965, p. 262.

opposed to the limitation of families where there are adequate reasons for such limitation. It also recognizes the value of married intercourse as a means of expressing the love of man and wife. The permitted method of control is the use of the 'safe period'. Intercourse during those days of the monthly cycle when the wife is unlikely to conceive is 'natural', whereas contraceptives interfere with nature and are, therefore, 'artificial'. If the use of the safe period were manifestly the best method of control, it might not be so important to argue about the use of the terms 'natural' and 'artificial'. But, in fact, the use of the safe period is open to many objections. Not all biologists admit that there is such a thing as a safe period. In any case, its use depends upon careful calculation, and this makes the method impracticable for uneducated people. Moreover, the restriction of intercourse to one part of the month, it is argued, is itself an artificial interference with the naturalness of the marriage relationship.

We must, then, consider whether the sharp distinction between contraceptives as 'artificial' and the use of the safe period as 'natural' is justified. The word 'artificial' in this context cannot presumably refer to the fact that contraception is a human invention. No embargo is placed on a multiplicity of manufactured compounds which are used by man for a variety of purposes, some of them connected with the functions of the body. Obviously the condemnation implied by the use of the word 'artificial' arises from the conviction that the use of contraceptives is a deliberate frustration of the purpose of nature.

This, however, is a judgement that fails to take into account the fact that nature itself frequently inhibits one function of a bi-functional activity. One obvious case of this is the inhibition, by means of hormones, of ovulation during pregnancy, thus eliminating the possibility of imposing a new pregnancy on top of the existing one. Because of this, intercourse during pregnancy may fulfil its relational role, but not its procreational function. The whole history of man's development is the story of his adaptation to circumstances and his invention of means of overcoming his physical limitations. This, surely, is his 'nature'. Why, then, should contraception, which can extend what nature does already, be called unnatural? May it not be that a deeper understanding of biology, and a closer relationship between it and theology, must lead to a reassessment of the position, particularly if the testimony of married Christians to the importance of the relational function of coitus is taken more fully into account?

The dubiety of the present Roman Catholic teaching becomes even more evident if the differences between animals and human beings are closely examined. The capacity to reproduce among the lower mammals is limited to certain seasons – in some cases the season during which the animal is said to be 'on heat' occurs annually, in other cases more frequently. Further, sexual activity is confined to these periods, and rarely takes place except when fertilization is possible. Among the animals, then, with the exception of certain apes and monkeys which more closely resemble human beings, conception is the sole purpose of mating and the latter cannot take place except when the former is possible. Even so, the fecundity of most animal species is high compared with human beings. Among humans the number of off-spring is comparatively small, as it must be in view of the fact that children require infinitely more parental care than animals. Yet sexual intercourse is not restricted by the hormone mechanisms which determine the breeding seasons in the animal kingdom. In short, to put the matter simply and crudely, a married couple have a lot more sex than is needed to conceive off-spring. We have arrived again at the point already made. If the experience of married Christians is that this 'balance of sexuality' plays an immensely significant part in strengthening marriage, and therefore in making them better parents, should not the emphasis on the primacy of procreation, almost to the exclusion of all else, be reconsidered?

It is against this biological background that Elizabeth Daugherty asks, 'Why do we call secondary the ends of the sexual act which have been accorded in fullness only to us, and why do we call primary the end that we share with the lower animals?'[1]

I have now set forth some of the arguments which are integral to the present debate on contraception. There are, I believe, two reasons why a larger measure of Christian understanding and agreement is urgently necessary.

The first reason is that the present disagreement is bound to impair the progress of ecumenical relationships and united action to help a needy world. The new spirit of cordial fellowship between Protestants and Roman Catholics is a wonderful develop-

[1] ibid., p. 110.

ment which already has made possible a great extension of co-operative enterprise. Divided judgement on a matter so basic as the method of controlling population is bound to be an impediment to progress in those very areas where the need of the world is so apparent, and where Christians can only speak with authority if they speak unitedly.

There is no need to repeat here the now familiar facts about the explosive rate of population increase which threatens the whole future of mankind. The tragedy is that the dire effects of population pressure are felt most acutely in those countries where already poverty and malnutrition are widespread. The concluding sentence of the final essay by Sir Julian Huxley in the symposium entitled *Our Crowded Planet*, sums up the conclusion of a host of well-informed observers: 'The control of population is, I am quite certain, a prerequisite for any radical improvement in the human lot.'[1] Among the priorities in the attack on this problem is clear agreement among Christians about the acceptable means of control.

But if the first reason why Christian agreement is important has to do with large-scale issues, the second arises out of the personal needs and sufferings of hard-pressed individuals. Life is full of occasions of suffering. Some of these occasions are unavoidable, and indeed it would be wrong to avoid them. It is also true that the person who is too much exempt from life's trials can become flabby in character and ineffective in his Christian witness. But there is no virtue in suffering for its own sake. Moreover, morality is concerned, among other things, with human happiness. What deeply disturbs many Christians about the present Roman Catholic teaching on contraception is the amount of sheer misery it is causing. Very many Roman Catholics are sensitively aware of this. It is moving to discover Roman Catholic priests who feel a sense of agony because, loyally accepting the official position, as they must, they are powerless to help many who come to them for advice. Dr Anne Biezanek, the first Roman Catholic woman to open a birth-control clinic, in her book *All Things New* understandably vacillates between scornful impatience with the hierarchy of her own Church, and tender understanding of the very real difficulties confronting the theologians. But when she speaks of the spiritual dangers besetting the

[1] op.cit. p. 188.

woman who is driven to use contraceptives she lays bare a vast amount of raw suffering. If such a person is a devout Roman Catholic she finds herself spiritually isolated.

> Neither comfort nor sense nor hope is to be obtained from the exponents of her religion. In the pious literature that she has hitherto comforted herself by reading she will find statements like the following: 'The one who sins by lust . . . by practising contraception in any form . . . puts on the face of ingratitude. Is it any wonder that God has no place in Heaven for those who use His gifts to insult Him? Can anyone doubt that there has to be a Hell for those who throw God's gifts back into His face by their unrepented moral sins?' (*The Five Faces of Mortal Sin*, D. F. Miller, C.S.R. 1962.)
> In this atmosphere she finds all the moral props upon which she has hitherto supported her personality suddenly withdrawn. She experiences something akin to what the lepers of old must have felt when they first detected signs of the disease on their bodies.[1]

This kind of suffering cannot easily be contemplated, least of all by those who have begun to doubt the validity of the teaching which occasions it. What is involved in the present reappraisal is not merely the correction of intellectual error; it is the need to assuage the sufferings of increasing numbers of good Christians who are torn between loyalty to their Church and the real demands of life.

In the light of what I have written, it must be said that the publication in July 1968 of *Humanae Vitae* (the Encyclical Letter of Pope Paul VI on The Regulation of Birth) evokes a feeling of deep disappointment and dismay. The early pages of that encyclical raised hopes of a more enlightened and realistic approach. The Pope recognizes the new understanding of the value of conjugal love in marriage, and the scientific developments which have given man greater dominion over the forces of nature. He then asks:

> Could it not be admitted that the intention of a less abundant but more rationalized fecundity might transform a materially sterilizing intervention into a licit and wise control of birth? Could it not be admitted, that is, that the finality of procreation

[1] op. cit. Peter Smith, 1964, pp. 87–88.

pertains to the ensemble of conjugal life, rather than to its single acts? It is also asked whether, in view of the increased sense of responsibility of modern man, the moment has not come for him to entrust to his reason and his will, rather than to the biological rhythms of his organism, the task of regulating birth.[1]

The Holy Father then proceeds to acknowledge the value of the work done by the Study Commission instituted by Pope John XXIII in March 1963. The reports of that Commission were only unofficially released, but they indicate a clear majority in favour of a radical change in the Church's teaching. Nevertheless, the Pope felt compelled to reject the majority view of the Commission and to reiterate the traditional teaching of his Church.

Unhappily, the familiar arguments which an increasing number have come to regard as fallacious are supported by reference to the allegedly evil consequences of the use of birth control methods.

Upright men can even better convince themselves of the solid grounds on which the teaching of the Church in this field is based, if they care to reflect upon the consequences of methods of artificial birth control. Let them consider, first of all, how wide and easy a road would thus be opened up towards conjugal infidelity and the general lowering of morality. Not much experience is needed in order to know human weakness, and to understand that men, especially the young, who are so vulnerable on this point, have need of encouragement to be faithful to the moral law, so that they must not be offered some easy means of eluding its observance. It is also to be feared that the man, growing used to the employment of anti-conceptive practices, may finally lose respect for the woman and, no longer caring for her physical and psychological equilibrium, may come to the point of considering her as a mere instrument of selfish enjoyment, and no longer as his respected and beloved companion.[2]

This passage will seem so far removed from reality to many who have first-hand experience as to confirm the fear that it is almost too much to hope for a sound official judgement on such matters

[1] On the Regulation of Birth, p. 5.
[2] ibid., pp. 20–21.

from a Church so dominated by the kind of theology that celibate males have produced for centuries.

The publication of the Encyclical has been followed by an immense furore of debate all over the world, the dimensions of which must surely have caused some surprise in Vatican circles. Rebellious priests have been disciplined, and attempts have been made through pastoral letters and archiepiscopal utterances to soften the blow for Roman Catholics who are practising contraception by telling them that they must not stay away from the sacraments, but continually confess their sin and promise to do their best to keep the law. (The psychological consequences of this kind of tension really do not bear contemplation.)

The whole of this vast discussion must be seen as part of the crisis of authority which has been growing in all authoritarian institutions. It may be that *Humanae Vitae* marks a major turning-point in the history of Roman Catholicism. When Pope Paul rejected the principle of collegiality and fell back on the authority of his office, he was setting his face against the tide of history. That he did so with the deep sincerity and compassion which are characteristic of the man does not alter the fact that he was wrong. Those who have never been able to accept the concept of an authoritarian Church may take heart. The renewal and re-structuring of the Church – and not least the Church of Rome – will not happen overnight. The forces of conservative reaction are immensely strong, but the wind which bloweth where it listeth is rending with its destructive and creative force the structures which even a little while ago seemed monolithic and immutable. The words of Leo Pyle are apposite:

In human terms, the point of view of *Humanae Vitae* is insupportable. Its final, creaking, support is the monarchical papacy. It is for this reason that the debate must continue, for the papacy in its present form, now seen in its authoritarian reality, is at odds with the demands of the gospel, as we see these demands crying out for action and commitment in the world. The tragedy of the situation is relieved by the new possibilities it opens up, of a reformed Church manifesting in its life and involvement the possibility of a truly human redeemed existence.'[1]

[1] *Pope and Pill*, Leo Pyle, Darton, Longman and Todd, 1968, p. 236. This book contains a most useful documentation on the birth regulation debate.

One final point which must be briefly mentioned is the growing demand for contraceptive advice for young, unmarried people. This demand has been accelerated by the passing of the National Health Service (Family Planning) Act 1967 which enables local health authorities to provide services in connexion with family planning under the National Health Service. The Act does not restrict the giving of such services to married people. Many Christians have been exercised in their minds as to whether they could conscientiously work in Youth Advisory Centres where such advice is given to the unmarried. Obviously this is a matter on which individuals must follow their consciences. My own view is that it would be very unfortunate if there were not an active Christian participation in a form of service which is bound to expand in the coming days.

Abortion

The problem of abortion is extraordinarily complex, involving religious, ethical, legal, and medical considerations.

The absolutist view which regards the deliberate destruction of the newly-fertilized ovum as a form of murder is difficult to accept because there is so obvious a difference between the speck of matter which exists at that time, and a fully-developed human being. The fact that spontaneous natural abortion occurs so frequently in the early weeks of pregnancy increases the difficulty of believing that the embryo is a human being whose right to life must be safeguarded by a law which permits of no exceptions. On the other hand, if it is incontestably wrong to kill a child after it has been born, surely it must be regarded as equally wrong to dispose of the life of the foetus during the period immediately prior to birth when it is capable of an independent existence?

Is there any point between fertilization and birth at which the developing embryo becomes 'a living soul' with the same right to legal protection as is afforded by society to all its members? The answer is that any attempt to fix such a point must be purely arbitrary. Following fertilization, the ovum continues its journey down the Fallopian tube. On reaching the uterus about a week later it nidates, or implants itself in the lining, thus completing the process of conception. The foetus becomes a part of the body of the mother at the point of nidation, but scarcely more 'human' on that account than it was before. Thereafter, the only recognizable 'event' during the nine months of pregnancy prior to birth to which it might be possible to attach any ethical and legal significance in respect of the foetus is the time of 'quickening'. This is the point, roughly half way through pregnancy, more clearly discerned by some women than by others, when the embryo is first felt to move. It used to be held that the quickening of the embryo was the signal that the soul had entered the body. This belief resulted from the acceptance of a theory of 'animation' attributed to Aristotle. According to this theory, a few days after conception the foetus was informed by an animal soul, and later by a rational soul – between the thirtieth and fortieth day for a male, and between the sixtieth and eightieth day for a female. (Note that the evidences of male arrogance turn up in the oddest places.) This theory, which was accepted by Christian theologians, greatly affected the development of European law. In England, prior to 1837, abortion was a capital offence if it occurred after quickening; if before, the penalty was imprisonment, transportation, or whipping. Thereafter, however, the distinction disappeared from English statute law. The theory of animation is today widely regarded as merely speculative and irrelevant as a basis for moral and legal decision regarding the status and rights of the foetus.

In view of the impossibility of answering the age old riddle 'at what point does human life begin?', are we driven back to the necessity of accepting the absolutist position and making this the basis of a prohibitive law? An affirmative answer to that question would, in fact, be contrary to the Christian moral tradition, and would be generally unacceptable to the Christian conscience today. Although both Pope Pius XI (in *Casti Connubii* in 1930) and Pope Pius XII (in his address to Roman Catholic midwives in 1940) appeared to uphold the absolute inviolability of the foetus, in practice exceptions are possible, e.g. if the life of the mother is threatened by a ruptured Fallopian tube or uterus, either may be removed with the foetus inside it. If the basic consideration is the value and importance of human life, we are forced to recognize that during pregnancy two lives are involved; that of mother and child. To refuse abortion in all circumstances might well result, in some cases, in the frustration of the intention to uphold the sanctity of human life. An Anglican Report on the subject concluded that 'if we are to remain faithful to the (Christian) tradition, we have to assert, as normative, the general inviolability of the foetus; to defend, as a first principle, its right to live and develop; and then to lay the burden of proof to the contrary firmly on those who, in particular cases, would wish to extinguish that right on the ground that it was in conflict with another or others with a higher claim to recognition.'[1]

During the year 1967 there was intensive discussion about the law on abortion both within and beyond Parliament, culminating in the passing of the Abortion Act. The old law was based on the 1861 Offences Against the Person Act which prohibited abortion absolutely. A later Act of Parliament, the Infant Life (Preservation) Act 1929, provided that any person who caused the death of a child before it had an existence independent of its mother was not guilty of an offence if it were proved that he acted 'in good faith for the purpose only of preserving the life of the mother' (Section I).

In July 1938 Mr A. W. Bourne, an obstetric surgeon and gynaecologist, appeared at the Central Criminal Court on a charge of having illegally terminated the pregnancy of a girl who had been criminally assaulted at the age of 14 years and 9 months. Mr Bourne had deliberately informed the authorities of his action, and his defence was that he had acted in order to preserve the girl's life, and had therefore acted lawfully. He interpreted the phrase about preserving life liberally, his contention being that the girl would have suffered grievous damage to her mental health if the pregnancy had gone to term. Mr Justice McNaghten, who presided at the trial, expressed the view that the proviso contained in Section 1 (1) of the 1929 Act was implicit in the 1861 Act, and that unless the Crown had satisfied the jury that the defendant had not acted in good faith to preserve the life of the mother, he should be acquitted. The judge further argued that 'preserving the life' did not merely mean 'preserving from death' but should be taken to mean 'preserving from the prospect of being turned into a physical or mental wreck'.

This (and a similar judgement in the case of R. v. Newton and Sturge in 1958), was never tested on appeal, but was taken as defining the limits of legal abortion in England, until the recent

[1] *Abortion: An Ethical Discussion*, Church Information Office, 1965, pp. 31–2.

alterations were enacted. Under the new law, abortion is legal when two registered doctors (or one only in an emergency) genuinely believe:

Either that continuing the pregnancy would involve risk to the life of the woman, or injury to her physical or mental health, or injury to existing children in her family, greater than if she had an abortion;

Or that there is a substantial risk that the child when born would suffer from such physical or mental abnormalities as to be seriously handicapped. When the doctors decide whether the pregnancy might injure the woman's health, or that of her existing children, they may take into account her actual or reasonably foreseeable environment.

The Act lays down directions as to where terminations may be performed, and also includes a conscience clause to cover doctors who feel unable to perform the operation for religious and ethical reasons.

The drafting of such a measure as this is immensely difficult, even when the principles upon which it should be based are agreed. Opinion in the Churches was divided on the extent to which abortion should be legally permitted. The Methodist Church supported the Bill during its passage through Parliament in the hope that it would mitigate to some extent the serious problem of illegal abortion. Whilst some Christians believe that the law should disallow abortion absolutely, others hold that abortion should not be the concern of the law at all. The latter argue that it should be left to every individual woman to decide whether she wishes to go on with her pregnancy or not. It is pointed out that, whatever the law says, thousands of women are not going to be deterred in their desire to secure abortion. (Before the passing of the 1967 Act estimates of the number of illegal abortions in Britain varied between 15,000 and 250,000 a year.) It has been vigorously alleged by some protagonists of complete freedom that vast numbers of people are driven to the degradation and danger of back street operations in order that the upholders of so-called morality may keep their consciences clean. If it is impossible to eliminate abortion by law, would it not be much better for all concerned to recognize the fact and remove the legal restrictions so that the operations could be performed skilfully and hygenically by responsible persons? Unfortunately, however, the matter is not as simple as that. Even if all religious objections be set aside – and many, of course, would hold that there is no reason why they should be – there are medical and social reasons for the control of abortion by law. This is born out by the experience of other countries. Russia, Japan, Sweden, and East Germany are examples of countries where the removal of legal barriers to abortion has been succeeded by more restrictive measures. The reason for this has been that the policy of freedom from control has proved to have grave disadvantages. The removal of legal restrictions has resulted in a steep increase in the number of abortions and in widespread damage to the health of the women of the nation, with a consequent threat to the future of the country. It has also been shown that once a people has come to regard abortion rather lightly it is very difficult to alter that attitude of mind.

Sweden is sometimes cited as a country which has found a way round all the difficulties. Legal abortion is permitted for a number of reasons, medical, social, eugenic, and humanitarian. But the procedures are very strict, each case has to be submitted to a sub-committee of the National Board of Health, and, in fact, over 30 per cent of the applications are declined. In a Report issued by the Swedish Institute for Cultural Relations with Foreign Countries it is indicated that in 1962 (the last year referred to) a total of 3,205 legal abortions were performed. It was estimated in the 1930s that there were 20,000 illegal abortions a year. It can scarcely be the case that this number has been greatly reduced, and therefore it would appear that even in Sweden the greatest part of the problem of illegal abortion remains in spite of a very liberal law.

In the end the problem of illegal abortion can only be effectively tackled by means which can be broadly described as educational. We must find ways of reducing the number of unwanted pregnancies. The spread of contraceptive knowledge is essential, but it is the least important aspect of the matter. What is needed is a more resolute approach to the whole subject of sex education. It is also important that every effort should be made to allay the anxieties of those whose resort to abortion may be dictated by fear of pregnancy and childbirth, and the responsibilities of rearing children. In the meantime, the effects of the operation of the 1967 Act must be watched with the utmost care.

Emergent techniques

We have already observed in Chapter 6 that the speed of scientific and technological advance is one of the factors which has presented us with new ethical problems and with questions for which there is no precedent. So far in this chapter we have considered as separate subjects contraception and abortion. Developments in techniques of conception control may bring these two issues together. The main methods of contraception now widely used rely for their effectiveness on the prevention of fertilization. (I exempt from this consideration the intra-uterine devices, like the plastic coil, because, oddly enough, opinions differ as to precisely how these work.) Before long, however, an oral contraceptive may become available which will allow fertilization to occur, but will prevent nidation (i.e. the implantation of the fertilized ovum in the wall of the uterus). The fertilized ovum would pass out of the body as it normally would during the menstrual cycle if unfertilized. The introduction of such an agent would raise the question whether its action is abortive, and if so whether abortion at that very early stage is morally admissible as a means of family limitation. The technical medical reply that a woman cannot abort until after the ovum has attached itself to her body is scarcely likely to affect the issue which calls for ethical judgement.

Advances in surgery which now make the operation for sterilization safe and simple (and possibly, at least in the male, reversible) raise the question whether the operation should be used as one of the weapons in the fight against excessive population. In India, a positive answer has already been given to that question, and there is State propaganda in favour of sterilization. As a result of a request for guidance on the matter from Christian doctors and nurses in that country, a group was set up by the Archbishop of Canterbury. Its Report[1] deals with the issue with the fullness and competence we have come to expect from working parties of the Board for Social Responsibility of the National Assembly of the Church of England. It expressed the judgement that there is no place for compulsory sterilization imposed either penally, or for the protection of society, or for the genetic improvement of the race. But where, as in India, there is a desperate situation, and where normal methods of contraception are too

[1] *Sterilization: An Ethical Enquiry*, 1961.

expensive and too sophisticated, the Report could find no adequate grounds for condemning voluntary sterilization.

It is, however, in relation to the promotion rather than the
prevention of conception that some of the most teasing ethical
questions are likely to arise. Indeed, some of them face us already
as a result of the introduction of methods of artificial human
insemination. When, in the 1950s, the public began to be aware
that these techniques were being used and that already babies
had been born as a consequence, the Churches, as well as other
bodies, started to discuss some of the issues raised. On the use of
A.I.H. (artificial insemination by husband) there was general
agreement that the method might well be used by those who,
because of inability to carry through a full act of sexual intercourse, were childless. The main reservations were on the ground
that the inability to have intercourse might in some instances be
evidence of some deep-seated psychological trouble which could
unfit one or both of the partners for the responsibilities of parenthood; some were opposed to the use of masturbation as a means
of collecting the semen. Of these two reservations I judge the
former to be the weightier.

Christian judgement about A.I.D. (artificial insemination by
donor) was on the whole of a quite different kind. Whilst not
describing it as adultery, Christian spokesmen, with some exceptions, expressed the view that it is adulterous, in the sense
that it constitutes an adulteration of the seed, an invasion of the
exclusiveness of the sexual relationship of man and wife. This
judgement seems to find some endorsement from considerations
which arise out of the likely psychological consequences within the
family, and the potentially harmful effects upon the child of the
secrecy with which the facts of his parentage are surrounded.

Artificial insemination is a technique which was used in the
field of animal husbandry for some years before it was adopted
by human beings. There are, of course, other techniques which,
although they are at the moment confined to use among animals,
might become capable of human application. These include the
use of stored sperms, the transplantation and storage of fertilized
ova, the grafting of ovarian tissue, the induction of multiple
births, and the selection of sex. The possible use of these methods,
and the combination of them, could very greatly affect the pattern
of human reproduction in the future.

A likely reaction to such matters is one of distaste and even horror. Some may feel like saying, 'There are limits beyond which science ought not to go.' That indeed is true, but the question arises, 'What are those limits?' In view of the immense benefits, actual and potential, which science has bestowed on the human race, through the advent of effective methods of contraception, it would be foolish to dismiss as improper all the other possible developments to which I have referred. On the other hand, just because science shows us how to do certain things, it does not follow that we ought to do them. The moral, theological, medical, legal, and other factors in each situation must be carefully weighed as the situation arises, or, better still, even before that, if we can discern the shape of things to come.

An attempt to do precisely that in relation to the matters just mentioned was made by a working group appointed by the British Council of Churches. Its Report[1] takes a searching look at the Christian doctrine of providence in the light of the developments under review. As to the criteria by which those developments are to be judged, these wise words are used: 'To what extent are the new powers, actual or potential, in human reproduction available for the fuller developing of the life of men as persons? Or, on the other hand, to what extent do they represent a threat to such truly personal life, perhaps particularly as it is found within the family?'[2] If those questions are regarded as the right ones to ask, then very clearly any technique which tends to turn men and women into 'breeding machines' is ruled out.

[1] *Human Reproduction*, 1962.
[2] op. cit., p. 31.

12 Penal practice

In CHAPTERS 7 and 8 we touched on the questions of the connexion between morality and the law, and of the meaning of responsibility. A number of difficulties were examined which lie behind one of the great matters of contemporary debate: the philosophy of penal practice and the reform of the penal system.

Concern about these matters has been deepened by the increase in the volume of at any rate certain types of crime. Once again, it is necessary to utter a caveat about drawing over-hasty conclusions from the statistics. They are affected by such factors as population increase, the sort of changes in the law referred to in Chapter 6, and even the attitudes of Chief Constables which may vary from place to place and time to time. It is probably not realized by many that roughly half the total number of convictions in all our courts are for motoring offences; and while, of course, some of these are serious, a great number relate to petty infringements of parking regulations. But however cautiously we approach the figures, they add up to a problem of vast dimensions.

Not the least of the distressing consequences of the volume of crime is the overcrowding of our prisons. However enlightened the ideas of the prison staff may be, the reform of the system they have to operate is obviously made difficult if not impossible when men are crowded two, or even three, into a single cell. All the problems of internal discipline are exacerbated. No wonder one prison officer when I questioned him about the incidence of homosexual practices in prison replied, 'We prefer not to know about that.'

In spite of considerable progress in recent years in our approach to the problems of the penal system, it has to be admitted that we still do not know what to do about the recidivists who spend most of their lives in and out of prison. There is a widespread feeling that Britain has not kept pace with some more enlightened countries in her approach to the treatment of offenders.

These are some of the factors which have led to considerable public interest in the basic questions about the aim of the penal system and the reforms that are needed if it is to be made more effective.

The purpose of penal action

Behind the working of the penal system lie three fairly obvious aims: retribution, deterrence, and reformation. Something must also be said about restitution which has only recently begun to be emphasized. We shall look at each of these in turn.

a) *Retribution*

The idea of revenge is as old as human history. To this day the motive behind many a savage deed is that of the man who has vowed 'to get his own back' on someone who has done him wrong. The Christian ethic finds no place for any such crude concept of vengeance: 'do not seek revenge, but leave a place for divine retribution; for there is a text which reads, "Justice is mine, says the Lord, I will repay".'[1]

In contrast with this crude concept of personal vengeance stands that of retributive justice meted out by society. For as long as men have grouped themselves together in families, clans, tribes, and societies, it has been found necessary to lay down laws of behaviour and to prescribe punishments for those who break the law. Those punishments have been administered in the name of the whole community by persons authorized so to act, and their purpose has been two-fold. In the first place punishment was thought of as a means whereby society cleansed and protected itself against the infection of the offender's sin. Then again it was the way by which society demonstrated its abhorrence of the offence and its allegiance to the established order of things.

[1] Romans 12:19.

This concept of retribution as right and necessary still plays a considerable part in determining the form and function of our penal system. In his evidence to the Royal Commission on Capital Punishment Lord Denning put the matter thus:

The punishment for grave crimes should adequately reflect the revulsion felt by the great majority of citizens for them. It is a mistake to consider the object of punishment as being deterrent or reformative or preventive and nothing else. The ultimate justification of any punishment is not that it is a deterrent but that it is the emphatic denunciation by the community of the crime.[1]

The actual working out in practice of the principle of retributive justice is beset with formidable difficulties. When a court has pronounced a man guilty of an offence, the question of the appropriate sentence has to be decided. A certain number of offences carry a fixed penalty, but for the rest, English law has been content to lay down a maximum penalty, leaving the court free to impose any lesser sentence which it may deem fit. We have noted earlier the problem of deciding with any precision the real degree of a man's personal responsibility for his actions. Two men may have committed identical crimes, but the culpability of one may be much greater than that of the other. When sentence has been passed, that is the end of the court's responsibility. It is those who are then responsible for carrying out the sentence who are likely to be most aware of the effects of the various kinds of punishment on those who are convicted. Inevitably, too, those effects will vary according to the personality of the individuals concerned. In some cases it is probable that the members of the offender's family suffer more than he does himself, and one is bound to ask what justice there is in that. There is the further point that if one of the objectives of punishment is to bring home to a man the wrongness of what he has done, there can be no guarantee that the desired result will be achieved. Unduly harsh treatment may produce a bitter feeling of animosity against society, and the use of any sort of force may encourage the view that violence pays provided one takes care to keep the upper hand.

[1] *The Royal Commission on Capital Punishment*, H.M.S.O., 1953, para. 53.

b) *Deterrence*

One of the arguments frequently used in support of penal sanctions is that society has the right and duty to protect itself against the anti-social activities of those who threaten its well-being. Quite obviously the power of the law to inflict punishment on those who break it does have a deterrent effect, but the matter is not as simple as some people appear to think.

To begin with, no one knows how many potential criminals are deterred by fear of the consequences of breaking the law. We only hear about those who are not deterred. Even though capital punishment has been abolished in Britain, the belief lingers on that it is a uniquely effective deterrent, although there is no evidence to prove this. On the contrary, the experience of all the abolitionist countries is that the retention or otherwise of the capital sentence makes no discernible difference to the murder rate.

The fact that many people are not deterred from committing crimes by thought of the punishment which may ensue is not surprising when certain facts about crime are borne in mind. Many crimes are committed in moments when tempers flare or when the processes of rational thought are in abeyance. Few murderers, for example, calmly sit down and weigh up the likely consequences of their action before they commit the deed. Some criminals, of course, are of the calculating type. They probably reckon that they have a very good chance of escaping detection – and so they have, since more than half the crimes known to the police are never cleared up. In some cases people commit crimes in order to experience punishment. They are people with a morbid sense of guilt who are in need of psychiatric and spiritual help.

The objections to making deterrence the main aim of the penal system really began to be apparent after the middle of the last century. When Australia finally closed its doors to the import of convicts, England was forced to face the fact that it would have to live with its discharged prisoners. It became evident that there was a type of person, known as recidivist, who was obviously not deterred by punishment, but who returned again and again to prison. Some prisoners, far from being improved by imprisonment, were made more dangerous and anti-social by the experience of incarceration.

Although judges still sometimes impose exemplary sentences –
'I am determined to make an example of you in order to stamp
out this kind of behaviour; I sentence you to twenty years
imprisonment' – the morality of such harsh punishment is increasingly being challenged. Can it ever be right to use a person
in this way as a means to an end?

The Gladstone Committee, which reported in 1895, was set
up to try to provide forms of punishment which would successfully deter without producing harmful effects on those who were
subjected to it. The Report placed strong emphasis on the need
to try to reform the offender.

c) *Reformation*

It goes without saying that the crime problem would disappear if
all those with criminal tendencies were reformed. It is now the
confessed aim of the prison system in England to 'fit people to live
a good and useful life'. Whilst this idea is very attractive, it
raises, like the other elements which lie behind the aims of our
penal system, substantial questions, both moral and practical.
Forcible reformation is really a contradiction in terms. People
cannot be compelled to be virtuous, for goodness is essentially the
voluntary response of the free spirit. Attempts to force a human
personality into a prescribed mould – however excellent the
resulting shape may be supposed to be – can be grossly immoral.
We react instinctively against any kind of forcible brain-washing,
whether it is undertaken by communist police officers, or high-
pressure religious evangelists.

In practical terms it may be asked whether there can be any
real hope of transforming the character of an offender through
the experience of imprisonment, so long as our prisons remain
overcrowded and for the most part unsuited to the application of
modern ideas of penal treatment. The very fact that it is almost
impossible to provide adequate work for prisoners to do is in
itself an enormous liability.

d) *Restitution*

The Probation of Offenders Act provided for the payment of
compensation or damages, but it was rarely put into effect.
Any doubts there may have been about the legality of such
arrangements were cleared up by the Criminal Justice Act 1945.

Under this Act an offender may be ordered by the court to pay damages or compensation to the victim of his offence, though in courts of summary jurisdiction the maximum amount is fixed at £100.

There are, of course, difficulties in applying the principle of restitution. Some offenders have no means of paying what might be regarded as reasonable financial damages. In the case of grave offences the harm done may be greater than could be compensated for by the largest monetary payment. But in view of the fact that common justice demands that, wherever possible, some compensation should be made, and also that this is probably the best way of bringing home to the offender the seriousness of his offence, it is important that restitution should be regarded as an integral element in our penal system. The announcement of a State system of compensation is a tacit admission that the State bears some responsibility for the existence of crime.

A working party set up by the Free Church Federal Council prepared a memorandum for the Royal Commission on the Penal System in England and Wales which expressed the following judgements about the matters we have just reviewed:

1. It is our conviction that the paramount objective of the penal system should be the rehabilitation of the offender, both in his own interest and for the safety of the public. In the light of modern knowledge of the factors which predispose to delinquency we believe that this objective can only be achieved by positive measures of treatment designed to counteract the pressures which make for crime. Harsh measures of punishment which are designed to humiliate and degrade the offender have no place in a programme which aims at the improvement of his character. The emphasis should be on treatment rather than on punishment.

2. We realize that the principle of retribution cannot be eliminated at once. Penal reform cannot go too far ahead of public opinion. It is understandable that the law-abiding majority should feel indignation towards those who break the law, especially when security is threatened by violence. On the other hand, the reforms of recent years have shown that public opinion can be educated to see that the surest way of defending morality and good order is to reform the offender.

The creation of a climate of opinion favourable to the increasing application of reformative techniques is a task to which the nation should address itself and in which the Church should take a prominent part.

3. We do not rule out the deterrent effect of penal action altogether, but we are persuaded that any deterrent value which punishment has been supposed to contain will be preserved by more certain detection and conviction, even when the treatment prescribed for convicted offenders is beneficial. As citizens we are concerned about the increasing volume of crime, but we do not believe that crime waves are governed by the methods of punishment in operation at any given time. If the weight of the deterrent factor can be reduced, fuller attention can be given to the elimination of those factors in our society which are known to conduce towards delinquency.[1]

The judgements contained in the foregoing three paragraphs reflect a change in emphasis away from the idea of retribution and towards the idea of reformation. Does this mean that the notion of retributive justice must be abandoned and no longer regarded as an essential element in the Christian understanding of how offenders should be treated? At the philosophical level, the argument is often inconclusive. In the realm of practice, however, the issues become somewhat clearer. There are obvious dangers in eliminating the whole concept of retribution from our thinking on penal matters. Justice is immensely important, however difficult it may be to administer. In our attempts to be fair to the offender, we may be unfair to society. If the device of the indeterminate sentence is used, on the ground that only those in charge of the offender can judge when he is sufficiently reformed to be discharged, this may lead to unjust detention.

Precise agreement on the theory of penal practice is made more difficult by the fact that the traditional meaning of many of the terms employed is changing under the pressure of practical experience. It is not always clear exactly what is meant, for example, by the word 'punishment', and when punishment becomes treatment. In the end the crucial question is not the philosophical one but the practical one: What type of treatment produces the best results?

[1] *Penal Reform*, Free Church Council, 1965, pp. 9–10.

The reform of the penal system

In the light of the general principles already quoted, the Free Church Working Party proceeded to comment on a number of related matters. It drew attention to certain laws which seem to set aside the treasured principle of British law, that a person is to be regarded as innocent until he is proved guilty. An example is the case of a man loitering who may be required to satisfy the court that he had no criminal intent. This is a point which needs careful watching, for the law is bound to fall into disrepute if it appears to be interfering unnecessarily with the freedom and dignity of the individual. Sometimes during the court proceedings a person in the dock is humiliated by harsh rebukes and discourteous mode of address which can only undermine his self-respect.

The Free Church Council Report also drew attention to the need to stimulate fruitful co-operation between the police and the public. The shortage of police personnel is to be deplored. It is certainty of detection which is likely to prove the most effective deterrent to potential offenders. The government should be encouraged to maintain its opposition to suggestions that the police should be armed. To provide policemen with guns would only increase the idea of civil war between the criminals and society, and would do nothing to eliminate violence. The situation in the U.S.A. should serve as a warning. The murder rate there is six times higher than that of Britain, and in New York one sixth of the killings are the result of shootings by the police.

Partly because of concern about what appeared to be deteriorating relations between police and public, a group was set up by the Church of England's Board for Social Responsibility. Its Report[1] shows a sympathetic awareness of the fact that any group of people primarily concerned with human conduct is likely to become somewhat set apart from the life of the community. There are parallels here between the police and ministers of religion. This means inevitably that the maintenance of law and order is regarded as the business of the police rather than the concern of the whole community.

A continuing group consisting of representatives of the police and the Churches has been set up to stimulate appropriate

[1] *Police: a Social Study*, Church Information Office, 1967.

regional and local activities. The responsibility of the Churches is described in the following terms:

> The Churches must carry some responsibility for the education of the public concerning the role and function of the police in modern society. They must work to ensure that the police have the support they need. In addition they must minister more effectively to policemen as such and take their part in ensuring that police organization and thinking are enlightened by those insights into social life and human good which the Christian faith gives and which are the common concern of policemen, ministers of religion, lawyers, and social workers. The functions of these groups of people are far from being identical but they have need of each other.[1]

There are many growing-points in the field of penal reform. The use of attendance centres should be encouraged. Experience on the Continent has shown that these can be a valuable means of dealing with offenders without the necessity of breaking up homes by removing persons from their social and domestic environments. There is need for more homes, and hostels for the training of young people who need a period away from their usual surroundings in which they have fallen into bad ways and disreputable company. Considerable improvements have been made in the after-care of discharged prisoners. Many a prisoner finds that his real problems begin when he is released and has to face the task of integrating himself into society again. Half-way houses, such as the Langley and Norman houses, have proved their worth. But they need more support. They face an acute problem in finding suitable staff for a work which is extremely demanding, and often disappointing.

The system known as 'probation' was described by the Economic and Social Council of the United Nations as 'one of the most important aspects of the development of a rational and social criminal policy'.[2] Probation developed from the old system of binding over to be of good behaviour. It began as a voluntary activity carried out by the Police Court Missionaries. It has now developed into a great system dealing with more than 60,000

---

[1] op. cit., pp. 67–8.
[2] Foreword to a Report on the *European Seminar on Probation*, London, 1952.

people on probation, and with 10,000 who have left penal institutions. It handles over 75,000 matrimonial problems every year, and makes more than 100,000 enquiries annually for the guidance of the courts.

The whole idea of probation still meets with opposition from those whose reaction is apt to be similar to the opening words of John St John's excellent study *Probation – the Second Chance*: 'Another let-off! What he needs is a bloody good thrashing – no blotting-paper in his trousers neither.'[1] But the probation system has helped great numbers of offenders to steer a course away from crime. Mr St John's concluding judgement upon it is worth quoting:

> Probation is designed precisely to make the offender become more responsible for his behaviour; it does in fact protect society, as well as offer practical and tolerant help to the offender, thus showing that in many cases the interest of the offender and society need not be in conflict. It offers a workable, intelligent reconciliation between the interests of both. Though it means overlooking the Home Office research unit's 'matched' comparison, I find it very difficult, too, not to believe that for the majority of offenders probation is more likely to boost responsibility and independence than does a stretch in prison. Probation, being founded on faith in the individual, is positive and avoids the sense of hopelessness that pervades most of our prisons and the special difficulties faced by the ex-prisoner in re-establishing himself – these erode the texture of responsibility as certainly as atomic radiation destroys the marrow in our bones.[2]

The problem of prison

The words just quoted echo the mounting criticism of prisons which is to be found in many of the recent books on penal reform. Much has been done to improve the prison system. The brutal conditions of a previous day have been greatly modified, a new type of humane officer has been attracted to the prison service, and the use of parole has been extended. The use of the open type

[1] Vista Books, 1961, p. 11.
[2] ibid., pp. 261–262.

of prison has encouraged a sense of responsibility in offenders who have qualified for transfer to them.[1]

Sington and Playfair, in their book *Crime, Punishment and Cure*,[2] challenge the assumption of most penal reformers that prison is an indispensable and potentially good institution. They believe that there can be no real solution to the problem of crime prevention as long as the prison system survives. Their concept of a truly constructive penal policy is set forth under five propositions.

The first of these is contained in John Stuart Mill's thesis that 'the only purpose for which power can rightfully be exercised over any member of a civilized community against his will is to prevent harm to others'.

The second proposition is that the law should concern itself only with preventing crime and not with punishing it.

The third proposition is that in order to prevent crime the forces of detection must be very greatly enlarged and improved. In so far as punishment may be necessary to prevent crime, methods other than imprisonment must be developed.

The fourth proposition is that more attention must be given to environmental factors and to the elimination of incentives to crime.

The final proposition is that when, for its own protection, society is compelled to deprive a person of his liberty, such a person should be regarded as neither responsible nor punishable. Everything possible should be done to re-fit him for life in the free world.

These propositions will sound revolutionary to some and others will regard them as irresponsible. They have, in fact, been strongly criticized, yet the authors have produced some cogent arguments and their references to forward-looking experiments being undertaken in Scandinavia, the U.S.A., West Germany, France, and elsewhere are impressive. There is need for a constant challenge to old established ideas and entrenched traditions and for more openness of mind on the part of the public to new notions of how the vast problem of crime might be more effectively tackled. In the search for better methods some risks must be taken, just as employers of labour must sometimes be willing

---

[1] For a useful comparison see Chapter 5, entitled 'Prisons of Yesterday and Prisons of Today' in *The English Penal System*, W. A. Elkin, Penguin, 1957.

[2] Secker and Warburg, 1965.

to run a risk if a discharged prisoner is to be given a job and a chance to prove himself.

The possibility of turning the penal system in the direction of reformation should appeal particularly to Christians. They already play a not unimportant role in such key positions as prison chaplains and visitors, in the prison and probation services, and in the manning of the homes and hostels already referred to. But the whole Christian community must be encouraged to share in the thinking and discussion about penal reform which is so lively an issue at the present time. Sir Winston Churchill, when he was Home Secretary, set the tone for such discussion in the following wise and measured words:

> The mood and temper of the public in regard to the treatment of crime and criminals is one of the most unfailing tests of the civilization of any country. A calm dispassionate recognition of the rights of the accused and even of the convicted criminal against the State; a constant heart-searching of all charged with the deed of punishment; tireless efforts towards the discovery of regenerative processes; unfailing faith that there is a treasure, if you can find it, in the heart of every man. These are the symbols which in the treatment of crime and criminals make and measure the stored-up strength of a nation and are sign and proof of the living virtue in it.

13 Politics and economics

The nature of politics

A FEW WEEKS before Nigeria became independent I made a tour of the Eastern and Western regions. Everywhere I was met by crowds of friendly and ebullient people. They were full of hope and excited expectation as they looked to the future. There might be doubts in the minds of some about the soundness of the country's federal structure, and fears about the tribal antagonisms which simmered under the surface of the nation's life, but none of these things were allowed to mar the impression of a people facing a great future.

There was, however, one disturbing point which recurred again and again at public meetings and in private conversation. When I appealed for Christian involvement in the political life of the country, there were dark allegations about corruption. 'Since the only way to enter politics is to bribe your way in, is the Christian justified in doing so?' was a typical question. The more I learned about the facts, the more difficult I found it to answer.

All too soon the Nigerian Federation was to be torn apart by the bloody conflict which followed the Biafran breakaway. The secrets of stable government and democratic co-operation are often bought at a very heavy price. It would be both foolish and unfair to expect the young nations of Africa to achieve overnight the refinements of political understanding which the older nations of the West have built up over centuries. And in any case, Europe has in this present century known violence as terrible as anything that has happened in Africa.

The question asked by the Nigerian Christians does, however, state with peculiar force a perennial problem which none of us can escape. The kaleidoscope of history provides examples of situations in which the Church has exercised tremendous political power, whilst at other times it has retreated from the world, urging its members to keep their hands clean. No one reading this book can doubt the writer's conviction that Christians must be involved in politics, and this is certainly the view to which the British Churches subscribe. There is abundant evidence for this in their teaching and their structures, at least at the headquarters level. But as we saw in the chapter on the transition from theory to practice, the acceptance of such an involvement exposes the Christian to tensions and difficulties which are an ineluctable part of the situation of the Church-in-the-world.

We must now look rather more carefully at the nature of politics so that we may understand more fully our responsibilities and justify our acceptance of them.

The practice of politics arises from the fact that man is a social being. Each one of us is aware of his existence as an individual, but when we stop to ask how we come to be what we are, then we are immediately aware of the profound truth of Emerson's saying: 'No man is the whole of himself, his friends are the rest of him.' The name I bear was given to me by others, as were certain in-built features both of weakness and strength. I am only able to speak because others gave me words, and vast numbers of people have contributed to those processes of thought and the varied experiences which have helped to form my character. The meals I eat, the journeys I make, the goods I buy, this book which I write, all testify to my dependence upon others. The mysterious fact of individuality is obvious enough; but no less obvious is the fact that 'we are members one of another'.

The word 'politics' is derived from the Greek word *polis*, meaning city, and refers to the way the social life of man is organized and governed. The dual fact that man is both a separate person and a member of society poses the central problem of politics, which is how to keep a right balance between the rights of the individual and the welfare of the community to which he belongs. The solution to the problem can never be final and fixed, for the proper balance is something which must be maintained amidst the flux and fever of ever changing situations. The Christian citizen must be concerned to keep a creative tension between the two extremes, one of which sets the rights of the community before any consideration of individual welfare, and the other of which puts the individual at the centre.

The attempt to maintain the kind of tension just referred to is inevitably an extremely complex business, and this is why the political arena is full of the noise and clamour of contending factions. The kind of balance a man tries to strike will very much depend on his basic philosophy of life, his understanding of what we are, and what we are here for. Extreme individualism takes the view that I am here to look after my own interests first and foremost, and therefore anything which gets in my way, or any person who thwarts my designs, must be ruthlessly crushed. Extreme collectivism on the other hand makes the power of the State absolute. The Marxist doctrine regards a man as a unit whose true fulfilment is found in the progress of the community which is so much greater than himself. A political system built on either of these philosophies can bring very great hurt to individual persons. Individualism run riot produces cut-throat competition and the exploitation of the poor by the rich. Doctrinaire collectivism can ride rough shod over personal liberties and cast a pall of colourless conformity over what should be the rich, diversified life in which individuals are able to express their own personalities and take their own initiatives.

The Christian approach

Has Christian faith any specific contribution to make to the working out of a balanced political philosophy? Only an affirmative answer can do justice to the content of the New Testament, and enable the Christian to hold with consistency that the whole of life is subject to the over-ruling providence of God.

It may sound strange to those who are still minded 'to keep politics out of religion' to say that our Lord was crucified because of His political views. Nevertheless, if the term political is given its broadest – though still strictly accurate – meaning, this is true. The relationship between the subject Jewish people and their Roman overlords was a political issue if ever there was one.

Jesus opposed the idea of rebellion, and talked openly about the duty of loving our enemy. He acknowledged the authority of Caesar, though He stated clearly that even Caesar is subject to God.[1] This was a message calculated to offend both sides.

St Paul also taught the duty of obedience to higher authority.[2] The authority of the State is ordained by God for the restraining of wickedness and the encouragement of the good life. If, however, the State requires from a man what his conscience cannot allow, then the Christian's duty is to disobey. The Book of Revelation is written against the background of religious persecution. The Roman Empire is seen as the enemy of God's people who are exhorted to resist. Later on, when the Roman Empire became officially Christian, the Church itself became politically powerful. It began to use the methods of coercion which it had condemned when they were employed against it by the State. This abuse of power was one of the factors which led to the Protestant Reformation.

In England, where a State Church was created with the Sovereign as its earthly head, there was the same temptation for the Church to use temporal power to enforce religious conformity. Against this abuse of power the nonconformist Churches struggled until religious freedom was achieved towards the end of the nineteenth century.

The Evangelical Revival of the eighteenth century greatly strengthened the forces of nonconformity. John Wesley was not only a great evangelist, but his concern for individual souls led him inexorably to espouse all kinds of social reforms. Wesley himself was, inevitably, to a large extent imprisoned within the political thought-forms of his day, and his position would seem to many of his present-day followers extremely conservative. But he set in motion a movement which led to social and political reforms of a far-reaching character. An estimate of the effect and extent of this great evangelical awakening on the social and political life of the country is given in J. Wesley Bready's *England Before and After Wesley*. Not all his judgements would be accepted by students of the period, but he is right to emphasize Wesley's pragmatism. The essentially practical nature of John Wesley's religious faith is brought out in this passage:

[1] See Matthew 22:15–21.
[2] See Romans 13:1–10.

Pivotal however to Wesley's religion as was that creative faith, which needs must issue in works of service and love, he would tolerate no mouthing of cant phrases, no vain repetitions of theological formulae. 'I find more profit in sermons on either good tempers, or good works,' he protests, 'than in what are vulgarly called "Gospel sermons". The term has now become a mere cant word: I wish none of our society would use it. It has no determinate meaning. Let but a pert, self-sufficient animal, that has neither sense nor grace, bawl out something about Christ, or his blood, or justification by faith, and his hearers cry out, "What a fine Gospel sermon!" We know no Gospel without salvation from sin.'

Neither would Wesley countenance any individualistic, exclusive, monopolistic interpretation of religion. To him religion was the be-all and end-all of life, and to exclude it from any department of human affairs was to maim and deform it. No man, no creed, no class, therefore, dare call upon God for puny, selfish ends. 'Christianity,' he continually taught, 'is essentially a social religion,' and, 'to turn it into a solitary religion is indeed to destroy it.' In the *Preface* to the first Methodist Hymn Book (1739) Wesley wrote: 'The Gospel of Christ knows no religion but *social*, no holiness but *social holiness*. This commandment have we from Christ, that he who love God love his brother also.'[1]

A group of evangelical churchmen known as the Clapham Sect exercised a considerable influence in Parliament and beyond in the late eighteenth century. They were led by Wilberforce, Thomas Clarkson, Henry Thornton, and others. In his perhaps rather too fulsome study of their many-sided achievements E. M. Howse says:

Because of the Clapham Sect England's policies and England's actions became more humane and more enlightened. Indeed, Clapham influence extended beyond England. Spain, Portugal, France, Holland, Sweden, Russia, and, at the international conferences, still other countries, were led by pressure from Clapham to actions they would not otherwise have taken. No peace negotiation, no council of the period, escaped the

[1] Hodder and Stoughton, 1939, p. 202.

influence of the Clapham Sect. Amiens, Paris, Vienna, Aix-la-Chapelle, and Verona were all bombarded by Clapham letters and Clapham pamphlets; and sometimes persuaded by speeches and documents carefully planned by Clapham 'Cabinet Councils', and painstakingly drafted by Clapham labourers. Castlereagh and Wellington were scarcely more ambassadors for England than for Clapham. It is unquestionable that Clapham passion and persistence and industry achieved what otherwise would have been unachieved.[1]

The social concern of these men was shared by Charles Kingsley, Bishop Gore and William Temple in the Anglican Church. Hugh Price Hughes and other Free Church exemplars of what came to be known as 'the non-conformist conscience', while differing in many respects from these Anglican leaders, insisted on the social importance of the gospel. The study of the Christian approach to politics reveals a variety of judgements about the particular policies to be adopted, and individual Christians have been and still are divided in their party loyalties. But all Christians who accept that politics are their business would agree that any political system or policy stands or falls by the extent to which it enables men to live their lives as God intends, or hinders the working out of that divine purpose.

The political parties

In what has just been said the Christian finds the criterion by which to judge all parties. The very fact that sincere Christians are to be found in different political parties is an indication that no party can claim a monopoly of truth and wisdom. The individual Christian will examine critically the programmes of all parties and give his support to whichever one seems most likely to serve both the welfare of society and the good of the individual. But the Christian will never give himself so completely to party allegiance that he equates a political programme with the Kingdom of God, or accepts uncritically all that the party says or does. Just because politicians are human and have to deal

[1] *Saints in Politics*, Allen and Unwin, 1953, p. 177.

with the often conflicting desires of all sorts of people and groups in a pluralist society, one elementary responsibility which the Christian citizen must accept is that of constant vigilance. There can be no escape from the tension between the ideal which the Christian desires and what is actually attainable in the given situation. That tension cannot be removed by attempts to create a 'Christian political party' which permits no compromise. Compromise is inevitable in a world such as this, and must often be accepted in order to get anything done at all. There are, of course, political parties which carry the word 'Christian' in their titles. The use of the word, however, does not relieve them from the necessity to grapple with the perplexity of situations in which issues appear in various shades of grey rather than with black and white clarity. The following comment provides an interesting illustration of this fact:

> With the division of Germany the political party known as the Christian Democratic Union was also divided. In the West it became the governing party; in the East it became one of the parties in the government bloc where under the leadership of Otto Nuschke it was clearly an anti-fascist party and stood for liberty when it saw the chance to do so, but as its newspaper *Mene Leit* perpetually demonstrates, it is in an equivocal position. It has, however, emerged as a focus of social Christian thinking not simply for Germany but for other countries as well.[1]

Politics are concerned with power and the structures of power: they are the way things get done. In this field supremely we have to recognize the truth which emerged so clearly in our discussion of Christian ethics that we have no neat answers to many of the tangled problems confronting us. Alan Booth has cogently argued that the Christian who is anxious to affect the course of events in the world does not begin with a few carefully selected 'biblical principles' which dictate all the answers to the practical problems. Rather he begins with the situation and tries to understand it. Booth speaks of the gospel as primarily in the indicative rather than the imperative mood.

[1] Stanley G. Evans, *The Social Hope of the Christian Church*, Hodder & Stoughton, 1965, p. 201.

It has been convincingly shown that all the early preaching of the gospel, recorded in the Acts of the Apostles and the Epistles of Saint Paul, was in the form of the announcement of events believed to have radically altered the conditions of human life. We have only to repeat to ourselves the basic creeds of the Church to notice that they affirm facts and events and new situations rather than principles of conduct. The whole of this present study has involved an attempt to be loyal to this perception of the truth, and to free our thinking from that somewhat secularized and diluted version of Christianity which conceives it merely in terms of a structure of rules of respectable behaviour. But of course this does not in any way alter the fact that Christian truth does indeed impose on us the duties of response in obedient and appropriate ways of living. The Epistles, which begin with great theological assertions, end with very practical instructions about what is and what is not the way of life in the situation revealed by the gospel. The point is rather that Christian behaviour and decision is always determined by a new and clearer picture of where we stand, what we are and where we are going rather than by general laws. It is the way of responding appropriately to the real situation as revealed by Christ, and it is in this sense a way of freedom rather than of legalism. The gospel releases us from a prison of delusions and false views into the light of truth and in that light we can walk without stumbling.[1]

I have already referred to the work of the social responsibility departments and boards of the Churches which seek to bring a Christian influence to bear upon the processes of parliamentary debate and decision. What of the more local and personal responsibilities of the Christian?

Exercise of social responsibility at the local level does not involve local miniatures of the national-level pattern. Direct consultation with Government Ministries, for example, cannot be duplicated on a smaller scale. There is need for a two-way traffic of comment between the national and the local levels, and for the provision of information about the grounds on which judgements have been, or are to be, made. Christian

---

[1] *Christians and Power Politics*, S.C.M. Press, 1961, pp. 118-9.

judgements firmly expressed at the national level are properly discounted by experienced politicians if they are aware that there is no strong and informed support from the Christian community at the local level.

But there is in addition, and equally important, a definite local responsibility. The point that Christian judgements and constructive criticism should be addressed to the level at which decision is made applies to those many matters of local concern on which decision is made locally. The local Christian community has a responsibility for the welfare of the area in which it is set. It is at this level that the Church has least equipped itself to shoulder its responsibility, mainly because the method of the working group has not yet taken root, and candid and regular dialogue on particular issues between Christian and non-Christian laymen is rare.[1]

The Statement just quoted concludes as follows:

According to his opportunity and ability, the Christian should participate actively in the work of his trade union or professional association. He will strive to take an intelligent interest in local and national political affairs, so that he may use his vote responsibly, and will therefore read a good newspaper. Some will be drawn to full participation in the work of local constituency associations, and may have the opportunity to serve as councillors or as Members of Parliament. Those who accept this call are undertaking a particularly valuable responsibility.

Economics

If politics represent one aspect of man's organized life in society, economics represent another. Much of what we have said about the one applies to the other. The economy is that intricate network of activities and relationships within which men and women earn their living and help to supply each other's needs and wants.

In every age the pattern of human life, personal and social, has been shaped to a very great extent by the necessity to earn a

[1] *Declaration of the Methodist Church on Social and Political Responsibility.*

living. In many parts of Africa today, among comparatively primitive tribal communities, the actual length of the week is determined by the frequency of the meetings of the local market. Some villages have a five day week, others a week lasting nine days. Life is geared to the producing, selling, and buying of the necessities of a fairly simple existence.

The same necessities dictate the pattern of our lives in the more complicated industrialized nations of the West. Men have to live where their place of work is located, and this is in turn determined by the nature of that work. The complex and inter-related processes of modern industry, and the growth of secondary and tertiary industries (the work done at one or more removes from the raw materials, and in the administration of commercial undertakings) have given rise to the growth of huge urban conurbations. In order to escape from the industrial areas of the cities, those who can afford to do so move out to the suburbs. Thus there have been created the huge commuter populations and the network of transport facilities which in London carry hundreds of thousands of people daily.

It would be difficult to exaggerate the extent to which our lives are dominated by the various factors which go to make up the processes of industry. The range of available employment is vastly greater than it was in the days when England was largely rural. The variety of foods and goods displayed in our shops is almost endless. Indeed, one of the problems of the Londoner travelling abroad is to know what to buy as souvenirs for the members of his family. He may purchase some trinket which he regards as absolutely unique, only to discover that he could have obtained it from one of the stores in Oxford Street.

Just because we are ourselves a part of this great social and economic order, it is easy enough to lose sight of certain fundamental facts. One of these is that men work in order to satisfy the demands of their fellows. There is no point in producing articles for which there is no demand. Another fact is that the sort of demands we make depend to some extent on the kind of life we want to have, or think we ought to have. It is, of course, also true that we can't have all that we want. Many, indeed, are denied even the bare necessities of life. But even in the wealthy nations where it is possible to satisfy the desire for sophisticated pleasures and all kinds of cultural amenities over and above the basic necessities of food and clothing, there are limits to what at any particular time the economy can provide. So choices have to be made. We can have more motorways, or better schools and hospitals, or the very latest nuclear weapons. But we cannot have them all. Again, in terms of working hours, we could choose between shorter daily hours and shorter vacations, or longer working days and extended vacations.

A healthy economy depends upon a proper balance between three basic factors: nature, labour, and capital. The resources of nature seem almost unlimited, but it is important to remember that they are not. Vance Packard, in his very striking book *The Wastemakers*, looks critically at the American way of life and warns that even in that land of plenty the pattern of consumption should cause grave concern:

> The average American family throws away about 750 metal cans each year. In the Orient, a family lucky enough to gain possession of a metal can treasures it and puts it to work in some way, if only as a flower pot.
>
> When the President's Materials Policy Commission surveyed United States consumption patterns in the early fifties, it concluded that 'the United States' appetite for materials is Gargantuan – and so far insatiable'. It found that each individual man, woman, and child was using up an average of eighteen tons of materials a year.
>
> Other estimates have suggested that the average American requires, for his style of life, ten times as much raw materials – not counting food – as the average citizen of the rest of the free world. Only in America would a housewife hop into a two-ton vehicle and drive downtown to buy the thumbtacks that she forgot to buy on her regular shopping trip. And only in America do people in midwinter warm themselves almost entirely by the wasteful method of burning thousands of gallons of oil to heat up a house rather than by getting much of their warmth by wearing warm clothing.
>
> The virgin continent that American settlers fell heir to a mere three centuries ago is being stripped of its material riches at an ever-accelerating rate. This wealth has made chronic optimists of the people of the United States. There has been so much wealth that they have come to assume there

will always be more where that came from. As an American, Rowland Howard, observed in the last century, 'You never miss the water till the well runs dry.'

Today, however, the weight of the evidence does not support much optimism. Even by the early fifties, the Materials Policy Commission was observing: 'The plain fact seems to be that we have skimmed the cream of our resources as we now understand them.' Since then the skimming has cut down into the milk still further. Today, Americans are consuming considerably more materials than they produce.[1]

The importance of the second basic factor in a healthy economy, namely labour, is abundantly evident. Sound labour relations are essential if any industry is to thrive, and where they are lacking, damage can be done not only to many individuals but to the whole fabric of a nation's life.

Capital, the third factor, may be likened to the seed which the farmer keeps back in order to be able to produce further harvests in the future. It is a vital part of any industrial economy. If we look at the newly-created African States, it is obvious that one of their crying needs, if they are to begin to achieve their dream of industrial development, is the investment of capital which will provide them with the initial impetus which their own unaided resources cannot furnish.

The 1968 Lambeth Conference of the Anglican Communion discussed a number of aspects of social and political change. Its general approach to some of these and to the question of how the mission of the Church is to be conceived is reflected in Resolution 19 which reads:

a) that, recognizing that for the foreseeable future the greater part of the earth will retain agrarian forms of society, the provinces of the Anglican Communion co-operate with the World Council of Churches and other agencies to carry out the regional surveys necessary to determine specific technological and other development needs in both agrarian and industrial areas;
and further, that the local Church in agrarian communities be urged to promote or co-operate in appropriate political,

[1] Longmans, 1961, pp. 195–196.

economic, and social development projects as its witness to the gospel of the incarnate Lord; and that in both agrarian and industrial areas the structures of the Church, devised for static and pre-industrial societies, be renewed for more effective impact on rapidly changing societies.

b) that the normal pattern for the missionary structure of the Church be that of ecumenical action and that every use be made of consultants from the social sciences and related fields.

c) that the Church increasingly call on the skills of full-time professionals in such fields as social work, community organization, education, recreational activities, and the mass media, and that they be regarded as members of the integral staff of the Church.

d) that the Church increasingly work for social goals which really benefit human beings, e.g. in housing, education, health, and adequate wages, using both secular agencies and, where appropriate, its own social agencies.

e) that the Church increasingly give itself seriously to the redeployment of resources of men and money so as to take the initiatives that effective mission requires both at home and abroad.

f) that, in consequence of the last recommendation, a serious study be made of existing buildings and the planning of new ones.[1]

Whilst the processes of economic change are subject to certain elementary laws – such as that we can't consistently spend more than we earn – it must be recognized that economic laws are not blind forces disposing of human destinies as the gods on Mount Olympus were thought to do. At the heart of all economic change lies the fact of human choice and decision. What sort of a society do we want, and how do we arrange the available possibilities in our list of priorities?

Issues requiring Christian judgement

Quite evidently these are questions which are of vital concern to the Christian, but they are rather vague and general. Let us, then, try to pinpoint some of the specific issues on which a

[1] The Lambeth Conference 1968: Resolutions and Reports, S.P.C.K. and Seabury Press, 1968, pp. 34–35.

Christian judgement is required if we are to move with any confidence in the complex field of economic discussion.

a) *Our attitude to the material*

The history of Christian thought about the material world has been bedevilled by the gnostic dualism which crept into the Greek world from the Orient. Its influence makes itself felt in the New Testament, but only emerges fully in the later manifestations of harsh asceticism of which 'the pillar saints' were notable examples. For them the road of redemption was a pathway of escape, and the pursuit of holiness led them into a literal renunciation of the world and all its works and ways. The material was evil, and so they mortified the flesh in order that the flowers of the spirit might bloom in the soul.

The real seed-bed of Christian thinking on this matter is the naturalism of the Old Testament. If one may presume to suggest one reason why God chose the Jews to be the vehicle of His supreme revelation, it is surely to be found in this characteristic element in their thinking. The narrative of the Creation is punctuated with the assertion that God saw the things He had made and pronounced them good. Just as in Chapter 9 we found this to be the starting-point of Christian thinking about sex, so now we must see it as the foundation of a proper understanding of the significance of the whole universe of material things. When God sent His Son to share our earthly lot He gave to us a view of life which, whilst it embraces a reality beyond the bounds of time and space, clothes the material elements of our present existence also with divine meaning. There is, therefore, a theological justification for our concern for man's material welfare, and a truly Christian motive for a full involvement in the discussion of economic affairs.

b) *The importance of relationships*

There is something seriously wrong with that attitude to work which sees it only as a necessary evil, and which grudgingly regards the hours of daily labour as a means of earning money so that the rest of life, which is reckoned to be the real part of it, can be enjoyed. We do in fact spend a considerable part of our life at work, and happy is the man who finds satisfaction in his daily task – a satisfaction balanced by full enjoyment of leisure time also.

But if daily work is to be a satisfying part of a whole and well-balanced life, the atmosphere in which that work is done is very important. I have already referred to the need for good labour relations. These are often marred by tensions between management and workers. The history of these tensions often runs far back into an unhappy past. The memories of old injustices and exploitation linger on, and if the past offences of capitalist owners were grave, present-day trade unionists often show a regrettable unwillingness to leave the past behind.

Much can be done by changes in the system. Sin, like righteousness, is not just a personal thing, it is a social fact: it gets itself organized. A worker in a factory was asked what he made. His answer was, 'S.D. twenty-fours.' When asked what this article was, and where it went when it left the factory, he had no idea. And he had been on the same job for nine years. The whole trend towards depersonalization in vast industrial organizations is to be deplored, and every effort must be made to give to individuals a meaningful place in the total process. The introduction of works councils and joint industrial committees which give to the workers a share in the direction of industry are moves along the right lines. A man may operate a machine, but he must never be treated as a machine.

The other side of this coin, of course, is the willingness of workers to accept a responsible attitude towards their work. This is where the Christian emphasis on vocation comes in. The Christian will not only do his job to the very best of his ability, but he will be a centre of goodwill, a peacemaker, contributing powerfully to good relations between the persons who are his fellow-workers. Whilst there is a real ministry for the industrial chaplain, the greater part of the Church's ministry to industry must be exercised by Christian workers who themselves belong to the priesthood of all believers.

The vast majority of jobs in which men are engaged offer a valuable contribution to the life of the community, and no false distinctions must be made between the service given by the business executive and the refuse collector. There are, however, some forms of employment which add nothing of value to the life of the community. No Christian, for example, could engage with a good conscience in the production of pornography. There are, on the other hand, many forms of service which at the present time deserve to be regarded as priorities by all who are concerned for the welfare of the community. Among these may be included the police and probation services, and the nursing and teaching professions.

c) *Private or public ownership*
The Declaration of the Methodist Church on a Christian View of Industry in Relation to the Social Order states that the principles which ought to be made manifest in the social order are Freedom, Justice, and Co-operation. But does freedom imply the right to the private ownership of the means of production? The Declaration rehearses the arguments for and against thus:

> Those who defend the private ownership of industry contend that it is more enterprising and efficient than any form of public ownership could be. They argue that developments in Communist countries indicate that centralized State capitalism can be more arbitrary and unjust than controlled private enterprise. They contend that the actual working of nationalized industries in Great Britain shows wide variations in economic efficiency, internal harmony, and concern for the general consumer. They fear that public ownership means bureaucracy, the stifling of personal initiative and creative ambition, and the curtailment of individual freedom. Those who defend public ownership reply that in fact there is as much scope therein for enterprise and initiative for salaried management as there is for salaried management in large-scale private industry. They maintain that planning the national economy for the public good can be secured only through some measure of public ownership. They assert that there are wide variations in economic efficiency, internal harmony, and concern for the general consumer in the practical working of private enterprise. It may be that, in order to render service to the community, a publicly owned enterprise does not make profit the sole criterion of efficiency, but particular economic loss is outweighed by general social gain.[1]

[1] *Declarations*, pp. 38–9.

The Declaration, recognizing that we have in fact a mixed economy, and that opinion is divided within the Methodist Church, was not able to go further than the words of a previous Statement written in 1934:

Where the abolition of economic poverty, the establishment of economic security, and the satisfying of the sense of justice and the furtherance of corporate responsibility in the realm of industry are believed, in any particular case, to be substantially furthered by the transfer of the ownership of the means of production from private to public hands, or by the retention of private control, a convincing claim would thereby be made on the Christian mind.[1]

d) *Fair distribution*

Leaving aside what a man receives in gifts, or what he may come by dishonestly, his income will consist of reward for whatever he has contributed to the community. That reward will be largely in the form of money which long ago replaced the clumsy method of barter as a convenient means of measuring economic value and exchanging goods and services. The money will be paid as wages or salary for work done; or as rent for the use of land or property; or as interest on loans; or as profit which is paid to those who undertake business risks.

The greatest of all the ethical problems in the economic field is how to secure a fair distribution of the total wealth of a nation. In nineteenth-century England the capitalist system produced extremes of wealth and poverty which were an obvious denial of basic justice. Many of those who worked hardest were almost starving, while some who lived a life of leisure and luxury did little if anything to justify their existence. Capitalism has taken various forms, but its basic features are the recognition of the right to private property, freedom of business enterprises, and liberty of choice by the consumers.

It is comparatively easy to engage in spirited debate about the merits and demerits of capitalism and socialism. Often such debate is confused because the protagonists have not defined clearly

[1] ibid., p. 39.

exactly how they are using the terms. The Christian cannot accept the extreme form of capitalist theory that would allow almost unlimited freedom to the individual to the ownership of property and the pursuit of enterprises which may be harmful to the rest of society. Equally, however, if the State assumes too rigid a control over the economic and social life of men and women this can lead to injustice, the infringements of personal liberty, and the stifling of those individual initiatives which are of great importance if the economy is to make progress.

There are no easy answers to the problems of justice in the distribution of the fruits of industry. The Welfare State represents a great economic and social revolution. The State has undertaken by taxation to fix a ceiling to incomes, and by social benefits and services to reduce the inequalities which once separated by a great gulf the rich from the poor. The system is far from perfect and many injustices remain, but the importance of the ideals which fired the architects of the Welfare State cannot be over-stressed. The concept of a society in which none shall be poor and in which the stronger shall help to bear the burdens of the weaker is one which must appeal to all Christians who are bidden 'Bear ye one another's burdens and so fulfil the law of Christ'.[1]

One general point I feel bound to make concerning the discussion of economic questions. This has to do with the technical jargon used by the experts. Every discipline must, of course, have its own vocabulary, and those who wish to enter into intelligent discussion must take the trouble to learn the necessary words. When, however, we are considering the sort of economic crises which blow up from time to time, and which affect the lives of ordinary people, it ought to be possible to make the main issues plainer than some of the experts seem capable of doing. If the economists feel that this is unfair to them, they really must try harder to get over to the common man what it is they are trying to say.

e) *Advertising*

The advertising of the products of industry has itself become a vast industry. It is interesting to note the amounts spent by various well-known firms on advertising. The following examples

[1] Galatians 6:2.

refer to expenditure on press and television advertising in the year 1961:

Bovril Ltd	£217,000
Castrol Ltd	£600,000
Hoover Ltd (washing machines)	£900,000
Interflora	£50,000
Renault Ltd	£240,000

At the end of their examination of the advertising undertaken by a number of selected firms,[1] Ralph Harris and Arthur Seldon state a number of conclusions. Some enterprises may not need much advertising, but others could not have established themselves without it. Advertising often leads to improvements in the product or service being recommended, or in competing products. Sometimes advertising can arrest or even reverse the contraction of a market. Again, it has led to the use of market research to discover why goods sell or fail to interest the public. The concluding observation is:

Finally, and not least, there seems to be a clear conclusion that although it may be wasteful because it is not yet a scientific instrument and although it may sometimes excite demand by improper appeals to fear, greed, envy, or by cynical exploitation of sex, advertising is yet one of the most dynamic influences in making the economy progressive. It is difficult to visualize a substitute for it that not only avoids its weaknesses but also embodies its advantages.[2]

This seems a fair and balanced judgement. Obviously advertising provides a helpful service to the community in the shape of information. Most people haven't the time to hunt out all the information which they need to enable them to decide what goods to buy. The advertiser presents the details in an easily assimilated form. One basic ethical requirement is that the information provided shall be true. A less easily determined point is the amount of information which may be regarded as necessary. It may, for example, be true that Lady X washes with a certain

[1] *Advertising in Action*, Hutchinson, 1962.
[2] op. cit., p. 335.

soap, but is it necessary that I should know this? It may increase my pleasure to know that I am sharing my soap with this distinguished member of the aristocracy, or it may not if she happens to be a person whom I don't particularly like.

It is, of course, at this point that the provision of information begins to merge with the other function of advertising, which is to persuade. Here there is need for vigilance. Some advertisements offend against good taste. More important than this is the possible effect on public attitudes of the kind of reiterated appeal to acquisitiveness which characterizes so much advertising. It is perhaps possible to exaggerate the dangers of persuasion, for there is much wisdom in the points made again by Harris and Seldon:

> The critics, including some economists, seem to have lost their sense of humour about persuasive appeals that exploit vanity and selfishness and shamefully contain no details of chemical or technical performance. The ordinary shopper has kept his head much better. How often is he fooled? Does he buy a second dose of the purchase to which he is led by an 'irrational' advertisement? It is the satisfaction derived from the product that brings him back for more. Often it is not so much the advertising that sells the product as the product that carries the advertising. Uninformative but amusing advertising may catch the eye, but it does not sell the goods. Let us not take such advertising so seriously. Standing by itself, it is far less effective than its critics – and its users – think.[1]

---

[1] *Advertising and the Public*, The Institute of Economic Affairs, 1962, p. 81.

14 International questions

THERE WAS a Scottish preacher who began his sermon by saying, 'I propose to preach about man, sin, and judgement, with, if time allows, some comments on the world in general.' It can only be hoped that time did not allow. Comments by Christians about the world in general are not likely to shed much light on contemporary problems. Alan Booth, in a closely reasoned study of Christian responsibility in relation to international questions, recognizes that we need some criterion or standing-ground unless we are to become playthings of the historical process, but goes on to assert that Christianity makes its best contribution when 'instead of insisting on eternal and unchangeable moral principle claiming an *a priori* authority, (it) offers to give further illumination to our understanding of what we actually see going on in history. This contribution is then made in the indicative rather than the imperative mood, or rather the imperatives are seen to arise naturally from our appreciation of the indicatives.'[1] It is a perceptive comment. In the area of international affairs vague and ill-defined moralizings are most obviously futile; comment must be factual, realistic and specific.

Having written this, I am acutely aware of the impossibility of dealing adequately in a brief chapter with any one of the many issues that call for comment. The reader must accept what follows as a lead-in to the subjects mentioned. Closer study of them may be pursued in the books referred to in the footnotes.

[1] *Not Only Peace*, S.C.M. Press, 1967, pp. 54–55.

Poverty

Poverty is a comparative term, and the quotation of statistics can obscure rather than reveal the true state of affairs. Nevertheless, when all proper allowance has been made for differences in the purchasing power of money and the actual needs of those who live in various parts of the world, the figures show the stark contrast between the haves and the have-nots. The average Briton spends as much on tobacco as the average Indian spends altogether. The Western nations have their economic difficulties, but compared with Asia, Africa, and Latin America, they are immensely wealthy. They have 90 per cent of its income, 90 per cent of its gold reserves, 95 per cent of its scientific knowledge, 70 per cent of its meat, and 80 per cent of its protein.

A baby born in Britain today may be expected to live until the year 2040, but a Haitian baby born at the same time will probably be dead by the end of the century.

About 72 per cent of the earth's inhabitants live in the developing regions of the world. The developing countries have increased their exports by nearly 6 per cent each year since 1960, but prices have fallen at the rate of 0·2 per cent annually. Every developing country has to compete for capital with 114 others. Exports from the rich countries have been rising in volume by 7 per cent annually, and their prices have also been rising by 1 per cent each year.

A large amount of aid has been given to the developing countries by the wealthier nations over the past twenty years. In the last three years for which figures are available, the total amount has averaged £2,000 million a year. In 1966 the British Government fixed a ceiling for gross aid at £205 millions. The net total of aid from Britain for the next two or three years is unlikely to exceed £155 millions per year, and this amount, which is some 0·6 per cent of the Gross National Product, has been reduced in value by about 10 per cent through devaluation. The British contribution to aid through voluntary agencies now exceeds £8 million per annum. This represents a great deal of very hard work and some generous giving, but it works out at only about ¾d to each poor person in the world.

The excellent report on *World Poverty and British Responsibility*, produced by a working party of the British Council of Churches,[1]

[1] S.C.M. Press, 1966.

makes clear that the raising of money for relief and aid is a continuing obligation which the Churches must accept. Indeed, their efforts must be redoubled. Individuals also, especially the young and qualified, should consider whether they have a vocation to serve overseas for a short or long period. But the Report also shows that the war on want will not be won by voluntary efforts alone. The three ways of promoting economic development to which the Report refers are the provision of direct financial aid, the redirection and reorganization of the flows of international trade and investment, and the expansion of all kinds of technical co-operation. One of the conclusions of the working party was that 'since governments will only do what public opinion will support or demand, individuals can help by studying these problems and promoting discussion of them in their Churches, in study groups, in political activity, and in conversation with friends.'[1]

Andrew Shonfield begins his expert study of the problems and methods of economic aid with the words, 'The assumption from which this book starts is that there is now widespread agreement about the need for a bigger effort to raise living standards in the undeveloped countries.'[2] That assumption is justified, but it must be recognized that arguments are still advanced by some who have reservations. It is sometimes said that the only help that is successful in the long term is self-help. The dispensing of charity by the wealthier nations is likely to sap the springs of initiative in the poorer countries. This argument overlooks the fact that there is no real likelihood that many of the very poor countries will be able to take the first steps towards prosperity unless they are given an initial impetus by the provision of capital and tools for the first phases of the battle. In other words the pump must be primed.

Another hesitation which some people feel springs from doubts about whether wealth brings either happiness or peace. They point to the suicide and divorce rates in the developed countries, and to the incidence of neuroses, and they ask whether we would not be well advised to leave the poor people as they are. They also draw attention to the fact that it is the wealthy nations that are able to afford the heavy armaments which imperil the safety of mankind.

[1] op. cit., p. 62.
[2] *The Attack on World Poverty*, Chatto and Windus, 1960, p. IX.

No one in his senses supposes that wealth leads automatically to happiness, or to peace. On the other hand, to argue that poverty is a pleasure is absurd. Not only does it cause a vast amount of suffering, but it helps to create those tensions which increase the threat of open conflict. An honest Christian examination of the facts leads irresistibly to the conclusion admirably stated by Edward Rogers:

> The gates of Hell will not be stormed and the Kingdom of God established on earth when all men have a reasonable expectation of an annual income of two hundred dollars. It is not the word of God for all time, nor all his word for this time, but it is surely part of what he is saying to his world and his Church from the midst of the turmoil of events; a light shining on the path to the next stage of our social pilgrimage.[1]

Hunger

There is a story that has already become part of the mythology of the age of automation. It is said that a group of men gathered a vast amount of statistical material about a forthcoming horse-race and fed it into a computer to learn who the winner would be. The answer came back: a horse.

We may arrange the statistical facts about world hunger as we will, and always the main conclusion must be that the sufferers are individual people. Hunger is one of the partners in a dreadful dance. The other partners include poverty, disease, squalor, ignorance, and apathy. It is a dance of death.

Hunger, like poverty, is not a simple word. It takes many forms, and causes various diseases. A man may be technically hungry when he is so full that he couldn't eat another mouthful; but he is full of the wrong things and suffering from dietary monotony. In order to maintain the human body in good health there must be a balance of many elements in the intake of food. Quality, not just quantity, is important.

As with the statistics about poverty, the figures relating to hunger need to be handled with care. If food consumption is measured in terms of average calorie intake, it must be realized that the actual needs of men and women vary according to

[1] *Living Standards*, S.C.M. Press, 1964, p. 120.

climatic and other conditions. Nevertheless, the broad outline of the geography of hunger is clear enough. The maps are being drawn with increasing precision, and they tell their sorry tale. Whereas the average daily supply of calories per head is over 3,000 in the U.S.A., Britain, Australia, and similar countries, the average in Brazil, West Africa, Egypt, and elsewhere is below 2,600; and in most of Africa and Asia it is less than 2,200. There is a depressing correspondence between the food map and maps which indicate the distribution of wealth and the infant mortality and life expectation rates. For example, the infant mortality rate is 24 for every thousand live births in the United Kingdom, and 113 in India.

No elaborate appeal to the Scriptures is necessary to prove that the feeding of the hungry is a basic Christian duty. Let Colin Morris make the point for us again. He is essentially right when he urges us to establish the correct Christian order in our priorities. 'Only when we cease to worry about strategies for the survival of the Church and bend all our attention to finding strategies for the survival of hungry little men can theology come alive again.'[1]

Unfortunately, we cannot assume that the experts are all agreed about the strategies. Estimates both of the situation confronting us and of the measures needed to meet it vary. The Paddock brothers write out of a vast experience of the undeveloped countries (they would insist that to call some of them 'developing countries', which is the current jargon, is to misrepresent the facts). Their sombre conclusion is that the population-food collision is inevitable. Nothing which can conceivably be done, they assert, can prevent the fulfilment of their dire prophecy: 'Ten years from now parts of the undeveloped world will be suffering from famine. In fifteen years the famines will be catastrophic and revolutions and social turmoil and economic upheavals will sweep areas of Asia, Africa, and Latin America.'[2]

There are, of course, all sorts of things that must be done in the face of this serious situation. The search for synthetic foods must be stepped up; more food must be produced from the sea; methods of desalinization must be improved; agricultural research must be encouraged; methods of fertilization and irrigation must be more widely employed; unused land must be used; and the policies of

---

[1] *Include Me Out!*, p. 99.
[2] W. & P. Paddock, *Famine 1975!* Weidenfeld and Nicolson, 1968.

governments must be rationalized. The Paddock brothers examine all these possibilities, and they note what is already being done, often in the face of enormous difficulties. Their conclusion is always the same: there is not enough time left for really effective action.

These two authors write from an American standpoint. Their estimates and forecasts could be seriously astray. Certainly, the viability of their ultimate proposals will be challenged by many. They believe that only the U.S.A. has the resources and the will to take decisive action to avert calamity. They argue that the United States must be ready to adopt the military method of 'triage'. The term refers to the device used on the battlefield whereby the wounded are divided into three classes:

1) Those so seriously wounded that they will die regardless of the treatment given them.

2) The 'walking wounded' who, though they suffer much, will be able to survive without assistance.

3) Those who can be saved only if given immediate care.

Applying this method of classification to the hungry nations, a list is produced of those whom it will be worth trying to save, and those who will eventually win through on their own. The rest must be left to their fate. Most people will recoil from this harsh and terrible analysis. But it is advanced by men who have a concern. It would, therefore, be wrong to dismiss their warnings without paying the most careful attention to the facts, or the alleged facts, on which their thesis is built.

A very different attitude is adopted by another American writer, Dr Frederick Wertham. Writing about what he calls 'the Malthus Myth', he asserts that hunger is a political, not a biological fact. 'Mass starvation is not made in bedchambers but in council chambers.'[1] 'For Malthus and the neo-Malthusians, overpopulation means overcopulation. But a surplus population is never absolute. It is always relative to other factors of production, distribution and social organization. It is relative also to occupation, sex and age.'[2] 'People are not poor because they are superfluous, they are superfluous because they are poor.'[3]

[1] *A Sign for Cain*, Robert Hale, 1968, p. 100.
[2] ibid., p. 101.
[3] ibid., p. 102.

The Rev. T. R. Malthus was an eighteenth-century English clergyman who propounded the theory that population grows faster than food production. The former increases in geometric progression, the latter in arithmetical progression. The only factors which can counteract this discrepancy between the number of mouths to be fed and the food available are abstinence from sexual intercourse, pestilence, and war. Malthus believed that the only remedy for the evil conditions in society was not to change the conditions, but to limit the number of people.

According to Wertham there are nine main defects in the Malthusian theory, and these he summarizes as follows:

1. It views population growth abstractly as a process independent of more fundamental social developments.
2. It underestimates natural resources.
3. It underestimates the enormous existing and potential progress of science and its power to create means to influence nature, e.g. atomic energy.
4. It is not neutral or socially progressive, but is intimately linked to a reactionary status quoism.
5. It is linked to racism and 'leading power' claims and privileges.
6. It devaluates human life as such and debases human sexuality.
7. It prevents the recognition and remedy of basic social problems by substituting biological (sexual) for sociological reasoning for their solution.
8. It is incompatible with both modern scientific biology and social science.
9. It has served extensively as an excuse and justification for hidden violence, domestic and foreign, and also indirectly for overt violence.[1]

It is obviously important that the discussion of rival theories should continue. But it is even more obvious that we must not sit with folded hands until the experts compose their differences. The war on want must be fought on many fronts, and every possibility of mitigating the lot of the hungry must be eagerly seized. It may well be that the Malthusian theory has been used

[1] ibid., p. 111.

as a smokescreen to cover the unwillingness of peoples and governments to face up to the social determinants of inequalities and the need for social change. Nevertheless, to deny that planned parenthood must be part of an overall policy to deal with our present situation is to fly in the face of all the facts.

Population

The facts about population are formidable. Though world population has been increasing gradually for many centuries, the present century has witnessed a phenomenal growth in the size of the world family. The rate of increase has itself accelerated alarmingly. The whole situation has been described as 'Noah's new flood'. This time it is a flood of people, and its consequences could be even more disastrous than those of the ancient flood were said to have been.

Precise population statistics are an impossibility for all sorts of reasons. The total number of people alive is bound to change from moment to moment. Lest anyone should assume, however, that the figures currently quoted by the demographic experts are alarmist exaggerations, it must be noted that almost always when the facts are more fully known, earlier estimates turn out to have erred on the side of under-statement. In 1947 there was a drought in Afghanistan. In connexion with a relief programme an attempt was made to estimate the size of the Afghan population. The Afghan government said it was 10 millions, the British replied that it certainly was not more than 7 millions. A later census revealed that both figures were too low. Today the population of that country exceeds 15 millions. Estimates made in recent years to forecast the size of the United States population by the end of this century vary from 263 millions to 338 millions. But in the early 1940s the experts were projecting a population of 165 millions for the year 2000. This figure was exceeded more than a decade ago. Recent estimates of 6,000 million as the size of the world population in the year 2000 are now being revised to something nearer 7,000 millions – well over twice the present population.

It is not easy to imagine what these astronomical figures mean. It helps a little, perhaps, to realize that the number of people in India increases each year by something like the population of the Greater London area.

The main reason for the emergence of this new and potentially calamitous factor in the history of the human race is simply stated by Richard M. Fagley: 'The chief cause of the mounting pressures of population is the beneficent and spectacular progress in modern medical science and its application to public health programmes in the less developed countries. It is this which causes the dramatic declines in mortality, the main factor in the upsurge . . . it has also had some effect in raising birth rates as well, though the changes here do not compare with the dramatic lowering of death rates.'[1] It is estimated that the world death rate per thousand fell from 25 in 1935 to 16 in 1965. The corresponding figures for Asia are 33 and 20.

The precise correlation between expanding population and the related factors of hunger, poverty, and disease may not be easily determined, but on any kind of interpretation the need for the greatest possible stress on planned, responsible parenthood seems plain. Millions of mothers still die an early death, exhausted by excessive child-bearing. Vast numbers of children die in infancy because they cannot be properly cared for. They are denied the basic rights of a human being. Along with all the other efforts to improve living conditions must go the kind of education which prevents the prodigal use of our powers of procreation.

Race

The Second Assembly of the World Council of Churches meeting in Evanston in 1954 declared that 'any form of segregation based on race, colour or ethnic origin is contrary to the Gospel and is incompatible with the Christian doctrine of man and with the nature of Christ'. It also urged the Churches 'to renounce all forms of segregation or discrimination and to work for their abolition within their own life and within society'. This clear judgement was reaffirmed in a resolution endorsed by the Fourth Assembly of the W.C.C. meeting in Uppsala in 1968:

Racism is a blatant denial of the Christian Faith. It denies the effectiveness of the reconciling work of Jesus Christ, through whose love all human diversities lose their decisive significance;

[1] *The Population Explosion and Christian Responsibility*, O.U.P., 1960, pp. 36–37.

it denies our common humanity in creation and our belief that all men are made in God's image; it falsely asserts that we find our significance in terms of racial identity rather than in Jesus Christ. In these terms our Assembly has reasserted the radical opposition of the World Council of Churches to all forms of racism and the basis upon which it calls upon Christians and all men of goodwill to work for the complete elimination of racial injustice.

The biblical basis of this declaration is clear. The Old Testament moves steadily away from the exclusive nationalism of the Jewish people. They have been signally blessed by God, but the great prophets see this as something to be shared. 'I will give you as a light to the nations that my salvation may reach to the end of the earth.'[1] In the New Testament the gospel is universal. Our Lord said, 'Whoever does the will of God is my brother, my sister, my mother.'[2] St Paul declared, 'For indeed we were all brought into one body by baptism, in the one Spirit, whether we are Jews or Greeks, whether slaves or free men.'[3]

It has become increasingly apparent that the race question constitutes an explosive threat to the peace and order of society, and even to the whole future of mankind. It underlies outbreaks of violence in various parts of the world. There is every indication that the future division of the world will be between the white, wealthy nations on the one hand, and the coloured poor nations on the other. It is not a pattern to be contemplated with complacency.

In Britain the growing argument about immigration has forced us to look squarely at what we feel and at what we believe about this issue. We now have nearly a million coloured immigrants from the Commonwealth living in Britain. Large numbers of these are concentrated in areas of big cities like London, Birmingham, Bradford, and Leeds. Reactions to this situation on the part of white Britishers has varied between sentimental exhortations to the effect that 'we are all the same underneath', which is untrue, to violent demands that all immigrants should be sent home, which is senseless.

[1] Isaiah 49:6.
[2] Mark 3:35.
[3] 1 Corinthians 12:13.

Three sorts of action are needed. The first of these is legislative. It is perfectly true that the hearts of men can't be changed by Act of Parliament, but the heartless can be restrained, and they ought to be. Moreover, if public opinion helps to make the law of the land, the law is in turn an instrument which affects public opinion. It is of great importance that our detestation of racial discrimination and our opposition to segregation should be reflected in the Statute Book.

The history of British legislation on this issue has not been an altogether happy one. The Commonwealth Immigrants Act 1968 which was rushed hastily through Parliament to deal with the problem created by the immigration of Asians from Kenya was condemned by the Churches as a racialist measure. The Government protested that this was not so, but the Act demonstrated, not for the first time, the gap that often separates intention from effect. The previous Commonwealth Immigrants Act which severely restricted the number of work permits available each year was not intended as an expression of colour prejudice, but it was interpreted as such abroad, particularly in the West Indies. In Britain the Churches criticized the measure because it was designed in economic terms to deal with what was and is essentially a social rather than an economic problem. If legislation is to help rather than hinder the movement towards racial integration, it must be based on a full knowledge of the facts of the situation both in this country and in the sending countries. At the time of writing, Parliament is considering the extension of the provision of the Race Relations Act which deals with public acts of discrimination and incitement to race hatred to the fields of employment, housing, and financial facilities. Beyond the sphere of specific legislation there is need for Government help for those areas where immigration has caused overcrowding both in houses and schools.

The second sort of action needed lies in the field of education. There is pressing necessity for realistic study and dissemination of the facts. Discrimination is prejudice in action and prejudice feeds on ignorance and fear. Many of the crude outbursts expressing opposition to Britain's immigration policy are based on a monumental ignorance of the facts. It is often alleged that the country is being swamped by coloured people; that they are taking jobs that ought to be available for white nationals; that immigrants have created slums; that they have caused an increase in the crime rate. None of these allegations can stand in the light of the facts. Coloured immigrants form less than 2 per cent of our population, and the number of immigrants in any one year is often equalled or exceeded by the number of emigrants leaving the country; the immigrants are making a most valuable and indeed quite essential contribution to the nation's economy and there are a great many vacancies still to be filled in the areas of employment where they usually work; slum conditions were with us before the immigrants started to arrive; and there is no evidence that the crime rate among coloured people in this country is greater than among the whites.

Hard facts on the sort of matters just mentioned are easily obtainable. But the roots of prejudice run deep, and some of the fallacies commonly held have to be examined in depth. There is the persistent belief that white people are superior to black particularly in the purity of blood and power of brain. A vast amount of biological bunkum has been talked on this subject. If everything can be blamed on nature, this is a convenient way of exonerating society from all responsibility. There are, of course, different types of blood, but they do not coincide with racial differences. If I were seriously ill my life might be saved by an infusion of blood from a particular black man, whereas the blood of a particular white man would be useless. As for brain power, it may be true that the average size of the brain of the American white is larger than that of the American negro. But there is no necessary connexion between intelligence and the size of the brain. Moreover, a survey indicated that the average size of the European brain is rather smaller than that of the average Japanese.

Apart from these considerations, it must be recognized that the measuring of intelligence is a very complex business. The UNESCO Statement on Race says:

It is now generally recognized that the intelligence tests do not in themselves enable us to differentiate safely between what is due to innate capacity and what is the result of environmental influences, training and education. Wherever it has been possible to make allowances for differences in environmental opportunities, the tests have shown essential similarity in mental characters among all human groups.

Whether we are considering physical characteristics such as height, or size of brain, or more subtle matters of temperament and disposition, we shall find that there are greater differences within any racial group than between racial groups. This does not mean, of course, that there are no differences between the races. The kind of differences that do exist and the right attitude towards them is very clearly described by Philip Mason:

> To me, then, it seems likely that there is a genetic element in the mental and temperamental differences which obviously exist between peoples. But all that this means is that there may be expected to be more people born with a particular kind of temperament in one group than in another; the way they are brought up will reflect this preponderance and accentuate and encourage the difference. Suppose that among the Welsh more people than among the English are born with an aptitude for music, it is likely that there will be more music heard in Welsh villages and more children will have a sense of tune and rhythm. There will be a genetic difference accentuated by upbringing. But surely here too we should expect to find nothing like such great differences between the general averages of races as there are between individuals, and the greater or lesser incidence of a particular quality in one group gives no ground for behaving to that group as though they were *all* different. It *might* be argued that everyone with blood-group B should be put in the same hospital, but it cannot be sensible to say that, because there are more Chinese than Englishmen with blood-group B, the Chinese and the English should be segregated. It *might* be argued that quick-tempered and imaginative people who like classical music should go in one suburb while those who prefer football matches to art galleries and seldom lose their temper are put in another; it may also be true that the Welsh include more of the former kind of person and the English more of the latter. But it is obviously not possible to divide the qualities neatly between Welsh and English, and it would be manifestly silly to put them in different housing estates.[1]

This leads to a consideration of the third sort of action which is needed. Christians must seize every opportunity for personal

[1] *Common Sense About Race*, Gollancz, 1961, pp. 100–101.

initiative and service in the promotion of good community relations. This will require understanding and patience. The problems of integration are real and are likely to remain acute for some time. Many of them will probably only be fully overcome when the second and third generations of immigrants have become accustomed to our ways and we to theirs.

There are now opportunities of service on the Liaison Committees which have been set up in areas where there is a heavy concentration of immigrants. Because of the shortage of housing, the setting up of Housing Associations can help to ease the situation of those in need of decent accommodation. Wherever opportunities exist Christians should welcome immigrants as visitors into their homes. House group discussions between people of different races could do much to deepen knowledge and dispel misunderstandings. So far as Church services are concerned, obviously coloured Christians cannot be prevented from worshipping God in their own way and in congregations that are predominantly or even exclusively coloured. But every effort must be made to secure the integration of worshippers and opportunities of leadership in British Churches must be given to coloured people.

The passage of time, however, will not lead automatically to an improvement in the situation. There are already those who have been with us long enough to resent being called immigrants. They regard themselves, rightly, as Britishers. The real issue here is the depth and sincerity of our desire to build a truly multi-racial community in Britain. This will not come about on its own. It must be planned and worked for, and there must be a resolute determination that we will not tolerate the idea of second-class citizens in Britain.

Peace and war

The willingness of men to use violence as a means of enforcing their will or attempting to settle disputes has been one of the causes of unending wars. There have not been more than about 300 war-free years during the last 3,500 years of world history. It is part of the tragedy of humanity that, though nations are divided on many issues, they seem agreed on the disastrous thesis that in the last resort the use of violence is justified as a means of 'defence'. I put the word in quotation marks because, of course, with the increasing sophistication of the weapons of war, defence becomes less and less feasible.

Christians are agreed that war is contrary to the spirit, teaching, and purpose of our Lord. The command to love our neighbours must not be narrowly interpreted as applying only to personal relationships. We are called to be the makers of peace, and no Christian doubts for one moment that peace is the will of God. The followers of Christ have been, and still are, divided in their understanding of how these general principles and convictions are to be worked out in the world of harsh realities, where peace so often seems an idle pipe dream.

The Christian non-pacifist believes that there may be occasions when war is the lesser of two evils. The making of peace involves a concern for justice, for there can be no durable peace without justice. If, therefore, the stability of a just and orderly society is threatened by the unprovoked aggression of an enemy bent on destruction, it may be necessary to go to war to ensure the preservation of the values which are more precious than life itself.

The pacifist Christian believes that obedience to Christ involves absolute dedication to the way of reconciling love exemplified in the cross of Christ. He does not reject all use of force, but the wholesale killing of men, women, and children which war involves is an evil so great as to blot out any good that might be hoped for by those who believe they are defending Christian values. He argues that there is no hope for the world unless the nations renounce war, and that Christians must pioneer the movement towards that renunciation.

Like all divisions of judgement on important issues, this one has been a source of deep agony within the Christian fellowship. It is imperative that the quest for deeper understanding and greater unanimity should continue. Christians who in order to avoid conflict refuse to discuss the issues are guilty of grave dereliction of duty. One of the tests of the value and reality of Christian fellowship is its ability to hold together in creative tension those who advance differing views.

Although I have referred to the two main positions within the Christian Church on the subject of war, it would be wrong to suggest that all Christians can be neatly divided into two camps, pacifist and non-pacifist. There are a great number of questions which present agonizing dilemmas to many Christians, whether they tend to the one general view or the other. What about chemical warfare, for example? There are many non-pacifist Christians who would feel bound to judge that their conscience could not approve the use of bacteriological methods of attack on the enemy, however cogent the military arguments in favour might appear to be. Much more difficult is the question of Christian participation in the kind of peace-keeping operations mounted by the United Nations organization. At the present time the personnel required for such operations are recruited from the armed forces. Many pacifists are bound to be unhappy that they are precluded by this fact from participating in what is often an important and necessary exercise. Again, there are difficult questions about the extent to which the Christian can condone civil disobedience, and about the legal rights of those who, while not objecting to all war, conscientiously disapprove of particular wars. On the latter point the Christian doctrine of the just war clearly implies the duty to distinguish between one kind of war and another. But has the individual the right to make a judgement to the contrary if the 'lawful authority' has declared the war to be 'just'? There are no easy answers to these questions. Christians of every shade of opinion need to discuss them together.

It is happily true that there are wide areas of agreement between Christians, and indeed between Christians and non-Christians, about how the quest for peace should be pursued. Obviously it is part of the obligation of Christians to seek to understand and remove the causes of conflict, some of which we have mentioned earlier in this chapter.[1] Pacifists recognize that the path to peace is long and tortuous, and are willing to work with non-pacifists for the achievement of limited objectives. After all, the only objectives which are attainable are limited ones – the next short, faltering foot-step in the right direction – and half a loaf is better than no bread.

The range and depth of the concern of the Churches in the field of peace-making is reflected in the various resolutions of successive assemblies of the World Council of Churches, and more

---

[1] Among books which might be studied are *The Christian Faith and War in the Nuclear Age*, report of a study commission in the U.S.A., Abingdon Press, 1963, and:

Alan Booth, *Not Only Peace*, S.C.M. Press, 1967.

particularly in the Reports of the Commission of the Churches on International Affairs. The 1968 Report of that Commission deals with a great variety of issues, including disarmament, nuclear weapons testing, the peaceful uses of outer space and of atomic energy, U.N. peace-keeping activities, and the situations in Vietnam, the Middle East, and Nigeria.

The advent of nuclear weapons of mass destruction has opened up new and terrifying possibilities of calamity on a cosmic scale. It has also altered very considerably the factors which Christians have to weigh in the scales of moral judgement. Some indication of the new dimensions of horror which the use of the new weapons would unlease is conveyed in the statement that one thermo-nuclear bomb releases more destructive energy than that released by all the bombs dropped on Germany and Japan during the Second World War. The stark and awful fact is that there exist enough nuclear explosives to destroy the whole of the human race.

The Declaration of the Methodist Church on Peace and War sets forth the conditions of a 'just war' as traditionally defined by the Christian Church. These state that for a war to be a 'just war' in the Christian sense it must:

1) have been undertaken by a lawful authority;
2) have been undertaken for the vindication of an undoubted right that had been certainly infringed;
3) be a last resort, all peaceful means of settlement having failed;
4) offer the possibility of good to be achieved outweighing the evils that war would involve;
5) be waged with a reasonable hope of victory for justice;
6) be waged with a right intention;
7) use methods that are legitimate, i.e. in accordance with man's nature as a rational being, with Christian moral principles and international agreements.[1]

In the light of what we know about the destructive effects of the use of thermonuclear weapons, it is obvious that no war in which such devices are used can be described as 'just' in the terms of this definition. It is not possible to believe that such a war could ever 'offer the possibility of good to be achieved outweighing the evils

[1] *Declarations*, p. 56.

that war would involve' (No. 4 above). It is equally evident that such a war could never 'be waged with a reasonable hope of victory for justice' (No. 5 above), for justice can have no meaning in a world reduced to ashes. The realistic contemplation of what would be involved in a thermonuclear holocaust does in fact turn the whole of the definition of the just war into a purely academic recital to which no meaning can be attached. Little wonder, then, that the Declaration concludes that in war waged with nuclear weapons of mass destruction the 'just war' is impossible.

The practical implications of this judgement are not all entirely clear. If it is accepted – and it is difficult to see how on any Christian premises it could be rejected – then obviously the Church is committed to every means of seeking nuclear disarmament and of preventing the spread of nuclear weapons to those countries which do not yet possess them. Many Christians, however, draw a distinction between the morality of possession of nuclear weapons, and of their use. They believe in the deterrent value of such weapons and argue that, however unpleasant the phrase may sound, it is 'the balance of terror' which has prevented the outbreak of a third world war. Others will reply that this is mere speculation, and that there is no guarantee that thermonuclear weapons will not be used. Past history does not encourage a belief in the wisdom and sanity of either political or military leaders; and there is always the possibility that 'the button will be pressed by mistake'. Some distinguish between the smaller 'tactical' weapons in the nuclear armoury, and the strategic weapons which are capable of wiping out whole populations. This distinction might be regarded as valid by those who accept the just war doctrine. In practice, however, it is likely to be made meaningless by the almost inevitable tendency in wars between the great powers to escalate from the use of smaller to larger weapons.

There is much to discourage the peace-maker, not least the complexity of the issues confronting him. But for that very reason Christians must be always exhorting each other to keep alive the concern for peace. Unless mankind can agree to abolish war, there is no future for the race. Some Christians are called to be experts in the study of the complexities of international affairs. But the whole Christian community has a part to play.

It must ceaselessly challenge the morality of government policies. It must eschew the militaristic outlook that finds some sort of glory in the wretched business of war. It must set its face against the narrow nationalisms and partialities which embitter the relationships of peoples. It must preach the positive message that peace is possible, and that the search for it is creative and exciting. It must exemplify within its own fellowship the reconciling power of love. A divided Church is a living lie which invites unbelief.

15 Modern society and the Christian citizen

The secularization of society

ONE OF THE great theological questions of our day concerns the relationship between the sacred and the secular. Some popular attempts to elucidate the connexion tend to rob both terms of any specific meaning: for example, the assertion that religion and life are one requires some exposition before we can be sure whether we can accept it or not. Does it mean that the making of a cup of coffee is every bit as religious as singing a hymn, and if so, would it be right to replace Church services with coffee mornings? And, since the making of machine guns is part of life, is this religious too? I do not dispute the measure of truth in the statement that religion and life are one, but merely indicate that its meaning does not lie on the surface.

Other exponents of the relationship between sacred and secular speak as if the one were the enemy of the other. Some Christians seem to ascribe all our ills to the secularization of society. Some humanists allege that the Christian religion, with its other-worldly exercises, is irrational and consequently hinders men from making an intelligent analysis of their problems.

A number of writers have helped to clear a way through this unfortunate jungle of confusion by drawing a distinction between secularization and secularism. Harvey E. Cox has put the matter very lucidly. Arguing that secularization arises in large measure from the formative influence of biblical faith on the world, he says:

Secularization implies a historical process, almost certainly irreversible, in which society and culture are delivered from tutelage to religious control and closed metaphysical world-views. We have urged that it is basically a liberating development. Secularism, on the other hand, is the name for an ideology, a new closed world-view which functions very much like a new religion . . . Like any other *ism* it menaces the openness and freedom secularization has produced; it must therefore be watched carefully to prevent its becoming the ideology of a new establishment. It must be especially checked where it pretends not to be a world-view but nonetheless seeks to impose its ideology through the organs of the state.[1]

The view that the processes of secularization have their roots in the Bible is a sound one. The great prophetic tradition of biblical teaching looks out upon the whole world as the arena of the divine activity. Jesus illustrated His teaching with parables which were observations of the on-going life of the world about Him. Many of the pioneers of modern science were devout Christians whose explorations of the universe were undertaken for the glory of God. But having once set out in search of truth, the path must be followed wherever it leads. The pursuit of truth has often been hindered by those whose narrow religious views were challenged and upset by new knowledge. They held the very misleading opinion that theology is 'the queen of the sciences'. By 'theology' they meant their own particular religious views. This was entirely to misconceive the function of religion. The Church has no right at all to try to dictate the results of scientific or any other kind of investigation. It has, of course, a right and a duty on occasion to say what use should be made of those results, but that is a different matter. There is no such thing as Christian mathematics or Christian geography. In relation to all such matters the function of the Christian faith is to provide an attitude – one of reverence for truth and honest concern to establish the facts.

In practice this means that Christians will not regard the secular world as an alien place. To them the place of worship and the place of work will both be part of the real world. They will learn of God in both areas of experience, and what they learn in either will inform and infiltrate into the other. In other

[1] *The Secular City*, S.C.M. Press, 1965, pp. 20–21.

words, Christianity and citizenship will be inextricably linked in the person of the Christian citizen.

But if Christian worship and the secular life of the Christian are to inform and penetrate each other, the structures and organization of the Church must be such as to make this possible. The social responsibility boards, Christian citizenship departments, and similar agencies of the Churches are designed to help to achieve this end. In these days their agendas are long and lengthening. This is bound to be so for two reasons. One is that, though we recognize that God is at work in the secular world, so also is the power of evil. We need to be constantly on the alert to discover what God is doing, and where He would have us fight for the right against the wrong, and what tactics He would have us adopt. The other reason why the agendas lengthen is that society is not a collection of unrelated bits but of interconnected parts. It is of more than semantic interest that the Christian Citizenship Department of the Methodist Church was formerly called Temperance and Social Welfare, and earlier still just Temperance. These changes in nomenclature indicate not only an enlargement of function but something of the logic of development in the Department's history. If you begin with a Christian concern about the evils of intemperance in the use of alcohol, you cannot for long remain ignorant of the other evils that spring from it or are related to it. Gambling is closely associated with drinking in the life of the community. Both can lead to criminal activities and so to imprisonment. Many prisoners come from broken homes, and domestic breakdown is a source of mental illness. The desire to escape from intolerable pressures is one of the causes of drug addiction. Already, since one thing leads to another, the agenda is assuming sizeable proportions.

The previous chapters in the second half of this book have dealt with specific areas of concern, and have gone into as much detail as space would allow. Now I propose, even more briefly, to make a selection from the many other items on which the Churches have sought to give guidance to their people. This, together with what has gone before, will, I hope, demonstrate the diversity and interest of the Church's social concern.

Temperance

Just as some people think of morality as relating only to sex, so others think of temperance as relating only to the use of alcohol. But temperance (or self-control) is part of what St Paul calls 'the harvest of the Spirit,'[1] and is a component in that strength of character which is required of the Christian in all the situations of life. The Christian virtue of temperance is rather different from that of the pagan Greeks who taught the value of moderation. Their proverb *Mèden agan* ('nothing too much') would rule out the passionate quest for righteousness to which Jesus exhorted His followers.[2]

The word 'temperance' has become particularly associated with the question of the right use of alcoholic drinks because of the temperance movement which had its rise during the latter part of the first half of the nineteenth century. Today the Temperance Council of the Christian Churches seeks to co-ordinate the temperance witness of the Anglican, Roman, and Free Churches. The member Churches of that Council are able to co-operate in the efforts which are made to secure and maintain effective legislative control of the drink trade, and to educate their constituents, and especially young people, in the nature of alcohol and the dangers of its use. The Churches are not all agreed about the propriety of, or need for, the appeal for total abstinence. Whilst all agree in condemning drunkenness, on the whole the Roman and Anglican Churches teach moderation in the use of alcohol, while the Free Churches, with varying degrees of emphasis, favour total abstinence. The Salvation Army insists on abstinence as a condition of membership. The Methodist Church 'appeals to all within its pastoral oversight to practise total abstinence from alcoholic beverages, not as a burdensome duty, but as a privilege of Christian service'.[3]

There is need for Christians who hold different views on the question of abstinence to look again at the facts. The easy assumption that temperance means 'moderation in all things' is superficial, because it obviously will not bear close examination. On the other hand, bigoted condemnation of moderates by abstainers

[1] Galations 5:22.
[2] Matthew 5:6.
[3] *Declarations*, p. 60.

is itself an offence against temperance. As I have said elsewhere:

As in every issue of this sort, there is great need for mutual respect and understanding between Christians of differing views. This is one of the points made by St Paul in Romans XIV. Inevitably we tend to accept without searching examination the beliefs and customs which belong to our religious, cultural, and social background. When either total abstainers or moderate drinkers say they cannot understand how anyone can hold a different view, they are confessing their ignorance. Looked at impartially it is clear that the Christian judgement about drink is not an easy one to make. Those who pretend that it is are probably either taking refuge in an unquestioned tradition or have overlooked some of the arguments which a full consideration must take into account.[1]

The Bible does not condemn the moderate use of wine. It mentions the Rechabites and the Nazarites who practised total abstinence, but does not suggest that their example should be universally adopted. There can be little doubt that our Lord used the table wine of His day, as His own words seem to imply: 'For John came, neither eating nor drinking, and they say, "He is possessed". The Son of Man came eating and drinking, and they say, "Look at Him! a glutton and a drinker".'[2] The wine used at the Last Supper was almost certainly fermented, since the meal took place seven months after the grape harvest. The Communion wine used by the early Church was certainly fermented, for Paul complained that some, through taking too much, had become intoxicated.[3]

In response to one particular situation St Paul did recommend abstinence both from meat and wine: 'It is a fine thing to abstain from eating meat or drinking wine, or doing anything which causes your brother's downfall.'[4] The Apostle, in saying this, had mainly in mind the fact that the faith of some of the newly-baptized Christians was being jeopardized by their being invited

---

[1] *Moderate Drinkers and Total Abstainers*, Epworth, 1963, p. 18.
[2] Matthew 11:18, 19.
[3] 1 Corinthians 9:21.
[4] Romans 14:21.

to eat meat which had been offered to idols. The principle of concern for our brother's welfare is, however, of perennial importance. The meat problem is no longer with us, but, by contrast, the drink problem is very much with us, and indeed has assumed proportions which make the Pauline approval of abstinence much more significant than it was originally.

As with all other ethical decisions, in this matter Christians have the basic responsibility of facing the facts. Britain spends well over £1,000 million annually on alcoholic drinks, and more than £20 million on their advertisement. The supporters of the drink trade can claim that it provides employment for a considerable number of people and that the tax on drink yields large sums for the national revenue. They would also argue that the moderate consumption of alcohol adds to the pleasures of life for vast numbers of people.

Unfortunately, there is a dark side to the picture. The connexion between the drinking of even quite small amounts of alcohol and road accidents has now been firmly established. The recognition of this connexion led to the passing of the Road Safety Act 1967 under which it is an offence to drive a car with more than 0·08 per cent of alcohol in the blood. The existence of this law has already saved many lives. The figure representing the blood/alcohol ratio which the law allows must not, however, be taken to imply that it is safe to drive with less than that amount. The fact is that any consumption of alcohol by drivers may increase the risk of accident.

The connexion between alcohol and crime, or the social disorders which lead to crime, has been traced often enough, and sufficiently underlines the fact that it is a dangerous commodity. The scientific verdict on it is that it is an addictive drug. Its effects on the nervous system are depressant. The medicinal and food values of alcoholic drinks are minimal.

The most melancholy fact about the drink problem is the existence of large numbers of alcoholics. These are to be distinguished from moderate social drinkers, and even from excessive drinkers.

Alcoholics are people with a disease that can be defined in medical terms and requires a proper regime of treatment. Alcoholics are addicted to alcohol. *Alcohol addicts* are unable spontaneously to give up drinking. Though they may go without a drink for a few days, or sometimes for even longer periods, inevitably they revert. The greater the need to stop drinking, the more difficult do they find it to do so. Besides this characteristic of the alcohol addict, that he cannot go for long without alcohol, he generally suffers from withdrawal symptoms – short lived (though often serious) physical or mental ill-effects which supervene when drinking is temporarily halted for a few days or even hours.[1]

The problem of alcoholism is growing. The World Health Organization estimated that there were 350,000 alcoholics in Britain, a quarter of whom showed physical and mental deterioration. Admittedly precise statistics on a matter of this kind are difficult to determine, but the substantial figure quoted is some indication of the size of the problem and the magnitude of the suffering involved.

There are, of course, many causes of alcoholism. Many alcoholics suffer from a personality disorder, and it seems likely that they would take refuge in the use of some other drug if alcohol were not available. On the other hand, it is naïve to pretend that the availability of alcohol and the strong social pressures to drink are not to some extent responsible for the incidence and growth of alcoholism. The Christian citizen is bound to recognize the importance of sound education among the young and of legislative controls over the sale of drink. Equally, he cannot escape the question, 'What sort of personal example is called for by the facts set out in the previous paragraphs?'

The total abstainer flies in the face of long-established tradition. He occupies a minority position. If he has been brought up in a home where total abstinence was very strongly advocated he may not find it easy to take an unbiassed view of the matter. But the bias is not all on one side. Non-abstaining Christians sometimes argue as if the majority were always right, which is a very dubious proposition. For my part the conclusion that total abstinence is a valid expression of concern for my neighbour seems entirely reasonable. Recent increases in convictions for drunkenness lend added weight to this judgement.

[1] Kessel and Walton, *Alcoholism*, Pelican, 1965, pp. 16–17.

Drug addiction

Recent years have seen a deepening anxiety in Britain and else-where about the growth of drug addiction. As I have already indicated, alcoholism is one form of drug addiction. It is often not recognized as such for the simple reason that alcohol, unlike heroin, cannabis, and other drugs, is socially acceptable.

One of the reasons why we face a problem of addiction to drugs is quite simply that drugs are available. Ours is a drug-taking society. It may well be that the medical profession relies, and has led the community to rely, too much on drugs as pallia-tives for all kinds of ills. On the other hand, the benefits which have come to us through the right use of drugs are enormous. Lives are saved, pain is relieved, and diseases are eradicated.

The range and variety of drugs is constantly being extended. It is therefore of the utmost importance that the manufacture and supply of drugs should be carefully controlled, and that the public should be educated to understand the benefits of right use and the dangers of abuse.

Dependence on drugs can be social, psychological, or physical, though in actual situations the various factors often overlap. A person may be described as socially dependent when he takes a drug of addiction mainly in order to conform to the behaviour pattern of his particular group. Psychological dependence indicates reliance on a drug for the production of a feeling of well-being. In the case of physical dependence there are physical symptoms, which can be very severe, when supplies of the drug are suddenly withdrawn.

The types of drugs currently causing concern include the amphetamines, which are stimulants taken as 'pep pills'; the barbiturates, which are sedatives, often taken as sleeping pills; the hallucinogens, like LSD, which cause considerable dis-turbance of the powers of perception; and the 'hard drugs', like heroin and cocaine, which produce all-round deterioration in the addict. In addition there is alcohol, to which reference has already been made; cannabis, usually smoked in reefer cigarettes, which produces a feeling of cheerful intoxication; and tobacco, which can cause lung cancer (the annual death rate from lung cancer with which cigarette smoking is clearly associated exceeds 30,000).

These drugs are all different in their effects, and dangerous in varying degrees. The full effects of some of them are not yet known. It is possible, for example, that cannabis has genetic effects. Certainly while this is in dispute, the very uncertainty constitutes sufficient reason for resisting the arguments of those who say that because it is not an offence to be in possession of alcohol, cannabis should not be subject to legal embargo. At the same time there is reason to doubt the wisdom of a law which ignores responsibility and intention, and makes simple unauthorized possession an offence.

In the nature of the case it is not possible to know exactly how many drug addicts there are. The total of known heroin addicts in Britain was 237 in 1963, 521 in 1965, and 849 in 1966. Prosecutions for the possession of cannabis rose from 17 in 1946 to 1,119 in 1966. The figures represent a comparatively small number of people, but that number is increasing. Also, the proportion of those whose addiction results from other than initially therapeutic treatment has risen rapidly.

These facts indicate a threefold need. The law relating to the manufacture and supply of drugs must be kept under constant scrutiny. Adequate provision must be made for the treatment of those who have become addicted. The educational task must be more resolutely tackled.

Beyond all this, however, lies a deeper consideration. Why do men and women become addicted to drugs? There are many reasons. Some seek to escape from their own inadequacies and from the pressures of life; others take drugs to enable them to face life's strains; others again experiment in order to explore new experiences. Whatever the cause, drugs are no real answer to the desire either to escape from life or to experience it more fully. They can be a dangerous delusion. The real challenge to Christians is to make good their claim that the secret of a full and satisfying life is to be found in obedience to the gospel.

Gambling

Many discussions of gambling are less than helpful because the participants do not begin by defining carefully what they understand by the term. The Declaration of the Methodist Church on the Gambling Problem begins:

By gambling, those practices are meant whose characteristic features are: a) a determination of the possession of money or value by an appeal to chance; b) the gains of the winners are made at the expense of the losers; and c) gain is secured without rendering in service or in value an equivalent of the gain obtained.

Gambling takes the following forms:

1) Gaming, or playing for money in a game of chance;
2) Betting, or staking money on a doubtful or uncertain event;
3) Lotteries and Sweepstakes, which may be defined as the distribution of prizes by lot or chance;
4) Gambling speculation. In the realm of finance and commerce there are transactions which have no relation to the legitimate production, marketing or distribution of goods, but are based upon the fluctuations of market prices and in essence consist of an attempt to gain through the loss of other people without rendering any commensurate service.[1]

Britain is, comparatively speaking, heavily addicted to gambling. The annual football pool turnover rose from £69 million in 1963 to £118 million in 1966. In April 1967 the Chancellor of the Exchequer based his estimate of the annual turnover for betting on horse racing and greyhound racing at £1200 million. The annual turnover on bingo clubs is probably between £30 million and £40 million. There are, of course, many other forms of commercial gambling, including gaming in clubs, gaming machines, and the sort of amusement machines operated in fun fairs.

All Churches condemn excessive gambling, but attitudes to controlled gambling differ. The Roman Catholic Church raises large sums of money for Church purposes by means of gambling. Although there have been distinguished Anglican opponents of gambling in all its forms, the Church of England on the whole does not teach that gambling is wrong in itself. The Declaration of the Methodist Church examines the question in the light of the Christian attitude to God and life, the nature of our relations in society and in the Church. It concludes that 'no sanction for gambling can be found in the Christian attitude to God and life. The claim that gambling is compatible with the Christian calling

[1] *Declarations*, p. 63.

shows confusion of thought, resting on false values and precedents drawn from sub-Christian and non-Christian levels of thought. Resort to gambling is a virtual denial of faith in God and an ordered universe, putting in its place an appeal to blind chance, prompted neither by love nor rectitude.'[1] The fact that this is a minority judgement within the Christian Churches neither disproves nor establishes its veracity. It does suggest, however, that there is need for Christians holding different views to examine each other's positions and to be willing to learn from one another.

The differences of judgement referred to do not preclude united action in the fields of legislation and education. Here the Churches' Council on Gambling commands the respect of the Anglican and Free Churches which it serves. The State recognizes the dangerous nature of the gambling habit by imposing legislative controls. It would have saved itself a great deal of trouble, particularly that caused by the proliferation of gaming clubs, if it had paid more attention to the Churches' Council when the Betting and Gaming Bill was being debated in Parliament.

The Churches' Council has been instrumental in launching in this country the organization known as Gamblers Anonymous. This is a much needed piece of outreach service to those compulsive gamblers who, because of their addiction, have made shipwreck of their lives. The very need for such an organization is part of the evidence which must be weighed in determining what is the right Christian attitude to gambling as a personal pursuit and a social phenomenon.

Sport

In view of the large place which sport occupies in our social life it is strange that more attention has not been paid to it from the standpoint of Christian ethics. Few people will doubt the value of games, both for participants and spectators. But there are aspects of organized sport which call for the careful scrutiny of those who believe that there is no part of life which is not subject to moral considerations.

The Methodist Declarations on Social Questions contain some incidental references to the subject. One of the grounds of objection to gambling is that it debases sportsmanship. The

[1] *Declarations*, p. 66.

Declarations on the Christian Observance of Sunday and on the Christian Significance and Use of Leisure refer in passing to sport. The most extensive reference comes in the Statement on the Treatment of Animals. This Statement deals with pest control, methods of trapping animals, the keeping of pets and farm animals, and the matter of experiments on animals. One section of the Statement deals with sports which involve the use or pursuit of animals. It says:

> The term 'sport' is taken to cover any physical activity in which pleasure is a primary motive. If the reduction of pests is a primary motive, it cannot be regarded as a sport. To seek enjoyment through the suffering of others – whether man or animal – cannot be justified. The effects on the participants and onlookers should not be ignored in any ethical considera-tion of blood sports. The judgement of the Conference is, therefore, that:
> 1. All sports which inevitably cause suffering to animals are to be condemned.
> 2. All sports which are harmful to the characters of the participants and degrading to the onlookers are to be condemned.[1]

The Department of Christian Citizenship of the Methodist Church has undertaken to look more closely at other aspects of sport which might require ethical judgement. Among such aspects are the prevalence of violence at some sporting occasions, and the effects of competition on international relations.

Sunday and leisure

The present century has seen a vast expansion in the leisure time of ordinary working people. Among the older ones there are still those who can remember when they worked from early morning till late at night, and apart from Sunday, had neither time nor resources for the enjoyment of leisurely pursuits. All this has been changed by the developing power of trade unions, the lifting of the material standards of living, and, more recently, the arrival of increasingly effective mechanization and automation.

[1] ibid, p. 134.

Christians sometimes seem to display a strange ambivalence in their attitude to leisure. Older Christians particularly are apt to sound scornful of labour-saving devices, as if there were virtue in work merely for the sake of it. They then go to Church and sing hymns about heaven which contain such lines as 'and then to rest for ever'. But if leisure is good in heaven there seems no reason why it should not also be good here below.

Perhaps, however, there are some good reasons for a measure of reserve about our increased leisure. It is a sound instinct which sees the good life as a balanced rhythm of work and leisure. Experience has shown that the devil finds work for idle hands to do, unless there has been some education and proper provision for leisure hours. There are those who dread retirement, and shrink from the thought of having 'time on their hands'. There are many grave social problems connected with the use, or misuse, of leisure time. The promise of a four-day working week which the enthusiastic apostles of automation hold out to us may not be as rosy as some have thought. The concluding words of a report on the subject need to be heeded. It stresses 'the imperfections of present knowledge of the economic and social aspects of automation, when compared with knowledge of the technical possibilities', and adds, 'It becomes more vital each year to extend knowledge of these aspects by research and exchange of experience, especially by case-histories of firms with automatic processes.'[1] One fact which should rightly cause concern is the introduction of shift work on account of the economic necessity to keep expensive machinery running all round the clock, and consequent disruptions in family life.

Proper areas for the exercise of Christian responsibility are the provision of adequate leisure time facilities for the various sections of the community; the maintenance of high standards in public entertainments; the improvement of housing conditions; the elimination of unemployment so that labour and leisure may be more equitably shared throughout the community; and the fight against every kind of commercial exploitation.

Another matter which is of special concern to the Christian is the preservation of Sunday as a different day. Traditionally, Sunday has been a different day from the other days of the week

---

[1] *Automation; A report on the technical trends and their impact on management and labour,* H.M.S.O., 1956, p. 81.

both because of those things which have been done on it and those which have not. For the Christian, Sunday has afforded special opportunities for the worship of God and for service. For Christians and for the whole community, Sunday has been a day when the normal work of the week has been largely laid aside.

The roots of Sunday observance go back into the Jewish custom of keeping the Sabbath as a special day. The Jews regarded this weekly rest day as a divine institution ordained by God from the beginning of things. The story of creation says that when God had made the whole universe, 'He rested on the seventh day from all his work which He had done. So God blessed the seventh day and hallowed it.'[1] This weekly observance came to be hedged about by a great clutter of restrictive rulings so that it was more of a burden than a blessing. Our Lord corrected this traditional approach when he said .'The Sabbath was made for the sake of man and not man for the Sabbath.'[2] At first the Christians observed the Jewish Sabbath, but when the faith spread into the Gentile world the practice grew up of keeping the first day of the week as a festival of worship and remembrance of Christ's resurrection.

The value of a weekly respite for the whole community has been amply proved, and Christians can make common cause with others in seeking to preserve Sunday as a day of rest and recreation. The Christian himself will also value the day because of the opportunities it brings of worship, service, and fellowship with God's people. But it must be recognized that the pattern of Sunday is changing, not least because the rest of the week has changed. For most people there is at least one other day – usually Saturday – when they are free from organized work. The liberal principle enunciated by Jesus must always be kept in mind.

What part does the law play in the safeguarding of Sunday? For many years the Statute Book of England has contained an odd assortment of archaic, anomalous, and inapplicable legislation on Sunday. No sensible person would argue for the retention of laws which no longer apply to our changed situation and which are not respected by the community. The trend in our time is towards a much more permissive law. Some Christians make the mistake of supposing that people can be forced by Act

[1] Gen. 2:2, 3.
[2] Mark 2:27.

of Parliament to worship God. Christians in Britain belong to a democracy, and cannot enforce their will on others by legislation. On the other hand, since they are part of a democracy, they have a right to claim that their voice be heard, especially since they are by no means alone in wanting to preserve the different character of Sunday.

In practice, it means that Sunday law must be a compromise. Among those who agree in wanting to keep Sunday 'different' there will be wide divergencies of judgement about just how different it should be. Certain general principles will be agreed by many. One is that the number of persons gainfully employed on Sundays should be kept to a minimum (the granting of some other holiday during the week is not an adequate compensation for a free Sunday, for this is a day when the whole family can be together). Another general principle is that we should interfere as little as possible with the rights of other people to spend Sunday as they wish.

So far as the Churches are concerned, it is a mistake to suppose that any fixed pattern of Sunday activity, however hallowed by tradition, is sacrosanct. Responsible experiment in adapting Church programmes to the needs of the worshipping community is to be encouraged. The concluding paragraph of William Hodgkins's study of the subject summarizes the kind of balanced Christian view that is needed:

> The Church must give considerable thought to the preservation of its Sunday, and in this can ask for the full support of social and religious leaders if at the same time it is prepared to present a programme of worship, religious education, and recreational activities which will appeal to the finest minds in the nation.[1]

Censorship

I once spent the weekend in the delightful home of an elderly couple who had a considerable number of unmarried daughters. The old man, feeling with some justification that there was no need for him to take any part in the domestic chores of the household, sat stolidly in the chimney corner and listened for

---

[1] *Sunday: Christian and Social Significance*, Independent Press, 1960, pp. 224–5.

hours on end to the radio. No doubt he absorbed a great deal of sheer inanity, but what amused me was his indignation at the broadcasting of a song which he described as 'downright indecent'. The offending lines were: 'Where will the baby's dimple be – on its chin or on its knee?' It seemed an innocent enough jingle to me, but the fact that the old man took strong exception to it illustrates the enormous difficulty of obtaining any clear consensus of public judgement on what constitutes a reasonable standard of good taste.

If it is a difficult task to determine what is commonly regarded as a reasonable standard of decency, it is even harder to settle the question as to the extent to which, if at all, the law should interfere with the freedom of writers and speakers. Freedom of expression is of enormous value, and it is a proper instinct which reacts strongly against attempts to interfere with or limit that freedom. We should be prepared to suffer a great deal before being willing to impose any kind of censorship. 'I dislike intensely what you say, but will defend to the death your right to say it' is a sound sentiment.

Most people, however, would agree that there are limits beyond which free expression must not be allowed to go. There is no censorship of books in this country, but legal action may be taken against matter judged to be obscene. Under the 1959 Obscene Publications Act, 'an article shall be deemed obscene if its effect or (where the article comprises two or more distinct items) the effect of any one of its items is, if taken as a whole, such as to tend to deprave or corrupt persons who are likely, having regard to all relevant circumstances, to read, see or hear the matter contained or embodied in it.' The application of this carefully worded criterion is notoriously difficult, and in the end judgement depends not so much on the letter of the law but on the prevailing views of society as reflected in the deliberations of the court.

Part of the difficulty of deciding about the extent to which freedom to publish should be curtailed is that we do not know with any certainty what are the causal connexions between pornographic books and anti-social behaviour, or even crime. The point is put before us very forcibly by Pamela Hansford Johnson in her book *On Iniquity*.[1] When she went to Chester to report on the appalling crimes known as the Moors Murders she

[1] Macmillan, 1967.

was impressed by the fact that the accused, Ian Brady and Esther Myra Hindley, were avid readers of pornographic books. Fifty-one such books were found in the place where they lived, and they were listed under the headings: Sado-masochistic, Titillatory, and Sado-Fascist. The question forces itself upon us: were these criminals corrupted by the books, or did they have the books because they were corrupt? The critics who suggested that this was a foolish question to ask were surely themselves distinctly foolish.

The problem of finding a satisfactory answer which can be made the basis of a reasonable law is underlined in a passage from Alec Craig's *The Banned Books of England*:

It would be, of course, a poor service to the cause of intellectual and artistic freedom which it is the purpose of this book to further, to assert that literature has no effect on conduct and morals. Indeed, one of the potential values of literature is that it does exercise a great influence; and the importance of freedom is that it allows the good to be distinguished from the bad. Admittedly great literature may have regrettable results on conduct where its unfortunate tendencies are not corrected by knowledge and an enlightened moral sense. In 1954 a cadet of the French military college of Saint-Cyr bullied his mistress into killing her little daughter – either as an *acte gratuit* or a ritual murder, probably the former. The young man's reading consisted largely of Andre Gide, Nietzsche, d'Annunzio and Jean-Paul Sartre, and these authors may have had a bad effect on his mind. But none of their works can be stigmatized as pornography and, whatever their intentions in writing, erotic stimulation was not among them. Their books are great literature. Is the world to be denied them because they may unbalance the immature mind or the personality with a propensity for evil? Certainly not; but something like this argument is sometimes put forward. One of the silliest contributions to the Lolita controversy came from Philip Toynbee who argued that the book should be suppressed if it could be shown that a single little girl was likely to be seduced as a result of its publication. This kind of criterion would ultimately rob the world of its literature because almost every great book, including the

Bible, must have been the cause of crime or misdoing at some time or other. Certainly in the past people have found encouragement in the Bible for witch burning and slave trading.[1]

Whatever may be said in defence of serious literary works of the kind which might be offensive to many ordinary readers, there is surely nothing to be said for a vast amount of hard-core pornography which makes no pretension either to literary merit or serious purpose. It is published with the sole intention of making money, and represents commercial exploitation of the most cynical kind. It is right that those who are responsible for this kind of trade should be subject to the sanctions of the law.

September 1968 saw the abolition of the censorship of stage plays by the Lord Chamberlain's office. The public now becomes the judge of what is good or bad theatre. It can exercise control by giving or withholding its patronage or, in the case of morally offensive plays, by invoking the obscenity laws.

The film industry imposes its own censorship, as do also the broadcasting authorities. In 1967 and 1968 consultations were held between representatives of the member Churches of the British Council of Churches and the BBC and ITA. Roman Catholics also participated. The purpose of these consultations was to discuss responsibility for the maintenance of high standards in broadcasting. Those who attended these consultations were agreed that broadcasting must not be allowed to come under the control of outside censorship, whether political, commercial, social, or religious. But there was also agreement on the need for the authorities to be very sensitive to and aware of public opinion. It is inevitable that risks have to be taken if creative talent is to be encouraged. Broadcasting which aimed merely at being 'safe' would be very dull indeed. Mistakes are bound to be made. But the Churches could help by taking a more positive part in the shaping of sound criteria of judgement. One of the consequences of these discussions has been the setting up of a small committee within the framework of the Social Responsibility Department of the British Council of Churches to explore the possibilities of continuing dialogue between the Churches and the BBC and ITA, and to have oversight of a pilot project in which Church-mounted groups undertake research and enquiry into selected

[1] Allen and Unwin, 1962, p. 216.

programmes. It is very much to be hoped that this research will produce some firm conclusions about the effects of various sorts of programmes, and particularly those which contain what must surely by any standard of measurement be regarded as an excessive amount of violence. (Commenting on American television Frederick Wertham records that in one week, mostly in children's viewing time, one station showed 334 completed or attempted killings.[1])

Suicide and euthanasia

The suicide rate in England exceeds 5,000 per annum. The figures for attempted suicides are inevitably unreliable, but some estimates put the number as high as 30,000 per annum. In the past society has treated the suicide very harshly, denying him the ordinary rites of burial. The law has reflected this attitude. Suicide was a crime, and penalties included the forfeiture of lands and goods.

The revulsion against suicide is rooted in the instinct of self-preservation. The Church has always taught that it is wrong to take one's life, for only God can take away what He Himself has given. Augustine condemned suicide on three grounds: that it was a violation of the commandment 'Thou shalt not kill'; that it precluded any opportunity for repentance; and that it was an act of cowardice. The Church has recognized certain exceptions to this general condemnation, notably the kind of altruistic action taken by Captain Oates, who walked out into the blizzard in order to save his friends.

Recent years have seen a marked change in public and Christian attitudes to suicide. A deepening understanding of the reasons why people are led to such terrible action, and a recognition that often society is partly to be blamed, have led to a new sympathy for those who often suffer severely and in great loneliness. A number of ecological studies of suicide have been made. 'A reasonable conclusion is that while attributes of personality and experience predispose to suicide, these are developed by specific social conditions. Accordingly both psychological and social factors should be taken into account when framing a social policy on suicide.'[2]

[1] *A Sign for Cain*, p. 199.
[2] Norman St John-Stevas, *Life, Death and the Law*, Eyre and Spottiswoode, 1961, pp. 255-6.

Under the Suicide Act 1961 suicide and attempted suicide ceased to be crimes. It had come to be recognized that the law was ineffective as a deterrent. What it was in fact likely to do was to deter those contemplating suicide from seeking help. It also added to the misery of the relatives of the person who had committed or attempted suicide.

The change in the law received support from the Churches.[1] This fact does not indicate any complacent acceptance of suicide. On the contrary, there has been a growing desire to prevent the tragedy and help those whose situation has brought them to the verge of final despair. More research still into the causes of suicide is necessary, and more could be done to help doctors, ministers, and others to cope with the symptoms. The work of organizations like the Samaritans is giving lay folk an opportunity to exercise a very valuable ministry.

On the related question of euthanasia, the law of England remains unchanged. 'Euthanasia' comes from a Greek word meaning 'happy death', and is used to describe the killing of those suffering from incurable disease, old age, or serious malformation. If a doctor administers a fatal dose to a patient, whether or not consent has been given, he can be charged with murder. In practice, the harshness of the law in such cases is mitigated and juries have usually brought in verdicts of acquittal or of conviction of a lesser offence.

Officially the Churches have opposed any suggestion that euthanasia should be allowed by law. The Christian argument against euthanasia is similar to that against suicide. Individual Christians, however, have argued that voluntary euthanasia is not inconsistent with respect for life and personality, for quality of life is more important than mere 'length of days'. In cases of terrible pain in terminal illnesses, it surely would be merciful to grant to the patient the voluntary right to die.

It will be held by many that the force of this argument is reduced by the fact that increasingly the medical profession is able to alleviate pain by the use of drugs. Moreover, any concession which makes a breach in the principle of the sanctity of human life is dangerous, and opens up possibilities of exploitation and corrupt practice.

---

[1] See, for example, *Ought suicide to be a crime?*, Church Information Office, 1959.

It is, of course, recognized that in the actual practice of medicine doctors administer drugs to alleviate pain, knowing that in all probability the patient's life will be shortened thereby. This kind of medication would be justified by many Christian moralists on the ground that it involves the principle of double effect: that is to say, the main concern of the physician is the relief of suffering; the death of the patient is only a secondary effect. Dr Glanville Williams, who supports the legalization of voluntary euthanasia, is rather too harsh in his criticism of a moral distinction which seems reasonable enough:

> It is altogether too artificial to say that a doctor who gives an overdose of a narcotic having in the forefront of his mind the aim of ending his patient's existence is guilty of sin, while a doctor who gives the same overdose in the same circumstances in order to relieve pain is not guilty of sin, provided that he keeps his mind steadily off the consequence which his professional training teaches him is inevitable, namely the death of his patient. When you know that your conduct will have two consequences, one in itself good and one in itself evil, you are compelled as a moral agent to choose between acting and not acting by making a judgement of value, that is to say by deciding whether the good is more to be desired than the evil is to be avoided. If this is what the principle of double effect means, well and good; but if it means that the necessity of making a choice of values can be avoided merely by keeping your mind off one of the consequences, it can only encourage a hypocritical attitude towards moral problems.[1]

It seems inevitable that with the increasing possibilities of prolonging life there will be a growing demand for amendment of the law. It is important that the Churches should keep the issues here briefly stated under continuing review.

Spare-part surgery

Reference was made in Chapter 11 to a report on *Human Reproduction* which examined some of the emergent techniques, such as the grafting of ovary tissue, which may one day affect human conception and birth. This is only one of the many fields in which

[1] *The Sanctity of Life and the Criminal Law*, Faber, 1958, p. 286.

advances in medicine and surgery are raising profoundly important ethical issues. Another such field is that of so-called 'spare-part surgery'. The operation known as corneal grafting has been familiar to the public for a number of years, and through the Churches and in other ways individuals have been encouraged to bequeath their eyes for this purpose. The Human Tissues Act 1961 gave legality to this sort of transaction. Recently, however, surgery has taken a great leap forward in its ability to transplant hearts, lungs, and kidneys. Obviously there is still much to be learned in connexion with these techniques, in particular about methods of enabling the body to overcome its tendency to reject foreign matter. But in spite of some criticism that the medical men have yielded to the temptation to move too fast, the results of their work so far in this field leave no doubt that there is an expanding future for this sort of surgery. Some of the issues raised by the use of these techniques have already been discussed in Parliament, and the Renal Transplant Bill was introduced by Sir Gerald Nabarro to make legal the use of the kidneys of a deceased person unless he had while alive expressed any wish to the contrary.

Public anxiety has centred on the problem of deciding with certainty when a person is dead. This matter has come to prominence as a result of the formidable resources of apparatus and skilled knowledge which medicine has now acquired for the combating of death. We take it for granted that the primary duty of doctors and nurses is to seek the health of the patient and the preservation of his life. But in these days it is possible to prolong almost indefinitely the lives of some who would have died much sooner in earlier times. The problem becomes acute in cases where the patient is unconscious and never likely to be able to have any other than a 'vegetable' existence. At what point is it right just to allow that patient to die? Or consider the case of a patient who has been 'drowned' and to the lay observer appears to be 'dead'. It may be that a team of medical people, with all the latest apparatus of resuscitation, will succeed in bringing the patient back to life. After this he may 'die' several times again. How long should they continue their effort, and if in the end they fail, at what point can it be said that the patient really died?

These are simple – though not by any means imaginary – instances of the sort of problems which the medical profession faces.

Often the situations are much more complicated. But the questions raised have an obvious bearing on the matter of transplant surgery. When the layman considers the tests whereby we determine whether a person has died, he is apt to think simply in terms of whether the heart has stopped beating or not. But what of cases where the heart has been kept beating by artificial means within the body of a 'dead' patient while preparations are made for a transplant operation on another patient?

In all these matters a heavy burden rests on the medical profession and we may be profoundly thankful for the very high standards of integrity which exist among its members. But the sort of decisions that have to be made are not 'merely medical'. Dialogue and consultation between the profession and others skilled in ethical discussion is, therefore, to be encouraged. *Decisions about Life and Death* is the title of a Report of a group of doctors, moral theologians, and lawyers set up by the Church Assembly Board for Social Responsibility. On the general questions relating to the problem of how far medical treatment should go in striving to keep alive it has this to say:

> What, then, are the ingredients of decision? Some derive, obviously, from a consideration of the patient: his age and general condition; the nature of his disease; the availability and practicability of means of cure or of relief; his own wishes and belief. Some derive, in certain instances, from a consideration of his immediate kindred, and the relationship in which they stand to him. Some derive from the just interest of society: its immediate interests perhaps, where in an emergency there is acute shortage of beds, or of blood plasma, or of a rare medicine; and its long-term interests, among which are the preservation of certain beliefs about or attitudes towards the value of life, or of liberty, or of the integrity of the relationship between doctor and patient. Some derive from a consideration of the codes of ethics which govern the professional life of the doctor and nurse, and of others serving the patient in his need.[1]

The conclusion of this Report is that in a given case, medical treatment should not extend beyond the limits defined by one's basic understanding of human personality.

[1] Church Information Office, 1965, p. 18.

There is a further dimension of our subject which must be mentioned if only in terms of tabling an issue for further discussion. Many of the new ethical problems which have emerged in recent times spring out of man's capacity to manipulate his environment. But, as we saw when discussing new techniques affecting conception (Chapter 11), it is not only his environment which is increasingly within his control: man is beginning to be able to manipulate himself. Some of the drugs now in use are described as 'mind-bending'. The concept of medicine as merely the physical treatment of bodily ailments would be disowned by the medical profession today. Health and sickness are conditions of the whole man, and we are aware of the powerful inter-action of mind and body, for man is a psychosomatic unity.

These facts about the constitution of man and about developments in the field of medicine raise the question how far it is right to go in altering personality, whether intentionally or as the by-product of treatment aimed at the curing of a morbid condition. In particular, within the context of the discussion of spare-part surgery, we have to ask whether there are certain parts of the body which are sacrosanct because they represent 'the core of personality'. The two parts of the body which have been thought of as in a special sense enshrining the essence of a man's personality are, of course, the heart and the brain. Oddly enough, the testicles and ovaries which enable us to some extent to put our stamp on succeeding generations have not been thought of in this way. (I have commented on the ethics of artificial insemination and ovarian transplants in Chapter 11.)

In view of the mystical importance traditionally attached to the heart, one assumes that if our fathers could have envisaged such a thing as a heart transplant, they would have opposed it as an improper violation of personality. It is perhaps an indication of the more rational understanding prevailing today that there have been very few objections to heart transplants on that ground. Even the transplanting of a black man's heart into the body of a white man has been accepted without undue objection by countries and sections of the community notoriously colour-prejudiced. Most of the doubts expressed have been on the quite different ground that the medical risk may be too high, or that such operations might encourage doctors to be slightly less eager to preserve the life of a potential donor than they normally would be. But we recognize that a heart transplant has no effect on the personality of the recipient other than the incidental ones that might be expected to result from any effective therapy which removed a grave physical handicap.

What about brain surgery? We know that the removal of a small section of the brain can alleviate certain kinds of mental illness, and can indeed produce what can only be described as a change of personality. Supposing it became possible to transplant sections of the brain as it is now possible to transfer a heart from one person to another? It seems likely that this could bring about very considerable changes in personality. Could such an operation be regarded as morally right? It may be that the question is purely academic, and that surgery will never be able to perfect a method of achieving success in so delicate an operation. But he would be a rash prophet who ruled out the possibility altogether.

In a realm so hypothetical and uncertain one is justified in making only the most tentative judgement. A brain transplant operation would only be justified if, as in any other operation, the risks involved were thought to be justified by the chance of success. There would also have to be a reasonable expectation that the person receiving the transplant would be able to live a fuller and more balanced life. Presumably a brain transplant would only be considered in cases of severe mental derangement. If the objection were raised that it is not right to change a man's personality, the Christian is bound to answer that, as long as the change is for the better, he is wholeheartedly in favour of it. If the objection is raised that such changes are only right when brought about by spiritual means, the answer surely is that this limits the ways whereby God works, and we must not set any limits to the operation of divine providence. If the objection is raised that the only personality change which the Christian can approve is that which proceeds from voluntary acceptance by the individual of the means of change, then two things may be said. One is that indeed no one should be forced against his will to undergo brain surgery. The other is that, in the nature of the case, there might well be those incapable of giving consent who might be brought to sanity by such surgery. In such cases it would surely be right for others to decide on their behalf.

Yet there is another side to the question of brain transplants. The effects upon the future life of the patient could not be fully understood until the first operation had been attempted; and the surgeon who performed this first, experimental transplant would be taking on a grave responsibility. Even if the operations were originally performed under strict control, there is the possibility that, once learnt, the technique would be misused. As we saw in the section on responsibility and mental sickness (pp. 106–9), there can be no precise definition of insanity. And one has only to think of reports from Russia of writers whose ideas do not conform to those of the State being committed to mental hospitals to realize that the judgement of a man as 'insane' can be inaccurately applied for what we would regard as wrong ends.

It is, perhaps, appropriate that our consideration of some aspects of the art of moral judgement should end abruptly and in the middle of the discussion of a problem that is emerging as a result of the rapid developments in this swiftly-moving age of amazing achievements. The agendas of Church committees on social questions are not likely to be lacking in items in the foreseeable future. There is always an affirmative answer to the familiar question 'Any other business?' Christians are often in doubt about the right way to take. But they need have no doubts about the fact that the search for it is God's business; and as He has called us to share in it, He will keep His promise that 'he who seeks finds'.[1]

[1] Matthew 7:8.

Appendix

The Following subjects are suggested as useful themes for those who wish to discuss in groups or write essays on some of the issues raised in the various chapters.

Chapter 1. 'Living the good life consists in keeping a few simple rules.' Discuss.

Chapter 2. Comment on the basic questions concerning Christian morality contained in the quotation from the Report on *Sex and Morality*.

Chapter 3. What is the difference between descriptive and prescriptive ethics? Elaborate by means of an example.

Chapter 4. Give an account of the meaning of natural law and comment on the usefulness of the concept.

Chapter 5. 'The unique thing about the Christian ethic is not its text, but its context.' Do you agree?

Chapter 6. What are some of the main reasons for moral confusion in the modern world, and what significance do you attach to them?

Chapter 7. To what extent should the law seek to enforce morality?

Chapter 8. What are the factors which may qualify the concept of personal moral responsibility?

Chapter 9. How can the Churches effectively present the Christian social witness?

Chapter 10. How would you define chastity?

Chapter 11. What ethical issues are raised by the use of contraceptives?

Chapter 12. Should the main aim of the penal system be the punishment of the offender?

Chapter 13. Justify the Christian concern about politics and economics.

Chapter 14. What are some of the practical ways in which the Churches can help to lift the burdens of the poor and hungry of the world?

Chapter 15. Comment on the problem of addiction in its various forms.

Index

Index of biblical quotations